BRITAIN AND EUROPE AT A CROSSROADS

The Politics of Anxiety and Transformation

Andrew Ryder

First published in Great Britain in 2022 by

Bristol University Press
University of Bristol
1-9 Old Park Hill
Bristol
BS2 8BB
UK
t: +44 (0)117 954 5940
e: bup-info@bristol.ac.uk

Details of international sales and distribution partners are available at bristoluniversitypress.co.uk

© Bristol University Press 2022

British Library Cataloguing in Publication Data
A catalogue record for this book is available from the British Library

ISBN 978-1-5292-0053-9 paperback
ISBN 978-1-5292-0051-5 hardcover
ISBN 978-1-5292-0054-6 ePub
ISBN 978-1-5292-0052-2 ePdf

The right of Andrew Ryder to be identified as author of this work has been asserted by him in accordance with the Copyright, Designs and Patents Act 1988.

All rights reserved: no part of this publication may be reproduced, stored in a retrieval system, or transmitted in any form or by any means, electronic, mechanical, photocopying, recording, or otherwise without the prior permission of Bristol University Press.

Every reasonable effort has been made to obtain permission to reproduce copyrighted material. If, however, anyone knows of an oversight, please contact the publisher.

The statements and opinions contained within this publication are solely those of the author and not of the University of Bristol or Bristol University Press. The University of Bristol and Bristol University Press disclaim responsibility for any injury to persons or property resulting from any material published in this publication.

Bristol University Press works to counter discrimination on grounds of gender, race, disability, age and sexuality.

Cover design: blu inc, Bristol
Front cover image: amesy/iStock

I dedicate the book to my partner
Henrietta and son Arthur

Contents

List of Tables	vi
List of Abbreviations	vii
Note on the Author	viii
Acknowledgements	ix
Preface	xi
Introduction: Paradigm Shift, Reflexivity and Securitization	1
1 Brexit Nationalism: History, Crisis and Identity	17
2 The Road to Brexit	41
3 Politics in Focus: The Conservatives	63
4 Politics in Focus: Labour	87
5 The Nationalists: Exclusionary and Civic	109
6 Brexit: Views from Europe	129
7 Boris Johnson: Getting Brexit Done?	145
8 Antidotes to Brexit	165
Bibliography	183
Index	223

List of Tables

I.1	Argumentative topoi	11
I.2	Discourse analysis tools, language focus and rhetorical strategies	12
1.1	Public views on societal issues	31
3.1	Meaningful votes and next steps	83

List of Abbreviations

CDA	Critical discourse analysis
CoE	Council of Europe
DHA	Discourse historical approach
DUP	Democratic Unionist Party
ECSC	European Coal and Steel Community
EEC	European Economic Community
EFTA	European Free Trade Association
EU	European Union
IPSO	Independent Press Standards Organisation
NCA	National Crime Agency
SNP	Scottish National Party
TUC	Trades Union Congress
UKIP	UK Independence Party
WTO	World Trade Organization

Note on the Author

Andrew Ryder is an Associate Professor in the department for Sociology and Social Policy at the Corvinus University Budapest and Visiting Professor at Eötvös Loránd University Budapest. Andrew has a long track record of activism for social justice.

Acknowledgements

I should like to thank Professor Emeritus György Lengyel of the Corvinus University, Professor Joanna Richardson of De Montfort University and Stephen Wenham and Caroline Astley of Bristol University Press for comments, feedback and encouragement.

Preface

We live in an age of chaos, anxiety and deep change. The trilateral balance between the state, markets and civil society has been unbalanced, with the market emerging as dominant (Foucault, 2008). It is in this context that Brexit should be judged; a goal of this book is to identify means by which equilibrium can be achieved. The book adopts a critical approach to understanding Brexit and seeks to gain insights into how British society is recalibrating itself in a historic moment of paradigm shift, where Britain is emulating the new neoliberal turn of the United States, by forging a more laissez-faire form of capitalism aligned with populist nationalism. This outlook is termed Brexit nationalism, a conception of Brexit that sees it as a national rebirth and the renewal of perceived essences of Britishness, centred on political, economic and cultural sovereignty and chauvinism. This book charts the trajectory of Brexit by dissecting speech acts of elite actors through discourse analysis at key moments in the Brexit process and chronicles the shifts and turns of a changing society. Central to this analysis is the securitization of speech, a politics of fear where anxiety and concerns about external threats and entities spur an emergency politics of radical change, which in the case of Brexit is reactive and illiberal and can be viewed as part of the populist phenomenon. While reactive sections of the elite, in politics, business and the media, have championed Brexit, there has been a countermovement by mainstream, liberal and radical elements of society, who through desecuritization have sought to highlight the dangers to pluralism in a revolutionary moment of time. This book provides insights into the speech acts, rationale and strategy of the two sides of the debate in Brexit discourse.

Through discourse analysis, the book traces speech acts and key moments in Brexit within the wider sociological, historical and cultural context of Britain and more broadly Europe. It offers antidotes to Brexit nationalism by arguing that transformative change and solutions to the ills of British society, most notably economic inequality, resentments and a sense of alienation, can be secured by building change on aspects of tradition in terms of parliamentary democracy and past social policy regimes – in other words, the British tradition of 'pouring new wine into old bottles'. Consequently, the book advocates the renewal of representative democracy with deliberative democracy centred on an egalitarian and redistributive discourse.

Introduction: Paradigm Shift, Reflexivity and Securitization

'Suicide!' This utterance came from an MP as their fellows voted in support of Article 50, with 494 to 122 voting in favour of approving the European Union (Notification of Withdrawal) Bill on 8 February 2017, basically the formal start of the process of Britain leaving the European Union (EU). This decision had been preceded by the referendum result on 23 June 2016, when the British public voted by 52 to 48 per cent to exit the EU, a decision termed as 'Brexit', a portmanteau of 'British' and 'exit'.

'Brexit was a war. We won.' So proclaimed arch Brexit donor and campaigner Arron Banks (quoted in Cadwalladr, 2017). Nigel Farage, leader of the UK Independence Party that had done so much to provoke the establishment into holding a referendum, was in a triumphalist mood. On the day of the referendum, he declared in a media address that '[t]he Eurosceptic genie is out of the bottle and it will now not be put back' (quoted in Martin, 2016). He then stated: 'The EU's finished, the EU's dead.' Donald Trump, soon to be president of the United States, proclaimed to reporters the day after the referendum result that Brexit was a 'great thing' (Parker, 2016). Donald Tusk, the President of the European Council, sounded a more apocalyptic note. In an interview with the German newspaper *Bild*, he remarked: 'As a historian I fear that Brexit could be the beginning of the destruction of not only the EU but also of western political civilization in its entirety' (Charter, 2016). In an interview with the *Guardian*, the former Liberal Democrat leader Paddy Ashdown revealed that upon hearing the referendum result he turned to his wife and said, 'it's not our country anymore' (Williams, 2016).

As is evident from the previous statements, Brexit is one of the most important and contentious decisions in recent British history. It will no doubt be the source of discussion and reflection for generations to come, having huge implications for every facet of life in Britain. This book focuses on the historical, social, cultural and political factors that influenced Britain to take its decision to leave the EU but also explores what the consequences might be in the wake of that decision.

Thomas Kuhn (1962) describes how at pivotal points in history, through scientific innovation or tension, a dominant view is challenged in a process of paradigm shift. When things are in a state of flux and contestation, a revolutionary phase can even be reached wherein a new viewpoint and understanding can become the established and dominant paradigm. But this in turn triggers new challenges and so the cycle of change and challenge starts again. Such cycles can, I believe, be applied to cultural, political and economic contestation, upheaval and reorientation. It is my contention that Brexit presents such a moment in British history: a change in mindset and the prospect of a new social, economic and cultural model. As will become evident, the financial crisis of 2008, austerity and the ever-intensifying effects of globalization (in terms of its impact on competitiveness and cultural certainties) culminated in profound tensions being played out in the body politic and, consequently, a surge of populist nationalism centred on the 2016 referendum. Furthermore, Brexit is part of a wider global phenomenon, what has been described as a 'populist moment' that has seen populist national surges across Europe. This same moment is also fundamentally changing the way politics is done in countries such as Britain and the United States, as a consequence of Brexit and Trump respectively. In Hungary and Poland authoritarian populism has consolidated its grip on power and it appears to be waiting in the wings in countries such as France and Germany.

Brubaker (2017) may be right to suggest that several independent crises have converged in recent years to create a perfect storm, given that populism thrives on crisis and emergency. A key area of concern for this book is where established political actors and elites are being challenged by paradigm shifts in a time of profound crisis. Another pertinent question is whether the political parties are undergoing or will undergo profound transformation. To help answer this, much of the book focuses on the flow of political discourse and provides historical and linguistic context and insight for this exploration. If language can shape structure and, conversely, structure can shape language, by probing the discourse around Brexit we can gain insights into the changing character of British politics and society and the extent and nature of any paradigm shift. This point is explored in more depth later in the Introduction.

Favell (2017, 198) argues that Brexit is a multilayered and multidimensional phenomenon, which sees the intersection of many social, political and cultural processes. He concludes that '[t]he possibility of identifying clearly and unambiguously its overall sociological significance, as well as its significance for sociology would be frivolous at best.' I have some sympathy with these comments, having now spent a number of years surveying and seeking to decipher the events surrounding Brexit. However, as a sociologist myself I realize that despite the near impossibility of clearly and categorically mapping out an understanding of an increasingly complex lifeworld, it is nonetheless something important and worth pursuing – especially so in the case of Brexit, which provides deep insights into the economic, social and cultural composition of Britain during troubled times. As a critical and reflexive sociologist, I start the investigation by searching in myself, for I agree with Beck (2000) who contends that the conflict and tensions of society are also to be encountered within our own biographies – we each contain a clash of cultures.

Reflexivity

Pierre Bourdieu (1990a) asserted that the author should defy the academic traditions of scientism and positivism by not sanitizing the 'I' from their narrative. As Wodak and Meyer (2001, xxvi) note: 'Calling oneself "critical" implies explicit ethical standards: an intention to make one's position, research interests and values explicit and one's criteria as transparent as possible, without feeling the need to apologise for the critical stance of one's work.' Through a process of epistemic reflexivity, the author should seek to identify their position in the 'field', a structured system of social positions that defines the situation of its occupants (Maton, 2003). The field is an arena where struggles and contests occur over the distribution of resources. By identifying my position in the field the reader can detect how my position, life experiences and viewpoints might have shaped the narrative of this book.

The following autobiographical outline describes my 'self-concept' – the set of values, purposes and conceptions that an individual acquires through a variety of social structures, and that continues to evolve throughout their life. Gross (2008) remarks on how the narrative character of a self-conception is expressed and embodied through the stories that the individual tells him/herself and others about the development of his/her life. It can provide an important tool to understand the mindset of an author, a useful aid in weighing and interpreting authorial assessments of intellectual ideas and philosophies and their relationship to the context of society, a task this book aims to achieve.

I was raised on one of those nondescript housing estates that sprang up in the 1960s. Its newness and modernity meant it lacked character and was not invested with the strong sense of tradition and identity to be found in more established and historical settlements. For my parents, though, it presented a great advance. They had come, as with many others on the estate, from humble working-class origins. Entry into the neat, semi-detached three-bedroom houses presented a social advance where they and others like them felt themselves now to be middle class. Life was comfortable for me and my peers, with family cars, holidays abroad and everyone's father seeming to have a stable job. Yet coinciding with my entry into adolescence I could sense change; the industrial action and economic decline of the late 1970s promoted talk of the 'British malaise' and the election of Margaret Thatcher in 1979 heralded a process of radical change. I recoiled from Thatcherism, maybe having been one of the beneficiaries of 'the glorious thirty' (Les Trentes Glorieuses) a postwar age of rising living standards. I was resentful of a paradigm shift that seemed to be unravelling the certainties and securities that I had grown up with.

The election campaign of 1983 heightened my teenage interest in politics. I was inspired by Tony Benn and the socialist insurgency he led within the Labour movement. At university in Wales, I operated within what might be termed 'hard left' factions of the Labour Party. In 1985, while a student, I was threatened alongside sixteen others with the high court action of tortious conspiracy and a fine of 300,000 pounds for my part in organizing protests against the construction of a nuclear bunker in Carmarthen. The protest had led to serious delays in construction and the local authority having to contract a security firm to repel protestors.

With time, I drifted from radical left politics. In part the influence of local Labour politics in Wales taught me that the Labour Party worked better as a broad church rather than being riven by factionalism. I was also influenced by the 'new realism' of the Labour leader Neil Kinnock, which favoured a more pragmatic approach to politics within the party. I became a constituency party chairperson and was elected to the executive of the Welsh Labour Party. However, by the time I started my first job as a schoolteacher in 1990, I seemed to be disillusioned with Labour – a mood that became more pronounced with the anodyne policies of New Labour, where third-way politics embraced and shadowed the tenets of neoliberalism.

In the mid-1990s I worked for the British Council and relocated to Central Eastern Europe, where I was privileged to witness the optimism and hope in these countries during a period of transition from communism to liberal democracy. At the start of the twenty-first century, I returned to Britain to start a PhD in social policy and ended up establishing and working for a campaign alliance of Gypsies and Travellers lobbying for more Traveller sites. The campaign offered the warmth and fraternity that

I had once found in local Labour politics and through such grassroots action I was inspired to see how even the most disadvantaged communities could mobilize and seek transformative change, something I felt Labour could no longer achieve (Ryder, 2017). Although less enthused by Labour, I remained a member and in my Gypsy and Traveller advocacy work campaigned closely with Labour figures such as the trade unionist Rodney Bickerstaffe, who became a close mentor.

My work with Gypsies and Travellers also gave me insights into something more sinister: the politics of demagoguery. From 2003 the tabloid press ran a series of articles critical of Gypsy and Traveller unauthorized developments (sites without planning permission). One of the most notable features of the media campaign was the series of articles *The Sun* newspaper published with the headline 'Stamp on the Camps'. In 2005 Michael Howard, the leader of the Conservative Party, ran a highly populist electoral campaign which sought to surf the media demonization of Gypsies and Travellers and migrants. The Conservatives were advised in their campaign by Lynton Crosby, an Australian electoral strategist with a reputation for running divisive and controversial campaigns. Howard claimed that Gypsies and Travellers were benefitting from the Human Rights Act and a 'rights culture', which unfairly privileged a minority above the majority and offended the British sense of 'fair play' (Richardson and Ryder, 2012). The Gypsy and Traveller community was highly traumatized by the campaigning, which caused an increase in bullying of this community in schools, leading the Commission for Racial Equality to raise concerns. This incident seemed to present a turning point, showing that a mainstream party could play upon national identity and insecurity in a racialized context in order to mobilize support. Such emotive and manipulative campaigning has only become more evident in British politics. The development of this style of politics has held a deep fascination for me, having witnessed directly one of its first formulations. Brexit thus revived concerns and emotions I first felt in 2005.

In 2010 I returned to Hungary to start an academic career. In this work I sought to fuse my skills and experience in activism with policy formulation and academic knowledge production, becoming a critical researcher interested in participatory research and co-production with Roma communities. It was from Hungary that I witnessed the Brexit phenomenon unfold and concluded traits that I had witnessed in 2005 during the 'Stamp on the Camps' saga were evidently at work on a much greater scale. In the wake of the referendum, both major political parties seemed to be in a state of flux and change, with the Conservatives adopting positions that appeared greatly at odds with its 'one nation' traditions. Likewise, Labour under the leadership of Jeremy Corbyn seemed to be reinventing itself. While I have welcomed its embrace of grassroots activism and bolder policy outlines than those offered by New Labour, the party's ambiguous stance on the EU has been a cause of concern. Furthermore, I have found myself alienated by the excessive factionalism and utilization of binary codes within Labour.

In Hungary, where I have lived since 2010, the optimism of post-communist transition society has evaporated. Prime Minister Orbán has declared that Hungary is no longer a liberal democracy; migrants, especially Muslims, and civil society are perceived as presenting a risk and threat to Hungarian society (Pap, 2017). My world, like that of many others, seems to have been turned upside down through nationalist populism, irrationalism and xenophobia. I set out in part on the exercise of writing this book to try and make some sense of these events but also to see if there was a means by which alternative routes to change could be found which avoid the dangers of overt intolerance and division.

As already noted, I seek to view and interpret the events around Brexit through the lens of critical thinking. Critical thinking asserts that within politics, economics and culture oppressive forces dominate, primarily through the construction of a false consciousness. As a critical thinker, I see modern societies as being prone to chaos and dislocation through economic crisis, which is inherent to modern society and even more apparent in the twenty-first century. I believe that these contradictions and vulnerabilities have been expressed both culturally and politically in Brexit. Thus, part of the appeal of studying this subject is that it serves as a case study of a society in deep crisis. In the ensuing chaos and change that is and will be unleashed on Britain, the motivations, stratagems and manoeuvrings of the political class, especially as expressed in speech acts which articulate cultural and political perceptions and aspirations, are scrutinized and questioned in the book. I return to my self-concept in the final chapter.

Securitization and speech acts

An important point of discussion throughout this book are frames, theoretical constructs related to the conceptualization of situation types and their expression in language. Frames are shaped by culture, history and experience, and are essential in interpretation and the mobilization of resistance and/or action (Chilton, 2004). Shared frames are essential in bonding and networking large groups of people into political and social movements. Important frames in the Brexit debate have been shaped by securitization and desecuritization. Originally, securitization was a term employed in international relations to describe the framing and strategization of tensions between countries but has in recent years it been applied to domestic politics. Securitization describes how power elites are able to use speech acts to play upon or construct perceptions of insecurity and fear and thus mobilize and frame thought and action to the level of priority, an 'emergency politics' that sets aside the normal process of decision-making (Waever, 1995). The framing of a political problem in terms of extraordinary measures takes the politics of security beyond the boundaries of normal politics. Securitization is thus a unique phenomenon where, through speech acts, we construct an issue as a matter of security, survival and emergency. Late modernity seems to be punctuated by a series of crises and moments of epochal change, of which Brexit is one manifestation (Krzyżanowski, 2019). In Chapter 1, I discuss in more depth the nature of the crisis, but suffice to say the debates and polemic around change have been highly securitized, often centred on a discursive and polarizing 'us and them' frame.

In observing the trajectory of the course of events leading to the Brexit result, it is evident that steering speech acts that played upon notions and perceptions of insecurity were deployed by political figures and the media. After Article 50 was triggered, a two-year process of negotiation with the European Commission commenced and a new phase in the Brexit journey started. In that phase the arguments made by those wanting to leave the EU were rearticulated and expanded upon, but there was also a counter-discourse by forces opposed to Britain's exit or a hard Brexit. Did these counter-Brexit arguments resonate with the public? Were they able to parry the pro-Brexit camp's arguments, which critics claimed played upon identity and xenophobia? The answers to these questions provide important insights as to the cultural and social direction of Britain in the twenty-first century and are a central point of discussion in the book.

Ceyhan and Tsoukala (2002) note how the rhetorical framing of securitization centres on the socio-economic axis, where, for example, migration is referred to as the cause of unemployment, the rise of the informal economy and crisis of the welfare state. Secondly, the security factor is linked to the loss of control narrative associated with the issue of sovereignty, borders and both internal and external security. A third factor is linked to identity, where migrants are seen as a threat to national identity and demographic equilibrium. Finally, there is the political axis, where anti-immigrant, racist and xenophobic discourses are articulated. These dimensions have clearly been evident in the Brexit debate, where an 'us and them' lens has been utilized in the identification of an existential threat and is described in the book as 'Brexit nationalism'. The function and role of collective anxieties are defined in more detail in Chapter 1 and are a running thread of discussion throughout.

Foucault (2003) describes processes like securitization and the politics of risk as legitimizing technologies of hegemonic power. Balzacq (2005) contends that the speech act within securitization is a sustained strategic practice aimed at convincing a target audience to accept a frame (outlook), based on what it knows about the world. Thus, invoking Foucault's and Balzacq's notions of hegemonic power, it could be argued we have witnessed in the Brexit debate the subtle manipulation of public thought on identity and nationhood to further an agenda premised on achieving a new neoliberal order and the consolidation of power by existing economic, cultural and political elites. This book seeks to test the validity of such a hypothesis.

Jürgen Habermas (1989) defined the public sphere as a public network that shapes opinion and is distinct from the private sphere (family). Habermas argued that under advanced capitalism the discursive power of the public sphere had been emasculated through its colonization by the state and market, where standardized mass media has erased the capacity for critical thought and manipulated it to create a notion of consensus geared to the interests of elites. Thus, the populace is swayed by the communicative techniques of advertising and marketing, creating unthinking citizens. The media has been a powerful force in the politics of securitization and anxiety.

In contrast to securitization there is the 'fear of fear', in which fear can work as a counter-practice against processes of securitization. It can be viewed as a core part of liberal theory and practice that counters and thwarts a shift towards 'security' in its more extreme manifestations (Williams, 2011). A counter-public sphere capable of being autonomous offers hope for a counter-hegemonic discourse. Within the counter-public sphere, civil society and small, independent and alternative news sources are prominent social actors in desecuritization. This book has a critical dimension by seeking to ascertain the reluctance of sections of the public to accept securitized notions of Brexit because of perceived negative consequences for other values (desecuritization) or the development of critical consciousness – the ability to dissect and reject steering discourse centred on elite interests. Thus, the book seeks to identify where challenges to Brexit have emerged from within mainstream institutions but also from the counter-public sphere.

Discourse analysis

In Greco-Roman society the art of rhetoric and the power of speech were integral to politics, where orators were trained in persuasion, deception and distortion. The study of rhetoric may have declined but in an age of spin and 24/7 media, the practice of rhetoric is no less important or scientific. This book focuses on elite speech acts through discourse analysis, identifying points of convergence between political discourse and change, through a process of social production. Speech acts and discourse are context dependent and are both socially constituted and socially constitutive (Reisigl and Wodak, 2009). Language is thus a form of social action that generates knowledge, identities and social relations. The label 'discourse analysis' incorporates a wide range of approaches. Some have a narrow focus on language (micro-analysis), while discourse-theoretical approaches/critical discourse analysis adopt a more macro approach (Wiesner et al, 2017), as in this study. The approach adopted in this book towards discourse analysis is influenced by Foucault and his critical conception of hegemonic power, believing that 'power is everywhere' and embodied in discourse, knowledge and 'regimes of truth'. Hegemonic power is an instrument of subjugation. Even unsuspicious norms, such as autonomy, liberty or solidarity, can become impositions. Foucauldian approaches to discourse analysis entail a study of the practices and material and symbolic realities that enable a certain discourse – discourse meaning the structured and institutionalized way of speaking in which the rules of creation can be brought to light and can be the object of social analysis (Foucault, 2002). Foucauldian discourse analysis as guided by critical theory not only compares claims with (symbolic and material) reality but also reveals the (symbolic and material) obstacles that prevent these claims from becoming reality; in other words, a more sociological approach to discourses is adopted (Herzog, 2016).

Use is also made of critical discourse analysis (CDA). Thus, through consideration of speech acts and the employment of an interdisciplinary approach, the book attempts to describe the social processes and structures that give rise to the production of a speech act and to uncover the ideological assumptions that are hidden in our words. CDA helps to increase consciousness of how language contributes to domination and is therefore a step towards emancipation (Fairclough, 1989). CDA has the ability to uncover micro-shifts in language that signal larger critical shifts and so is a useful tool in revealing the discursive nature of social and cultural change, which is a central interest of the book, viewing Brexit as a form of paradigm shift. Much of the discussion centres on quotes from elite actors collected in the discourse plane (societal location) of politics and the media, but it is not interested in linguistic units per se, as might be the case with more traditional linguistic discourse analysis, but rather a multidimensional and multi-method approach (Wodak and Meyer, 2001). The form of CDA adopted is centred on argumentation, seeking to discover and understand the arguments (topoi) that framed Brexit and the means by which political actors try to justify and legitimize their opposition to opponents.

A critical form of discourse analysis seeks to tie speech to context and can, through a discourse historical approach, integrate historical background information into the interpretation of speech acts. The discourse historical approach triangulates historical and intertextual sources and the background of the social and political fields related to the macro and mezzo contextualization and micro analysis of text/speech, which can reveal the cumulative process of discursive change over time (Wodak, 2018). In other words, it attempts to integrate knowledge about historical sources and the background of the social and political fields in which discursive 'events' are embedded. Within the book, contextual notes are provided on the historical development of identity and politics in Britain. The book can also be said to make use of 'public discourse', an interpretative lens that enables the researcher to evaluate the instrumentality, effectiveness and significance of rhetoric. A key focus of such an approach is the analysis of controversy rather than either the rhetor or the text (Zarefsky, 2011). Thus, in the tradition of public discourse the book presents a series of key moments in the Brexit process, often marked by dissension and sharp polarization between political actors. Topoi, the key and recurrent lines and means of argument, are highlighted throughout and their historic origins and logic are discussed in relation to Brexit (Table I.1).

Language makes it possible to communicate about things past and future, possible and impossible, permissible and impermissible. Language in a political context often relies on key strategies centred on coercion, legitimization and delegitimization, and representation and misrepresentation (Chilton, 2004). Coercion entails speech acts backed by sanctions, warnings and threats and depends on the status and resources of the speaker in terms of the impact they have. Legitimization is closely linked to coercion, it establishes the right to be obeyed and heeded and involves arguments about voters' wants, ideological principles, charismatic leadership projection, boasting about performance and positive self-presentation. Delegitimization is centred on disparagement and involves speech acts of blaming, accusing and insulting. Representation and misrepresentation involve the control of information, which is in effect a matter of discourse control and can involve emphasis, omission, evasion and lying. These strategies are prominent in the story of Brexit and the speech acts it generated.

There are no rigid guidelines as to how to conduct discourse analysis and, in fact, in the literature there is a paucity of detailed instruction. To help the reader understand my methodology, Table I.2, coupled with Table I.1 outlines my approach.

Table I.1: Argumentative topoi

Common topics in arguments and strategies
i. Usefulness
ii. Uselessness, disadvantage
iii. Definition, name-interpretation
iv. Danger and threat
v. Humanitarianism
vi. Justice (equal rights/social justice)
vii. Responsibility (particular group to blame so they must find a solution)
viii. Burdening (too much)
ix. Finances (negative cost)
x. Reality
xi. Numbers (if numbers prove a topos specific action needed)
xii. Law and rightness
xiii. History (past teaches us certain actions have certain consequences)
xiv. Culture (because a culture is the way it is, problems arise)
xv. Abuse

Sources: Wodak and Meyer (2001) and Wodak (2018)

Topoi in the national corpus
i. National uniqueness
ii. Definition of the national role
iii. Modernization
iv. The EU as a national necessity

Topoi in the European corpus
i. Diversity in Europe
ii. European history and heritage
iii. European values
iv. European unity
v. Europe of various speeds
vi. Core and periphery
vii. European and national identity
viii. Europe as a future orientation
ix. Modernization (often taken to mean technocracy and the single market)
x. National mission in the EU
xi. Joining the EU at any cost
xii. Preferential treatment

Source: Zagar (2010)

In addition, we could add the topoi of:

xiii. Right Euroscepticism and fear of federalism and or migration
xiv. Hyperglobalism and belief economies should be set free from the EU
xv. Left Euroscepticism and fear of neoliberalism

Topoi of democracy
i. Will of the people (direct democracy)
ii. Orwellian manipulation of the people, reminiscent of the novel *1984*
iii. Representative democracy and judgement
iv. Elitist and hierarchical manipulation of the people

Topoi of resources
i. Redistribution/social justice
ii. Neoliberalism rewarding the wealth creators
iii. The topic of free trade and protectionism can invoke arguments i and ii as set out above

Table I.2: Discourse analysis tools, language focus and rhetorical strategies

Ad hominem	rebutting an argument by attacking the character, motive or other attribute of the person rather than the argument itself
Antithesis	the direct opposite of someone or something
Connotation	an idea or feeling that a word invokes for a person, in addition to its literal meaning
Contextualization	putting language items into a meaningful and real context, rather than being treated as isolated items of language
Critical discourse analysis	social processes and structures give rise to the production of a speech act (see discussion in main text)
Delegitimization	involves negative presentation involving acts of blaming, scape-goating, marginalizing, othering, attacking the moral character of some individual or group, attacking the rationality and sanity of the other; the extreme is to deny the humanness of the other
Doing and not just saying	ask not just what the speaker is saying, but what he or she is trying to do, keeping in mind that he or she may be trying to do more than one thing (Gee, 2011)
Discourse historical approach	intertextual relations of a text to history and society
Ethos	credibility of the author/speaker
Expression structures	volume, intonation, stress, pitch, silences, accents, laughing and prosody (patterns of stress and intonation in a language) also includes kinetic signals (hand movements, nods of the head, facial expressions, shift in gaze etc)
Exigency	a rhetorical call to action that compels the speaker to speak out
Face work	the ways in which we construct and preserve our self-images, or the image of someone else (Gee, 2011)
Fill in	what was said and the context in which it was said, what needs to be filled in to achieve clarity (Gee, 2011)
Genre	a wide and diverse set of genres can be found in political discourse: policy papers, leader's speech, ministerial speeches, government press releases or press conferences, parliamentary discourse (grand style of oratory), party manifestos, electoral speeches, informal interviews, speaking directly to the audience and low rhetoric (matter of fact), i.e. there is no alternative
Irony	to convey to the audience an incongruity that is often used as a tool of humour to deprecate or ridicule
Insinuation	innuendo/to infer; when the facts, or the way the facts are presented, are challenged, the originator of the discourse can readily deny any culpability
Interdiscursivity	relationship between discourses/genres

(continued)

Table I.2: Discourse analysis tools, language focus and rhetorical strategies (continued)

Kairos	timeliness of an action
Legitimation	authority a person has through tradition, law, custom, moral values, status and/or expertise or being a role model
Logos	the link between an argument and evidence; presentation of logical or quasi-logical arguments
Manichaean dichotomies	othering, delegitimization and polarization for example through pronouns 'we' versus 'them', an adversarial group or entity is construed as a threat to interests of the home group to generate fear (Cap, 2017)
Metaphors and idioms	contain archetypes with expressive and emotive power and have cultural resonance; can simplify complex points
Modals	the modal verb 'will' implies a strong sense of certainty and authority; 'Must' indicates urgency
Orientation to difference	can encompass the following strategies: *acknowledgement* of difference and openness towards it; *accentuation* of difference and polemic against it; attempt to go beyond difference, which can entail an explicit choice to *set aside difference* and focus on what is held in common, a rhetorical representation of a consensus *suppressing difference*
Pathos	appeals an author/speaker makes to the emotions of an audience, evoking or amplifying emotions among the public; can include blame and praise
Rationalization	goal orientation and arguing doing things in a certain way is appropriate to certain types of people
Reifying	creating stereotypes
Repetition	to make an idea clearer and more memorable
Syntax	grammatical structure of sentences; for example, passive forms lead to a focus on the action/result rather than the responsible agent

I indicate references to the tables with the highlighting of the aforementioned terms throughout the course of the book's discussion, defining and expanding upon some of those terms – in particular the topoi. This book is centred on a series of vignettes of language, highlighting important moments in the Brexit process. These linguistic vignettes are threaded together with broader contextual, cultural, historical, social and political discussion. At this point, I should inject an element of caution. Throughout the book, I seek to highlight shifts or the state of public opinion, but while speech acts can be important in shaping opinion it is not always a case of mechanical causality (Fairclough, 2003).

Analysis of the rhetoric around Brexit gives insights into the dynamics of the Brexit negotiations. As in all negotiations, language is of paramount importance in articulating aims and aspirations but also in critiquing the demands and offers of one's negotiating opponents. David Davis, a minister responsible for leading Brexit negotiations who later resigned, apparently compared the negotiations to a game of chess and even took some interest in wargaming activities (the simulation of conflicts to devise strategies) to inform his approach to Brexit (Shipman, 2017). Care is needed in taking rhetoric around the negotiations at face value; as is often the case in negotiation, excessive and exaggerated demands or threats (hard bargaining and bluff) are part of the stratagems to reach a compromise through concessions. The Brexit negotiations were the most important to take place for Britain in the postwar period – probably even more important than those leading to entry to the EU in 1973, as nearly five decades later Britain's economy and direction was so entwined with that of the rest of Europe that departure was clearly going to be more chaotic and radical than entry. With such high stakes, namely the economic wellbeing of Britain, its identity and relationship with the world, political reputations and perhaps even the future direction of the European Project, it was not surprising that emotions and tempers were strained in the negotiation process.

By following the trajectory, outcome and rhetoric of those negotiations, this book enables the reader to decide whether the British government pursued an astute and informed negotiating strategy. The ingredients for successful negotiations are said to be trust, positivity and strong relationships between the negotiating parties, preparation, research and securing of sound information to inform negotiating positions. In contrast, an overt reliance on hard bargaining, threat and accusations and insults are said to destabilize the preconditions for a successful outcome (Mnookin et al, 1996). This book should help the reader to decide within which category the Brexit negotiators are located.

Outline of the book

I aim to give a wide historical, sociological and political overview by focusing on Europhiles and Eurosceptics, as well as describing the Brexit referendum itself and the socio-economic and cultural fall-out, exploring the wider significance of these events, both in Europe and globally.

Chapter 1 gives an overview of nationalism, identity and the impact of the financial crisis, providing the contextual background to the discursive contestation centred on Brexit, and offering insights into a series of deep socio-economic, spatial and demographic cleavages that it revealed. Chapter 2 details the events that led to the referendum being held and follows the course of events and debate during the referendum and first stage of negotiations with the EU, with particular reference to how speech acts were securitized and desecuritized in what became known as 'project fear' and 'hate'. Chapter 3 reflects upon what became of 'one nation' and pro-EU conservatism. The chapter considers whether the Conservative Party is transforming itself into a new populist movement. Chapter 4 discusses the rationale for Labour's policy of 'constructive ambiguity' and the direction of Labour's stance towards Brexit under the leadership of Jeremy Corbyn. Chapter 5 considers how in response to Brexit a more civic-minded and inclusive form of nationalism is being developed in Scotland and Wales, in contrast to England where a resurgent English nationalism has aligned itself with nativism. Chapter 6 explores how representatives of the EU deployed the politics and rhetoric of 'fear of fear' to depict Brexit as an assault on social protections and economic stability premised on irrational and xenophobic sentiments. The chapter discusses how Brexit presents important dilemmas for the EU as to whether to maintain the status quo or embrace radical reform. Chapter 7 details the final stages of Brexit under the premiership of Boris Johnson and the impact upon the fortunes of the British political class, bringing together the trajectories of change chronicled in the preceding chapters. Chapter 8 argues that the European Project as an effective counterfoil to nationalist populism can only emerge if the vision of European supranationalism and cosmopolitanism is rekindled through the fusion of deliberative and participatory forms of democracy with representative democracy and a Europe-wide 'new deal' to stimulate growth and wealth redistribution.

1

Brexit Nationalism: History, Crisis and Identity

The Introduction set out the aim of this book to follow the trajectory of the Brexit process and the transformation of British politics by threading together speech acts centred on key moments and controversies in the Brexit process. This chapter sets out to provide some of the historical, social and cultural context for these events by exploring Britain's relationship with Europe and its place in the world, the impact of the financial crisis and how anxiety has come to the fore of political debate as a shaper of policy and identity. A large section of the chapter is concerned with historical details; this is important to enable the reader to understand the Brexit phenomenon, for where we are depends on where we have been (path dependency) and facilitates a discourse historical approach to the analysis of speech acts that follows. In describing historical, political and cultural developments, the chapter highlights a series of topoi and rhetorical devices outlined in Table I.1, which help describe the positions of argument taken up by a range of actors in different milieux.

British exceptionalism

Britain is frequently referred to as the 'awkward' member of the European Union (EU). For much of the postwar period, Britain's relationship with Europe has been ambivalent, indecisive or suspicious of the EU's intentions (George, 1998), a state of affairs that has great relevance to the present Brexit debate.

Winston Churchill, former prime minister and wartime leader, is regarded as a central force in the emergence of supranational European politics, having been instrumental in the formation of the Council of Europe (CoE) and the EU. In 1946 Churchill made his famous reference to building a 'United States of Europe', which might avert a future war through forms of economic integration but also greater political cooperation (topos of European unity). Yet Churchill and the Conservatives chose to distance themselves from the emerging European community that was initially based on the Schuman Plan to form the European Coal and Steel Community (ECSC). The ECSC was established in 1950 to centralize and regulate the coal and steel industries in Belgium, France, West Germany, Italy, Luxembourg and the Netherlands. The Attlee Labour government and then the Churchill government were perceived as being awkward and obstructive in the newly established CoE, leading politicians on the Continent to perceive that little headway could be made through the CoE, in turn giving them impetus to develop the ECSC (Crowson, 2011). The countries participating in the ECSC signed the Treaty of Rome in 1957, which established the European Economic Community (EEC). Its primary aim was to create a common market among its members through the elimination of most trade barriers and the establishment of a common external trade policy. Having excluded itself from the Treaty of Rome, in 1959 Britain set up the European Free Trade Association (EFTA), an intergovernmental entity consisting of Denmark, Norway, Sweden, Austria, Portugal and Switzerland. But EFTA lacked the economic and political muscle of the ECSC and EEC.

So Britain stood aloof from the ECSC and EEC. For Conservatives like Churchill, it was imperative that Britain should retain and continue to lead its empire. This sense of exceptionalism and being apart from Europe was also perhaps a product of Britain's pride at having stood alone against fascism at the start of the Second World War, eventually triumphing. The French economist and political advisor Jean Monnet, who was an architect of the Schuman plan and is considered a founding father of the EU, stated: 'I never understood why the British did not join. I came to the conclusion that it must have been because it was the price of victory – the illusion that you could maintain what you had, without change' (quoted in Ellison, 2012). There was also a perception that Britain's central ally and focus of foreign policy should be the United States, as reflected in what Churchill termed the 'Special Relationship' where Britain and the United States, as in the war, sought a common cause in promoting stability and liberal democratic values in the world. Britain's initial postwar policy has been described as the 'three circles' doctrine – a perception that the empire/commonwealth, Western Europe and the United States overlapped, with Britain being the common denominator and thus a world power. Britain's postwar deportment in the field of foreign policy can also be said to reflect the topos of national uniqueness, a belief that Britain was culturally set apart from Europe and had a special mediatory role to play in international affairs. Britain's distancing from European entities can also be characterized as attributable to the classical Anglo-Saxon notion of political order that emphasizes parliamentary democracy and external sovereignty; consequently, in this view there was no space for strong European transnational alignments (Cap, 2017).

The Suez Crisis was a turning point. Britain, under pressure from its key ally the United States, withdrew its military force from Egypt. This force had been sent there by Prime Minister Anthony Eden (1955–57) to reclaim the Suez Canal, which Gamal Abdel Nasser, the president of Egypt, had nationalized. The humiliated and disgraced Eden was replaced by Harold Macmillan (1957–63), but it was evident that Britain's pre-eminent place in the world had been greatly diminished. Britain now also realized that its dream of retaining an empire was forlorn, and in a reverse of the scramble for empire there was a rapid retreat from the colonies. In a landmark speech, entitled 'Winds of Change', addressed to the South African parliament in 1960, Macmillan unveiled Britain's commitment to decolonialization and an acknowledgement of national consciousness within the subject nations and their desire for independence. There was also a realization that the colonies were now liabilities due to the material and human cost of trying to maintain imperial power in the face of insurmountable opposition.

In a postcolonial and imperial age, what was to be Britain's place in the world? President Kennedy persuaded Macmillan to apply for membership of the EEC. Realizing the potential of this new grouping, the United States hoped its key ally, Britain, might be able to exert influence from within (Morphet, 2017). Political consensus – at least on the front benches of the main parties – for entry into the EEC grew. The President of France General Charles de Gaulle twice vetoed British applications (that in 1961 made by Macmillan and in 1967 by Wilson), fearing that Britain's special relationship with the United States might create a rift in the EEC. This caused some outrage but also seemed to confirm Britain's diminished place in the world. Later, France relented under President Pompidou and acquiesced to Britain's eventual accession. This initial rejection and coming late 'to the party' created resentment, as some in Britain felt they were playing second fiddle to the Franco-German axis, which was perceived to privilege these countries' interests. According to Tilford (2017a): 'In short, the British have never been able to wholeheartedly support a European project that they were not the leaders of. And it is this, as much as an aversion to sharing sovereignty, that explains the depth of antipathy to the EU.'

Conservative Prime Minister Edward Heath (1970–74) was motivated to take Britain into the EEC in 1973 in part because, as with many

'One Nation' Conservatives who had fought in the Second World War, he felt that the European Project could avert another war (Heath, 1998). Heath also believed that the business-focused EEC would offer a remedy to Britain's now weak and underperforming economy, another painful indicator of Britain's loss of place in the world (topos of Europe as future orientation/modernization/national necessity). Labour rejected the Schuman plan in 1950 because it feared that this might compromise nationalized control of steel and coal, challenging Heath on Britain's terms of entry to the EEC, which had been secured through a parliamentary mandate rather than a popular vote. Some Labour figures such as Tony Benn also deemed the EEC to be primarily a transnational capitalist project that could interfere with Britain's next phase of socialist transformation (topos of left Euroscepticism). In contrast, the social democratic and gradualist strands of the party were enthusiasts for the EEC. To maintain a semblance of unity, the Labour leader Harold Wilson promised a referendum if elected in the 1974 election and his minority government duly staged such a vote in 1975, where 67 per cent decided to remain. This overwhelming support may have reflected the fact that both of the two main party leaders, Heath and Wilson, were in agreement on Britain remaining but also the fact the media was overwhelmingly in support of this step. Yet, by staging the referendum, Britain revealed to its new European partners that it could be troublesome, a trend that repeated itself in the following decades.

During the first phase of her premiership, Margaret Thatcher (1979–90) was an enthusiastic supporter of the EEC, especially with its move to create a single market, which she believed would bolster free trade and the more laissez-faire economic approaches at the heart of her political philosophy (topos of modernization centred on the single market). But at the same time Thatcher revived a strong sense of nationalism and strongly disparaged what she labelled 'utopianism' in the possibility of the EU developing too far in the social dimension (Daddow et al, 2019). This resurgent nationalism was articulated in the famous Bruges speech in 1988, where Thatcher took exception to the idea of a European super-state, which she feared would emerge through growing talk and support for federalism and due to her realization that a single currency could presage this development (topos of right Euroscepticism and fear of federalism). However, under its reformist leader Neil Kinnock (1983–92) and through a topos of modernization, Labour embraced the European Project more enthusiastically, especially with the influence of European Commission President Jacques Delors, a socialist who actively promoted the social dimension through measures to protect workers' rights (Westlake, 2017). This not only drew the ire of Thatcher, who prided herself on having tamed the trade unions, but also that of the tabloid press: in response to the proposals promoted by Delors in 1990, The Sun newspaper carried the headline 'Up Yours Delors' (a rhyming play on words reflecting the coarse humour of the British press). Another feature of Britain's relationship with Europe was becoming more apparent: incessant demonization of European politics and Brussels in the print media.

Thatcher's hostility to Europe was one of the factors that prompted a leadership challenge by Michael Heseltine. Although the incumbent won, this left her mortally wounded and led ultimately to her resignation. Thatcher's successor, John Major (1990–97), was more pro-Europe but still secured opt-outs on the social chapter (EU protocol on social policy) and the single currency. Nonetheless, under Major the Conservative Party was bitterly divided over Europe. Conservative MPs, many of them supporters of Thatcher, were deeply concerned by the Maastricht Treaty of 1992, which heralded the political, monetary and economic union of what was now to be termed the European Union. Convergence criteria were also set through the treaty to enable economic and monetary union and the people of Europe became citizens of this new entity. For Eurosceptics, this meant a fundamental abdication of British sovereignty. So, Major faced a series of large rebellions from within his own party, which sapped his authority. In fact, the prime minister and his government's standing had been greatly compromised at an early stage, in September 1992, on what became known as Black Wednesday, when Britain was forced to withdraw the pound sterling from the European Exchange Rate Mechanism (a foundational step towards economic and monetary union) because of the weakness of that currency. This was perceived as a humiliating sign of Britain's weakness.

Divisions over Europe were a principle factor in the Conservatives' disastrous electoral performance in 1997. The New Labour government under Tony Blair (1997–2007) was more pro-Europe, joined the social chapter and proved to be a more conciliatory partner. However, Labour decided to remain outside the eurozone, thus consolidating the stance of the previous administration, which set limits on its integrationism and held that complete uniformity was not desirable (topos of a Europe of varying speeds). Conservative opposition leaders William Hague, Iain Duncan Smith and Michael Howard established a much more Eurosceptic position, defining themselves in contrast to Labour's perceived Europhilia but also reflecting the fact that the Thatcherite strand of thought in the party was again in the ascendancy. Hague (2001) had promised to save the pound by opposing Britain's entry into the euro and declared 'I will give you your country back', portending that if Labour secured a second term Britain 'would become a foreign land'. Howard accused the Labour government of planning to surrender Britain's borders to Brussels and stated that 'a small and crowded island' like Britain could not shoulder such a disproportionate burden (Bale, 2016).

Another prompt for a more Eurosceptic stance within the Conservative Party was the fact that Eurosceptic parties such as the UK Referendum Party and then the UK Independence Party (UKIP) seemed to be garnering more support, syphoning much of it from the Conservatives. Three successive election defeats, though, compelled the Conservatives to opt for an ostensibly more 'one nation' Conservativism in the form of David Cameron, prime minister from 2010 until his resignation in the aftermath of the Brexit vote in 2016. Successive rebellions on the subject of the EU arose among an increasingly militant and growing cabal of Eurosceptic Conservative MPs. In tandem, there was a dramatic rise in support for UKIP. These factors compelled Cameron to promise a referendum on Britain's membership of the EU if he won the 2015 election. Some observers feel that in this gesture he had taken note of Harold Wilson's stratagem of managing to bring a semblance of unity to his party by promising a referendum on Europe (Watt, 2012). Cameron achieved this objective and it was probably an important factor in securing, in 2015, the first Conservative majority government in twenty-three years. But, as will be discussed in Chapter 2, this move ultimately destroyed Cameron's premiership and, some would say, his political reputation too. Support for the EU in British politics was also tempered by the election of Jeremy Corbyn to the leadership of the Labour Party, a radical left Eurosceptic who by 2016 claimed to have become a reformist remainer. After the referendum, Corbyn at times appeared to argue that leaving the EU could be part of a transformative agenda (Asthana, 2017). A section of Corbyn supporters known as Lexiteers actively countenanced such a view in the promulgation of a topos of left Euroscepticism and fear of neoliberalism.

In this section, we have observed a series of competing topoi centred on national uniqueness, modernization, a two-speed Europe and left and right Euroscepticism being played out over the postwar period. A traditionalist section of the radical left sees the EU as being market driven, with the potential to interfere in and stall socialist policies in Britain. The radical right sees the EU as a federalist project under German and French hegemony, which threatens British identity and sovereignty. For the centre left, the EU is a civilizational project based on enlightenment values which promotes forms of solidarity and cosmopolitanism. The centre right deems the EU to be a pragmatic technocratic economic project which promotes economic, social and political stability and enables the freedom of movement of capital, goods, services and people (Susen, 2017).

It is evident that in the wake of the Brexit referendum the positions of the radical right and radical left came to the fore, given that different variants of Leave were the avowed official positions of the two main parties. As this brief summary of British postwar politics makes clear, Britain since the late 1940s has often been ill at ease with itself and unsure of its place in the world – and this anxiety has been reflected in various forms of Euroscepticism. For some commentators, the loss of empire and the retention of a sense of exceptionalism were driving forces in Britain's unease within the EU, which culminated in Brexit. As Boyle (2017) argues:

> The English have been unable to recognise how much of their society and its norms was constructed during the imperial period and in order to sustain empire, and have therefore been unable to mourn the empire's passing or to escape from the compulsion to recreate it. Over three centuries the needs of empire shaped England's systems of government, national and local, its Church, its schools and universities, the traditions of its armed and police forces, its youth movements, its sports, its BBC, its literature, and its cuisine. The end of empire meant the end of all this. And because England has been unable to acknowledge that loss, it has also been unable to acknowledge the end of English exceptionalism … The trauma of lost exceptionalism, the psychic legacy of empire, haunts the English to the present day, in the illusion that their country needs to find itself a global role.

Germany is another nation that had been shaped and moulded for much of the early twentieth century by a sense of exceptionalism and hegemony, with tragic consequences. However, defeat in war and challenges to a cultural identity fuelled by remorse and shame meant that Germany in the postwar period was perhaps more adept than Britain at exorcizing its demons by resorting to innovation and reinventing itself. British exceptionalism can be deemed a catalyst for Brexit nationalism (national rebirth and a chauvinistic bolstering of the perceived essences of Britishness and desire for forms of sovereignty). Britain's nostalgia for past glory, its reluctant acceptance of the EEC/EU and a propensity to challenge those bodies all set a tone that induced sentiments that were self-reinforcing and created a set of narrative frames that left little room for manoeuvre, leading to the critical juncture of Britain deciding to leave the EU (see Introduction for discussion of relevant frames).

The frames and aspirations of the British political elite have not been working in isolation; they have often reflected wider anxieties and frustrations related to diversity, security and a sense of distrust in the establishment, which are detailed in the rest of the chapter.

Crisis

Society has become increasingly marketized and can be described as a plutonomy, a society where wealth is controlled by a select few. As it is subject to economic cycles and lack of regulation, neoliberalism is prone to instability; the recession that followed the financial crisis in 2008 is central to understanding Brexit. As former Labour chancellor Alistair Darling remarked in the *Guardian* newspaper:

> The financial crisis clearly traumatised a lot of people, I think if you look at today's political situation, you can trace it back to events of 10 years ago, when people's faith in structures and authority was shaken ... A financial crisis became an economic crisis and that economic crisis became deeply political. The rhetoric was all about austerity. It's affected people's standard of living ... People felt, 'This is not my fault.' (Quoted in Treanor, 2017)

Cutbacks and austerity seemed to have reversed to unprecedented degrees what Karl Polanyi (1944) described as the 'Double Movement', that is, the push for social protection against laissez-faire marketization, which gained momentum in the first three decades of the postwar period. The postwar decades were shaped and guided by the tragedies and failures of the pre-war years. The Wall Street Crash of 1929 and the Great Depression of the 1930s clearly revealed the weakness and injustice of laissez-faire economic systems. In the case of Germany, a country grappling with tensions between the humiliation of defeat in the First World War and the strong residue of a bombastic imperialist culture of Wilhelmine Germany, anxiety trauma and crisis found expression in fascism, which in turn spurred the Second World War.

The postwar political elite reached a unique consensus by resolving to try and bring a degree of stability to the world and avert the dangers of recession and political extremism. These goals were achieved through a framework centred on forms of economic justice, which countenanced intervention and regulation based on Keynesian economic principles. A new economic approach was coupled with greater emphasis on human rights, through the establishment of the United Nations and its 1948 Universal Declaration of Human Rights. A liberal world order was nurtured to avert any resurgence of totalitarianism. This was a period when, in many Western societies, the state became a key economic driver through state ownership of major strategic industries, where full employment was a central goal and welfare states and social housing were developed through forms of progressive taxation (topos of finance – redistribution and social justice). The French economist Jean Fourastié (1979) called this time 'Les Trente Glorieuses', the glorious thirty, a gilded age from 1945 to 1975 in which living standards rose dramatically. Before the First World War the 1 per cent – the highest strata of the economic elite – received around a fifth of total income in both Britain and the United States. By 1950 that share had been cut by more than half (Saes and Zucman, 2014).

In 1973 the Organization of Arab Petroleum Exporting Countries proclaimed an oil embargo that targeted states, principally the United States, deemed to have supported Israel during the Yom Kippur War in 1967, when Israel occupied the remaining tracts of a free Palestine. This event is seen as a pivotal moment in the U-turn away from Les Trente Glorieuses, as increased oil prices led to inflation and stagnation (Jacobs, 2017). Equally, though the cost of the Vietnam War and fragmentation of the Bretton Woods agreement were principal factors in contributing to what was then the greatest economic crisis of the postwar period, which in addition to rampant inflation, witnessed very low or non-existent growth and mass unemployment. As social democracy unravelled in the 1970s, both Labour and Conservatives shifted to their respective left and right, presenting radical reform agendas.

Influenced and guided by the economic philosophy of economists such as Milton Friedman and Friedrich Hayek, the neoliberals argued that Keynesian economics and state interventionism weakened the economy by limiting the dynamism and freedom of competition in capitalism (Jones, 2012). For neoliberalism, whose policies were most clearly articulated through the politics of Reagan and Thatcher, this meant 'rolling back the state' through privatization and deregulation, and incentivizing entrepreneurialism by reducing the tax burden on the economic elite. This in turn led to a radical downsizing and marketization of the welfare system, in which the poor were vilified through a moral underclass discourse which pronounced poverty to be the result of fecklessness (Levitas, 1998). The consequence of these changes has been a reverse of the distribution of wealth away from the disadvantaged to the economic elites. Hence, the share of income and wealth as held by the top one per cent has returned to the pattern that prevailed before the First World War (Piketty, 2014).

The ascendancy of neoliberalism was bolstered through the disintegration of the communist system of the Soviet Union and a sense of triumphalism, as expressed in Francis Fukuyama's (1992) 'end of history' assertion, which contended that liberal democracy was the apotheosis of our socio-cultural evolution. This sense of triumphalism led to what Joseph Stiglitz (1998) termed market fundamentalism: an unquestioning faith in neoliberalism, which found shape in the policies of the World Bank and the International Monetary Fund. This new economic order coerced weaker and more vulnerable economies, especially in the developing world, to fall into line with the neoliberalism of the West (the Washington Consensus), which also permeated all forms of life through an audit culture and marketization of institutions and the public sphere (Brown, 2015).

In considering macro-economic, social and political developments, world-systems theory is an important tool in the analysis of the global situation. It divides the world into core countries, semi-periphery countries and periphery countries, with the core countries being hegemonic in the global economy and often the most wedded to capitalist principles (Wallerstein, 2000). Ironically, the migration of workers to Britain from countries on the semi-periphery was in part a catalyst for the Brexit debate. Brexit in itself can be seen as an attempt by core countries such as the United States and Britain to reorient their economic models in order to maintain an advantage over old and emerging competitors and thereby retain their hegemony in the core (hyperglobalism). These reorientations are prompted by the growing multipolarity of the world, where US and British dominance is in relative decline and the financial system and markets are increasingly unstable – hence, some core countries have been searching for alternative strategies. It is in the context of this troubled world order that Brexit takes place.

The financial crisis of 2008, which as noted earlier was a key stimulus for Brexit, was the product of an unregulated market. Polanyi (1944) felt that in the previous great crisis of capitalism in the 1930s and the (somewhat) resulting world war there would be a great transformation – a movement from the market towards democratic socialism. But Polanyi was also aware that in crisis economic elites were drawn to forms of authoritarianism as the best means of defending their interests. Might history be repeating itself? Do the emerging radical left movements, with their emphasis on activism and participation, such as Die Linke in Germany, Syriza in Greece, Podemos in Spain and most notably for the discussion in this book the UK Labour Party, represent the start of a great transformation and movement away from neoliberalism? Conversely, are the Conservatives and economic elite embracing populism? These are questions I return to later in the book, in particular Chapters 3, 4, 7 and 8.

Collective identity

Identity is simultaneously imposed by others and chosen by individuals as part of a sense of belonging. As Weekes (1990, 88) puts it, 'Identity is about belonging, about what you have in common with some people and what differentiates you from others. At its most basic, it gives you a sense of personal location, the stable core to your individuality. But it is also more about social relationships, your complex involvement with others.' Identity involves self-reflection, self-perception and agency. Simmel (1957) argues that individuals are not passive tools of culture but creative agents trying to work out the meaning of their lives, yet that social life is a struggle and process of tension between individuality and group identity. Bourdieu (1990b) develops this concept, positing that identity is formed through both socialization and interaction; self-experience and culture fuse and negotiate responses to events. Thus, Bourdieu's position involves acknowledging both the structures in which people negotiate their identity and the notion of autonomy and agency. The negotiation between biography and culture can produce mixed responses, but culture can be a more constant and patterned variable than personal biography. It could be argued, though, that such responses are more predictable in times of tension, when an individual might seek greater solace and protection in group identity (Woodward, 2002). Thus, an individual's response to events may be shaped by the nature of those events, but they may also find comfort and reassurance within a particular identity. As will become evident, challenge, crisis and the fluidity of identity may have played an important part in determining the decisions voters reached on Brexit.

Identity has offered a number of communities, particularly those suffering from marginalization and profound upheaval, something of an anchor and sense of certainty in a world that is in a state of flux produced by deindustrialization, globalization, mass communication and conflict (Woodward, 2000). These identities can be condensed into rigid and uniform sameness, where difference is despised (Young, 1999). Cohen (1995, 46) echoes this point: 'It has long been noticed that societies undergoing rapid, and therefore destabilizing, processes of change often generate atavistically some apparently traditional form, but impart to them meaning and implication appropriate to contemporary circumstances.'

The process related to identity formation in a time of crisis gives some explanation for what this book terms Brexit nationalism – an essentialized and reified conception of Brititish identity through nationalist populism. The postwar period witnessed large-scale migration to Britain from its former colonies, largely to fill a growing unskilled labour shortage. Britain became much less monocultural, but there was resistance and opposition to this new diversity (Rex, 1996). The Conservative politician Enoch Powell claimed in his infamous 'rivers of blood' speech in 1968 that diversity would lead to violent race conflicts, while small far-right political groupings such as the National Front emerged and later Thatcher talked about fears people had of the country being 'swamped' (orientation to difference – accentuation of difference and topos of burden). Despite these tensions, many assumed that Britain was a liberal and tolerant country at ease with its diversity.

For a significant part of the postwar period in Britain, notions of liberal democracy based on political equality and safeguards for the rights of individuals and minority groups meant the British state was prepared to promote certain forms of multiculturalism (Ashcroft and Bevir, 2018). In the early days of postwar diversity, policymakers through a topos of orientation to difference with an emphasis on suppression assumed that racism was caused by the 'strangeness' of an immigrant or ethnic group and that with the acculturation and eventual assimilation of these groups into majority culture, the problem would disappear (Anthias and Yuval-Davis, 1992). From the 1960s, it became evident that the 'melting pot' theory of assimilation did not work and was perhaps not the right way to counter racism. In 1966, then Home Secretary Roy Jenkins summarized this emerging policy change by defining integration through a topos of orientation to difference through openness to diversity. According to Jenkins, policy should entail 'not a flattening process of assimilation but equal opportunities accompanied by cultural diversity in an atmosphere of mutual tolerance' (quoted in Rex, 1996, 55). What was being espoused was a version of liberal 'tolerance' based on the assumption that there was a dominant cultural identity that incoming ethnic minorities had to adjust to, but that concessions could be made and with time and through education resentments based on ignorance could be eradicated. However, such multiculturalism was criticized for caricaturing ethnicity in a simplistic manner, presenting minority cultures as homogeneous, static and conflict free (Sarup, 1991). From the 1980s anti-racists sought to highlight and challenge institutional factors contributing to racism, but critics argued that this approach neglected gender and class issues, did not question the basic structures of the British economy and society, and could be essentialized and racist (Ladson-Billings and Gillborn, 2004).

Furthermore, the promotion of policies aimed at supporting particular minority ethnic groups and the celebration of minority cultures led to the exclusion of white communities, who perceived themselves as having an invisible culture and even as being 'cultureless'. In some cases this has triggered a white backlash – resentment and frustration from white marginalized groups jealous of the affirmative measures directed at ethnic groups (Hewitt, 2005). Some have denounced 'anti-racism' as 'political correctness', a pejorative term that implies some form of left-wing tyranny. However, it was the 9/11 terror attacks against the World Trade Center in New York and other targets that raised fears about Muslims and accentuated 'Islamophobia' (Kundnani, 2007), leading to a radical review of policy frameworks on diversity. The twenty-first century appears to have seen a return to assimilationist policies with the new agenda of 'Britishness' and 'integration' – Orientation to difference – suppressing difference (Bourne, 2007). Prevailing philosophies on diversity may thus have come full circle, as evidenced by vocal criticism of multiculturalism by political elites. A poll by Lord Ashcroft in 2016 (see Table I.2) indicated that 80 per cent of the poll sample who saw multiculturalism as a force for ill had voted Leave in the referendum.

British policies on diversity have either fallen into the trap of essentializing cultures, as collateral making white communities feel ignored, especially working-class ones living in close proximity to ethnic minorities; at the same time, they have given inadequate attention to class and cultural factors. Britain could, therefore, be accused of having failed to adequately challenge its sense of exceptionalism, nativism and chauvinism. Policy on diversity has been tokenistic or assimilatory and the underlying tensions in race relations have not only not been addressed but have been exacerbated in recent years through major socio-economic and cultural change.

Kaufman (2018) identifies immigration as the principal and most decisive factor for those voting Leave in the referendum. With the accession of Central Eastern European states into the EU, such as the Czech Republic, Poland, Hungary and Slovakia (2004) and Romania and Bulgaria (2008), migration from the EU to Britain greatly increased, rising from 15,000 in 2003 to 180,000 in 2015. Blair failed to implement EU directives to help local workers and protect them from cheap labourers coming in and was happy to satisfy the demands of industries desperate for low-skilled and low-paid labour (MacShane, 2017). In some communities, the number of EU migrants was now large and very visible to longstanding residents. In post-industrial towns already grappling with poverty and unemployment, there was a strong perception (topos of burden) that these new migrants were taking jobs or depressing wage levels and/or putting strain on local services such as schools and hospitals (Hearn, 2017).

Poverty and pressure on services in many communities was exacerbated by austerity measures introduced in the wake of the financial crisis in 2008. The coalition government of David Cameron instigated a series of massive cuts in public spending in government departments. With the exception of the National Health Service and Department for

International Development, departments faced on average real cuts of around 25 per cent over four years, and Communities and Local Government experienced a budget change of around 50 per cent (Gray and Barford, 2018). The rationale for these savage cuts was, according to then Chancellor of the Exchequer George Osborne, the risk of Britain following Greece and allowing debt to spiral out of control. However, the cases of Greece and Britain were very different, primarily because Britain was not part of the eurozone. The cuts defied conventional economic wisdom, which held that deficit spending was the most effective way to end a recession (Skidelsky, 2015).

For many communities the consequences of austerity were devastating, as services and welfare support were cut. In addition, the rhetoric of government and new means testing approaches seemed to demonize the poor and blame their predicament on idleness and fecklessness. Reduced benefits and bureaucratic flaws in the new welfare system have meant a growing number have been forced to go to foodbanks for charity donations as they have been suffering the indignity of food poverty. To soften the impact of these changes, Cameron unveiled his 'Big Society' agenda that would see radical decentralization and a new communitarianism in the form of greater levels of volunteering and community action (Smith and Jones, 2015). For some critics, the Big Society was coded language for the 'small state' and an attempt to get philanthropy to fill the growing vacuum left by a shrinking and depleted state (Ryder, 2017).

The simmering resentment of post-industrial austerity-hit communities led to large numbers being angry about migration, in contrast to the enthusiasm about diversity of the more materially fortunate liberal metropolitan elite (Seidler, 2018). In an insightful study into white working-class communities and support for the English Defence League – an anti-Muslim direct-action campaign – Winlow et al (2016) found that the decline of traditional industries and, correspondingly, working-class identities, denied communities a sense of purpose and guidance. This was a process accentuated by the drift of Labour politics into third-way neoliberalism, which sought to fill a vacuum in its radicalism by embracing liberal multiculturalism. Working-class constituencies seemed to be regarded as an embarrassment by Labour. As Winlow et al (2016) highlight, the incident where leading Labour politician Emily Thornberry posted a scornful picture of a house draped in English flags with a white van, which was construed by some as an example of the metropolitan elite sneering at white working-class men (Walsh, 2014). For some in working-class communities, none of the politicians from the mainstream parties seemed to speak for them or be interested in them. Cast adrift from traditional political frames that emphasized the need for intervention and redistribution, through forms of nativism sections of the working class identified Muslims and migrants as their proximal enemy, a resentment that ultimately reflected itself in support for Brexit.

Brexit nationalism thus presents a series of fissures, with poorer communities, especially in the North and Midlands, being more likely to have voted Leave than affluent/metropolitan areas that were more cosmopolitan in their outlook. Again reflecting class, the less educated were more likely to vote Leave than the educated and, finally, older voters were more likely to vote Leave than younger ones. Large numbers of Conservative supporters with more insular conceptions of English identity were also prominent in supporting Brexit. Lord Ashcroft, Conservative donor and pollster, conducted a survey after the referendum. The research assessed people's feelings about many of the major social issues in modern democracy. Critics of social causes that have generated forms of liberal progressivism, such as multiculturalism, feminism or environmentalism, were much more likely to vote Leave (see Table 1.1).

On the matter of class, a modicum of caution is needed. Brexiteers were able with some success to frame remainers as part of some metropolitan elite and that the North was a homogenized swathe of leavers, with large numbers of working-class people opting to leave (Drury, 2019). Danny Dorling (2016) has argued that the middle class (A, B and C1 categories) were instrumental in the Leave vote. The categories referred to are based on the National Readership Survey's system of categorizing social class. This divides the population into six categories – A, B, C1, C2, D and E – the first three taken to be 'middle class' and above, and the latter three 'working class'. The short definitions are: A – higher

Table 1.1: Public views on societal issues (how the UK voted on Thursday, 23 June 2016)

Respondents were asked if they thought of the following as being a force for good, a force for ill or a mixed blessing.
How did the people who thought the following were a force for ill vote in the referendum in 2016?   **Multiculturalism** – 81% Leave   **Feminism** – 78% Leave   **Immigration** – 80% Leave
How did the people who thought the following were a force for good vote in the referendum in 2016?   **Multiculturalism** – 71% Remain   **Feminism** – 62% Remain   **Immigration** – 79% Remain

Source: adapted from Ashcroft (2016)

managerial, administrative and professional; B – intermediate managerial, administrative and professional; C1 – supervisory, clerical and junior managerial, administrative and professional; C2 – skilled manual workers; D – semi-skilled and unskilled manual workers; E – state pensioners, casual and lowest grade workers, unemployed with state benefits only.

Some of the claims for the Brexit vote being driven by the middle class are problematized by inclusion of the C1 category of voters, which covers a range of occupations including secretaries, nurses, people working in sales, supervisors and full-time students who work part time. Such groups should not really be classified as middle class and their inclusion in such a category distorts the picture greatly if aggregated with A and B voters to make up the middle class (Butcher, 2019). It should also be noted that in the ABC1 range comprises 55 per cent of the population, as opposed to the lower classifications of C2DE at 45 per cent; the ABC1 categories are more likely to vote. The Leave vote comprised: 41 per cent of AB votes cast; 48 per cent of C1 votes; 62 per cent of C2 votes and 64 per cent of DE votes. Thus, a large majority of working-class and poor people's votes went for Leave. Also according to Butcher (2019), other figures show that 60 per cent of unemployed people's votes, 63 per cent of those by social renters and 70 per cent of those from people defined as without qualifications opted for Leave. It is therefore evident that Brexit represented a cross-class coalition. True, the middle classes and affluent have not been immune to anxiety stemming from economic crisis, hence being described by some as the 'squeezed middle', but their relatively high representation among the Leave vote suggests wider cultural factors were at play in mobilizing support for Brexit – linked to age, education and identity and a shared cross-class propensity to reactive identity. Approximately 60 per cent of the over-fifties voted Leave, in contrast to 70 per cent of 18 to 24-year-olds opting for Remain. The older voters could be described as the 'carriers of cultural legacy', generations that were socialized, indoctrinated and habituated in a particular cultural milieu. Perhaps, the imprint of British exceptionalism, empire and war was most evident among this demographic age group.

One of the most striking statistics that emerged as part of the Brexit result and which provides insights into identity and perceptions is that 72 per cent of those who see themselves as English voted Leave, compared with 43 per cent of those whose primary identity is British; perhaps uppermost for the former of these voters, Brexit was an assertion and defence of English monoculturalism. Since the late 1990s, a range of surveys has revealed that the small nation identities have gained substantial ground over Britishness, with British identifiers tending also to be Europhiles and those who define themselves as English much more likely to be Eurosceptic (Goodhart and

Kaufmann, 2016). Part of the reason for this mismatch might be attributed to critics from the left tending to believe that Britishness is an acceptable, multicultural form of patriotism, whereas Englishness is reactionary (Denham and Kenny, 2016). Conversely, it might be assumed that Englishness is perceived to be more 'white' and monocultural than notions of Britishness, but also unlike its Welsh and Scottish counterparts it lacks the civic sense of nationhood these Celtic identities possess. Yet national identity can be fluid and malleable. Thus, a challenge for progressives and the future of Britain/England is how English identity might be recast – a question I return to later in the book, in particular in Chapter 5.

Within the rubric of identity, a key dynamic in seeking explanations of Brexit has been the argument that the British, in particular the English, have a weak sense of European identity and therefore are less willing to endorse a supranational project like the EU. Since 1992, when a Eurobarometer survey asked citizens if they saw themselves more as members of their particular nationality or more as European, Britons have consistently demonstrated a weak sense of European identity (Carl et al, 2019). This might also be evidenced by the fact that 49 per cent of Leave voters said that the biggest reason for wanting to leave the EU was the principle that decisions about the UK should be taken in the UK. Likewise, fear of migrants is evidenced in the same data by the fact that 33 per cent of those who voted Leave believed it was the best chance for Britain to regain control over its borders (Salter, 2018). Evidence for the insularity of identity in Britain is revealed by data from the British Social Attitudes survey, which compares two cultural groups – libertarians who are in favour of diversity and authoritarians who support conformism. Of the authoritarian group, 72 per cent voted Leave, while only 21 per cent of libertarians did (Clery et al, 2016).

Much of the discussion so far has outlined how economic and cultural insecurity in the postwar period, especially in the 2010s, may have shaped the Brexit phenomenon and manifested itself in hostility and suspicion towards the EU and the perceived cultural and economic dangers of migration. Later in the book, primarily in Chapter 8, means of forging an inclusive national identity are discussed. Identity has been shaped by anxiety and insecurity and these forces and their entanglement with populism are considered in the next section.

Anxiety, populism and Brexit nationalism

Giddens terms the present age as one of 'reflexive modernity', where ordinary social actors feel that society has changed rapidly and that the future is uncertain. We thus live in an age unlike that of 'modernity', which was based on absolute truths and certainties (Giddens and Pierson, 1998). Koselleck (2004) contends that crisis in late modernity is entwined with the 'scope of experience' (everyday life, personal and collective memories of the past but constructed in the present) and the 'horizon of expectations' (perceptions of the future). Such is the speed and impact of change in modern times that society can face a crisis in aligning its experience of past and present. The Third Reich was the tragic consequence of such a process of dislocation and disorientation at its most extreme.

Rapid change and a sense of loss and threat are central dynamics in Brexit. Joschka Fischer (2017), German Green Party politician and former foreign minister, captured the nature of trauma of rapid change felt among the British: 'Britain appears to be undergoing not just a political and identity crisis, but also a crisis of confidence in its political and economic elites, which began with the 2008 global financial crisis.' But these problems actually go back even further than the financial crisis of 2008, as important as that was; they also have roots in a series of cultural, economic and political changes that took place in the postwar period, whose trajectory this chapter has detailed. In some respects, Britain could be said to have undergone a process of 'cultural trauma', where a collectivity feels they have been subjected to a profound trauma which leaves indelible scars upon their group consciousness, marking their memories forever and changing their future identity in fundamental and irrevocable ways (Alexander et al, 2004, 1). Such trauma does not always come from sudden change: dramatic change can happen over an extended timescale and sometimes only in the wake of that change does trauma appear (Erikson, 1995). Britain's response to its shifting place and sense of self in the postwar world reflects a collective mood of doubt, indecision and anxiety, all of which have contributed to the events of Brexit.

Rapid change and trauma have fed a discourse of what has been described as 'moral panic' and 'risk society'. Moral panics and a fear of 'folk devils' help to normalize mainstream institutions and values, where community voices (social guardians) who claim that they represent the majoritarian view based on tradition and/or established behaviour castigate those (folk devils) who are deemed to deviate from convention. Successful panics and acts of collective hysteria are able to find resonance with deeper historical, cultural and structural anxieties, which can reinforce boundary maintenance in a neurotic form of 'us' and 'them', described in this book as Manichaean dichotomies (Cohen, 2002). Although there is much overlap between concepts of risk society and moral panic in terms of the production of hysteria, risk discourse focuses on the fearful uncertainty of material hazards rather than moral regulation but is propelled by blame and polarization and accentuated by individualism (Garland, 2008). In recent times, migrants and the perceived cosmopolitanism of the EU have become powerful folk devils in the imagination of public discourse. Such hysteria and scapegoating create distractions and a sense of false consciousness or misconception with reference to the real causes of people's misfortune, thus shielding an elite who should face a crisis of legitimation as a result of their gross economic mismanagement (Young, 2011).

Hysteria and moral panics centred on migrants and the EU have been orchestrated by media editorial teams, aware that nativist news stories appeal to their readers. For such editors, fact and accuracy are secondary to sensationalism and galvanizing the emotions of readers, in a process that trivializes and devalues debate in the public sphere. This is a process Habermas (1989) described as the refeudalization of the public sphere (see the Introduction). Politicians have also orchestrated such nativist waves of emotion or surfed those created by the media. As Wodak (2015) observes, in crisis situations political elites and the media tend to reduce complex historical processes to snapshots, these construct Orwellian manipulation and trigger Manichaean dichotomies – in other words, elite-driven manipulation of the masses' actions and thoughts. Some would argue that such processes have been evident in Brexit.

Wider anxiety and trauma have been articulated through a global wave of populism where radical new frames of thought are being advanced. Centred on nativism, chauvinism and authoritarianism, such ideas manifested themselves in Britain through Brexit. In comments highly critical of the rhetoric and division generated by Brexit, former prime minister John Major remarked, 'I caution everyone to be wary of this kind of populism. It seems to be a mixture of bigotry, prejudice and intolerance. It scapegoats minorities. It is a poison in any political system – destroying civility and decency and understanding. Here in the UK we should give it short shrift, for it is not the people we are – nor the country we are' (quoted in Sculthorpe, 2017). The final discussion of the chapter assesses the validity of Major's assertion.

Despite the conservatism of those supporting Brexit on social issues such as migration and feminism and for some an insular and reactive sense of English identity, Brexit nationalism is tinged with a sense of radicalism that presents fundamental challenges to the established order and is, in this sense, part of the populist phenomenon. The key traits of populism involve a desire for a strong leader, who is charismatic, at times messianic, and willing to support issues popular with the masses despite offending the political and cultural sensibilities of elites. Populism appeals to the masses through speech acts that resonate with the emotions, including anger, of the masses. These can include forms of nativism and xenophobia. Populism is also an appeal to folkloric traditions and a desire to preserve and maintain idealized notions of national identity, which often encompass jingoism and bombast. Moreover, populism encompasses a form of paranoia where exaggeration, suspiciousness and conspiratorial fantasy are rife.

Populism is thus an outlook that lacks refinement and complexity; it is considered by some to be crude and simplistic. It voices the basest thoughts and anxieties of the masses, which in previous times might have been easily dismissed as demagoguery or opportunism. In this sense there is a repoliticization of topics intentionally or unintentionally ignored by political elites and dismissed as being atavistic or reactionary. At the centre of the populist phenomenon is a critique of the establishment and adulation of 'the people', who are portrayed as 'decent' and 'hardworking' and whose collective positions must prevail in all policy decisions – topos of will of the people. These 'good people and values' are defined in contrast to outsiders who present cultural and economic dangers – groups such as migrants and the political elite. The latter is deemed as distant, privileged and furthering their own interests at the expense of the masses but also accused of foisting alien and unwanted liberal and cosmopolitan narratives onto the people; they are basically characterized as 'selling out' their country – topos of elitism and hierarchy (Mudde and Kaltwasser, 2017).

Populism is not a new or novel phenomenon. Fascism in Europe in the 1930s reflected many of the traits of populism. Arendt (1973) felt that the economic and social dislocations of the interwar years had created the anomic anxiety of the masses that led to totalitarianism, where the masses were attracted by grand narrative solutions to the problems confronting them. The year 2016 might be comparable in some respects to 1848, in terms of the scale of the problem when nationalist and liberal uprisings took on the established political order of Europe; 2016/17 had the same quality of profound challenge but one centred on nationalist populism. Aside from the Brexit vote, there was the election of populist Donald Trump to the presidency in the United States; in Austria the far right nearly won the presidency; and there were fears that Wilders in Holland and Le Pen in France might triumph, joining the radical right's ascendancy seen in Hungary and Poland. Brexit nationalism clearly espouses many of the same characteristics of populism and was seen as a clarion call by the international populist far right. Controversial advisor to Trump, Steve Bannon, was apparently highly enthused by Brexit, as was Trump (Shipman, 2017).

Populism in the context of Britain was not an entirely new phenomenon but was generally at the fringes of political debate; however, forms of demagoguery had not been unknown in the mainstream. The charismatic leadership of Thatcher and some of her rhetoric centred on danger and a need for radical emergency measures against vested interests revealed populist traits. Successive governments, both Conservative and Labour, were aware of public anxieties on migration and appealed to those concerns through nativist speech acts. Through the media, politicians have either led, followed or surfed these nativist news cycles that demonize migrants or outsiders. This has also been articulated in ever-more draconian policies on migration, which together with governmental speech acts could be described as 'state-sponsored racism'. The consequences are that the media's disregard for truth on issues of race, identity and migration has now pervaded politics in what is termed 'post-truth politics' (Economist, 2016), where emotion trumps fact (Orwellian manipulation).

Having outlined the cultural fears and anxieties of the frames of Brexit nationalism, it is worthwhile to reflect on how that narrative views the political establishment, which in the populist tradition is another focus of ire and frustration. For much of its history, the British parliamentary system has been shaped by the concept of representative democracy as formulated by nineteenth-century political thinker Edmund Burke. Such a conception of democracy contends that those who are elected should take note of public opinion and be prepared to be influenced by voters, but ultimately they must reach decisions influenced by a range of factors including concepts of the greater good, protection of minorities and rational policy formulation (Sweeting and Copus, 2012).

The three-decade ascendancy of neoliberalism has caused tensions within representative democracy; the power of the market has weakened democracy, maximizing the influence of the market over the views of the masses and commodifying policy and politics to a degree where the pursuit and maximization of profit seems to be paramount. Thus, politics has become individualized and decontextualized and the shrinking of the state has been dictated by market logic rather than the needs of voters. Moreover, the declining need for work and populist exploitations of employment insecurities and fears threaten the elite basis of stable political systems in the twenty-first century (Higley, 2017).

As noted earlier in this chapter, austerity has done much to fragment communities but has also led to a deep distrust of the political class. People were aware that somehow the banks and elite economic interests had played a principal part in the financial crisis, but they were angered by the fact that politicians had failed to prevent such a crisis through regulation. People were further outraged that average citizens seemed to be paying the price of financial sector bailouts through cuts in services and welfare and through increased taxation. In the wake of the financial crisis, Cameron (2009), as opposition leader, exclaimed that the nation was 'all in it together'. Later, these words seemed hollow as under Cameron's premiership the rich seemed to keep their advantages and comforts. Indeed, members of the political class were themselves mired in sleaze and corruption centred on lobbying payments and fraudulent expense claims. A perception of elite contempt for democracy was reinforced during this time by the Chilcot Inquiry into Britain's decision to go to war in Iraq, which for many confirmed that Blair had taken Britain into conflict on the basis of a lie, due to false and misleading intelligence reports informing erroneous statements about weapons of mass destruction (Herring and Robinson, 2014).

A central charge against political elites is the accusation that they have used unelected bodies and technocratic institutions to depoliticize contested political issues (Mudde and Kaltwasser, 2017). This is particularly true for the EU. From its conception the EU has been an elite-driven project, with European political classes rarely entering into direct discussions with their electorates. As Habermas contends, during the decades that followed the Treaty of Rome, the liberal economic order, which was driving integration dynamics, was strong enough to create institutions from above. Habermas (2009, 80) describes the EU as an 'elite project above the heads of the people concerned and [which] continues to operate with the democratic deficits resulting from the essentially intergovernmental and bureaucratic character'. The low turnouts across Europe for elections to the European Parliament reflect the disinterest and lack of engagement between the EU and its citizens. In the European Parliament elections of 2014, average turnout in the 28 member states was 43 per cent, but in the UK it was 35 per cent, the Czech Republic saw 18 per cent and in Slovakia it was 13 per cent. This low turnout adds credibility to the following assertion of Giddens (2014, 4): 'It would be fair to say that, in spite of its many successes, the union has not put down emotional roots anywhere among its citizens.'

The bureaucratization of the EU was exacerbated by the financial crisis, which led to Germany bolstering its hegemony in Europe by placing limits and restraints on the spending and debt-making abilities of eurozone members through the 2012 European Fiscal Compact, an intergovernmental agreement that placed strict limitations on government spending and borrowing (Truger, 2013). Habermas (2012) concludes that the 2011 agreement, which led to the Fiscal Compact, implied that Merkel and Sarkozy intended to expand executive federalism or, as it can be termed, 'ordoliberalism' (use of institutional power to uphold market freedom) through threats and sanctions, thus disempowering governments. Elsewhere, Habermas (2009, 81) laments that never before 'has European politics been conducted in such a blatantly elitist and bureaucratic manner as on this occasion – the political class is sending the signal that it is the privilege of governments to decide the future destiny of Europe behind closed doors.'

To save the euro currency in this crisis there was a need for greater cohesion but decisions were made in secret, were not transparent and were often done in haste as Europe was in the midst of a financial meltdown. The German solution to the crisis, as in Britain, was austerity; cutbacks and financial restraints were placed on governments across Europe, defying the logic of deficit spending to escape recession. In this period of crisis, the EU could have demonstrated its relevance through bold and ambitious stimulatory economic projects to boost employment and training opportunities, but the conservative presidency of the European Commission under Jean-Claude Juncker seemed to offer only timid half measures (Ryder and Taba, 2018).

Forms of neoliberalism and ordoliberal bureaucracy and technocracy were factors alienating not just swathes of British voters but also voters across Europe and offered a useful target for the rhetoric of populism across Europe, which was scathing of allegedly self-interested and self-serving political elites at home and in Brussels. Populist frames were particularly provoked by the EU being perceived as an agent of migration and diversity, primarily through freedom of movement. Concerns about Europe and migration were inflamed a year before the Brexit referendum by the 2015 immigration crisis, where large numbers of refugees fled war-torn Syria, seeking refuge in Europe. Despite relatively few of these refugees coming to Britain and Britain not being in the Schengen Agreement – again reducing the chance of these refugees arriving on its shores – the crisis added to a sense of panic about migration and gave the impression to some that the EU was weak and defenceless and had no control over migration (Clegg, 2017).

Nonetheless, the EU seemed intractable on the question of reform to freedom of movement. Such recalcitrance stems in part from the fact that the free movement of people sits alongside the free movement of goods, services and capital and is thought of as a central pillar of the European Project and the topos of European unity, largely supported by business interests but also in harmony with the cosmopolitanism of some EU enthusiasts. Reluctance on the part of EU leaders to reform free movement was even evident when Cameron was seeking concessions in this area in the pre-referendum negotiations and holding up the threat of a disappointing negotiation outcome playing out badly with voters in the referendum. The EU held firm in part because of the fact that the EU's social policy dimension is limited in scope and recoils from interventionism and redistribution; migration is one of the few adjustment mechanisms to economic disparity, allowing workers in high-unemployment countries to move to member states that are booming (Crouch, 2017). Critics at both ends of the political spectrum have argued that in a time of profound crisis the EU and policymakers failed to construct meaningful responses to crisis. In the vacuum they left others to offer solutions, giving rise to Brexit nationalism and other forms of populism across Europe.

Conclusion

The economic crisis since 2008, malaise, anxiety and a crisis of identity were principal factors shaping speech acts and steering the Brexit debate. This chapter has set out the historical, social, cultural and political context for a series of topoi deployed around discourse on Britain's position in Europe. These will be referred to in the proceeding chapters, which dissect the development of Brexit. Longstanding tropes hostile to European unity meant pro-EU topoi could make limited headway; thus, indecision and uncertainty have been common features in postwar British relations with Europe.

2

The Road to Brexit

Context

This chapter follows the course of events and debate during the Brexit referendum and examines the initial negotiations and legislative attempts in Westminster to enable the Brexit process. The chapter gives an overview of the speech acts and associated stratagems that aimed to facilitate or to frustrate Brexit. It includes a number of vignettes, presenting some key or insightful moments in the campaign.

Referendums have often been tools of populist leaders who sense the value in being able to brandish a mandate based on the 'will of the people'. Roy Jenkins dismissed Harold Wilson's proposal to stage a referendum in 1975 by declaring such polls to be a 'device of dictators and demagogues' (quoted in Saunders, 2018). Referendums can be blunt instruments, where people's emotions can be manipulated and stirred through gimmicky and shallow forms of political campaigning. It could be argued this was the nature of the 2016 referendum.

In an event like a national poll or a potentially nation-defining moment such as the Brexit referendum, the emphasis is on politicians to turn the vote out, to motivate and mobilize their people to vote. In such circumstances the emotion, exaggeration and argumentation of speech acts become more pronounced than those of the everyday, and such features were clearly in evidence in the referendum campaign. Craig Oliver, Cameron's director of communications, acknowledges that allowing four months – the period from when a referendum date was set to the day of the poll itself – was insufficient to win a complex argument and educate the public, especially after decades of debate and negative reporting about the EU (Oliver, 2016). As will become evident, longstanding tropes on Britain's relations with Europe, set out in Chapter 1, were utilized and orchestrated in speech acts by political actors on both sides of the debate. Furthermore, desperate attempts to rouse core voters from each side were not conducive to a rational or coherent debate.

As noted in the previous chapter, Cameron had promised a referendum in 2013 if he were to win the next General Election. This was in order to constrain dissent in his own party on Europe and to limit the haemorrhaging of votes from the Conservatives to the UK Independence Party (UKIP). It also had the advantage of ensuring that Europe received little attention in the 2015 election, thus not fully exposing Conservative divisions on this issue. The strategy was probably a key factor helping to ensure the resulting Conservative victory of a thirty-seat parliamentary majority. But Cameron was now obliged to organize a referendum. Before that he had to try and renegotiate Britain's terms of EU membership.

Renegotiation

Initially, in the renegotiation Cameron focused on reform of freedom of movement. However, 2015 had been one of the most challenging years for the EU as it had to deal with the Syrian refugee crisis. There was a fear on the part of the EU that concessions on freedom of movement would lead to other member states, shaken by the refugee crisis, requesting the same right. Cameron did threaten to leave the EU, but his European counterparts apparently detected an element of bluff and felt he was desperate for a deal (Shipman, 2016).

Cameron eventually proposed what some considered a diluted response to migration, by calling for limitations on EU migrants claiming in work benefits. Tim Oliver, Cameron's close aide at the time, felt that at the end of the negotiations important concessions were achieved, with Britain now exempt from closer union, a target to reduce bureaucracy, protection for the pound alongside the euro and benefit restrictions reducing the pull factors for migrants (Oliver, 2016). However, the deal was attacked by the media. A *Daily Mail* editorial (2016) was scathing: 'They [Brussels] want a federalist pussycat, not a British lion. It's up to us to make sure that lion roars – because when it does, no one can beat us.' Three decades of Euroscepticism by politicians and the media had built up such a store of negativity that it was difficult for Cameron to forge a compromise in the real political world that could assuage inflated expectations and animosities.

By failing to secure a limit on actual migrant numbers, the negotiated deal did not manage to convince Boris Johnson and Michael Gove, high-profile cabinet members with influence in the media, to back Cameron and support Remain. Both were to become instrumental supporters of Leave. In his *Telegraph* column, Johnson (2016a) justified his stance partly through the topos of history and lessons to be learnt:

> There is only one way to get the change we need, and that is to vote to go, because all EU history shows that they only really listen to a population when it says No. The fundamental problem remains: that they have an ideal that we do not share. They want to create a truly federal union, *e pluribus unum*, when most British people do not.

The use of pronouns like 'they' and 'we' helps accentuate a mood of division and polarization, which Johnson's article plays upon by presenting the trope of the EU seeking to impose traditions and values which are considered alien (topos of hierarchy). Here the classic populist tactic of emphasizing boundaries between an 'in' group and 'out' group is evident. The securitizing argument that the EU posed an existential threat to British freedom and traditions was to be a prominent thread in the Leave frame. Later in the article, Johnson further develops the theme of outsider interference through the use of metaphor and by comparing the EU to an imperialist power stifling the autonomy of the 'we': 'We are seeing a slow and invisible process of legal colonisation, as the EU infiltrates just about every area of public policy.' The language in this sentence implies a level of subterfuge and lack of transparency on the part of the 'they'.

Towards the end of the article, Johnson opines: 'This is a moment for Britain to be brave, to reach out – not to hug the skirts of Nurse in Brussels, and refer all decisions to someone else.' He is gesturing towards notions of courage, implying that if the country fails to take this opportunity for 'self-rule', like a child, it will have failed a test of resolve and strength because of a sense of dependency on the authority of the EU – a rather masculinized view of the world, which dreads perceived emasculation. Such binary and polarizing narratives were to be a prominent feature of the referendum (Manichaean dichotomies).

Leave and Remain

The principal Leave groups were Vote Leave and Leave.EU. Vote Leave was headed by Dominic Cummings, often considered as a controversial and maverick character who had been forced to resign as an aide to Michael Gove while at the Department of Education. Despite his abrasive reputation, Cummings was said to be hesitant to focus overtly on migration at the start of the campaign, fearing Vote Leave might be tainted with forms of xenophobia and was thus keen to keep UKIP leader Nigel Farage at a safe distance (Shipman, 2016). Yet Cummings did not always shy away from controversy. At a Confederation of British Industry (CBI) conference in late 2015, Cummings organized two students to unfurl a banner stating that the CBI was the voice of Brussels, an act that involved setting up a fake company to gain credentials – actions that were denounced as 'grubby' by pro-EU campaigners (Dathan, 2015). This incident was an early indicator of the degree of risk and opportunism that Cummings was willing to inject into the campaign. Cameron himself released ministers from collective cabinet responsibility for the duration of the campaign, leading to a number of ministers joining Vote Leave, most prominent of whom were Michael Gove and Boris Johnson. The latter had recently finished his tenure as Mayor of London and was considered to have great electoral appeal. The Electoral Commission opted to endorse Vote Leave as the official representative of the Leave campaign.

Leave.EU was the second prominent group, largely centred on UKIP and its leader Nigel Farage. Farage resented efforts by Vote Leave to sideline him; he wanted his own platform and approached Arron Banks, a wealthy philanthropist and insurance businessman. Banks was to play an instrumental role in coordinating and funding Leave.EU and was influenced by the Trump style of campaigning, basically generating publicity through controversy. Banks (2017, 29) notes in his published account of Brexit how Trump was dismissed as stupid and dangerous but suggests that people were 'missing a trick. All over the world people are fed up with professional politicians. Outsiders are making the running ... being confrontational and provocative is the way ahead. We'll take some flak, but it will get people talking, engaging them in the campaign.' This approach was accentuated by newspapers like the *Guardian* often playing into his hands by fanning the winds of controversy with their outrage. Reflecting the populist mood of the time, Banks (2017, 179) declared: 'We are fighting the establishment, not gagging to be part of it and that's why our supporters love us.' A sense that Leave campaigners were outside of and 'up against' the establishment gave campaigners such as Banks an air of rebelliousness that appealed to those frustrated by the status quo. Leave campaigners and Leave-supporting news outlets framed the 'establishment' as having vested interests in a vote to remain – 547 articles mentioned the 'establishment', while 636 mentioned 'elites' (Moore and Ramsey, 2017). A significant divide was clearly opening up within the British establishment, given that associations like the CBI supported Remain and were at odds with those who believed Brexit would be a catalyst to deregulation and greater competitivity (hyperglobalism). The 'establishment' was painted as either naive multiculturalists, a privileged metropolitan elite and or an uncaring cabal within the economic elite who welcomed migration and free movement because of the cheap labour they provided and who cared little for the social, economic and cultural implications.

The Remain campaign was headed by a group called Stronger In. The Conservatives had initially thought of running their own campaign and were not sure of the merits of a cross-party campaign. Stronger In was dominated by Conservatives, despite being coordinated by the Labour politician Will Smith. Part of the reason for Conservatives' overt influence in Stronger In was a consequence of the decision to keep the Conservative Party machine neutral in the referendum because of deep Tory divisions on this issue. This meant that £7 million which could have been spent under Electoral Commission rules on the cause of Remain was never used, because the Conservative Party machine was kept in a neutral mode to avoid internal strife. Hence, Stronger In was not able to develop a more neutral and independent voice as it was the only national vehicle Cameron could work through (Shipman, 2016).

Data analysis based on regression analysis indicated that two groups, labelled 'hearts' and 'heads', were both susceptible to the economic risk argument of leaving the EU. Thus, it was resolved that the key focus of the Remain campaign was to be the economic risks associated with Leave. This stance was enhanced by the fact that Cameron and Osborne felt the referendum would be a replay of the Scottish independence reference in 2014, in which the nationalists had lost because of the Remain campaign's focus on economic fears (Oliver, 2016). It could be said that such a 'fear'-focused campaign was shaped by the tactics of Lynton Crosby, which tended to play upon anxiety, repeating core messages in simple soundbites and slogans that a sympathetic and compliant media normally latched onto and amplified. However, the strategic mistake was not realizing that the referendum was being organized in an environment where the print media, who were usually allied with Crosby and the Conservatives in acting as sirens of concern, were in this case on the other side of the political fence. As Craig Oliver (2016) noted, he and his fellow campaigners discovered what it was like to be Ed Miliband, the Labour leader who had been vilified by the media. If the tabloids had supported Remain, Cameron probably would have won.

As the interim Labour leader in 2015, Harriet Harman set up a separate Labour remain campaign group. People felt it had been a mistake to campaign with the Conservatives on the referendum in Scotland, holding this decision partly responsible for Labour losing all but one of its Scottish parliamentary seats. The campaign was headed by former minister Alan

Johnson but his leadership was considered lacklustre in its focus on the economic merits of the existing relationship and what he considered the huge dangers of exiting the EU. The lack of a visionary voice was compounded by the fact that Corbyn did not seem enthusiastic in his support of the EU. Although Corbyn had been a Eurosceptic, consistently voting against further integration, as leader he now argued Britain should remain. Corbyn's support was not unconditional; he sought reform of the EU from within, but critics felt he did not clearly articulate the nature of those desired reforms. Corbyn, therefore, like many Remainers, tempered his statements with qualified support, whereas the Leavers were more dynamic and assertive in the language they used to articulate the benefits of Leave. In part because of what happened in Scotland and his being suspicious of the motives the Conservatives had in staging the referendum, Corbyn refused to share a platform with Cameron and was ultimately held to have been a marginal figure in the referendum (McSmith, 2016). Polling showed that many Labour supporters did not know what position their party had on the referendum. A campaign memo from Stronger In indicated that only about half of Labour voters realized their party was in favour of staying in the EU, with the rest thinking it was split or believing it was a party of Brexit (Mason, 2016). It could be argued that the lacklustre campaigning of Johnson and Corbyn failed to deliver what some would have hoped from Labour: an idealistic and galvanizing frame that could have mobilized Labour voters.

Labour and Conservative positions, from those who wanted to remain and those seeking exit, were shaped by the historic contextual frames of the postwar period where opinions ranged between cautious support and outright hostility for the European project (see Chapter 1). Narrow frames that at times begrudgingly welcomed the economic merits of the single market and which foresaw life outside it as a disaster were juxtaposed with frames that emphasized the bureaucratic dangers of federalism; harking back to forms of nostalgia by promising a renewed Britain were themes at the centre of the campaign. The dominance of such frames over decades in political discourse and the print media squeezed out the possibilities for more informed, rational and even visionary debate.

The Referendum campaign

Cameron utilized a topos of danger for the Remain campaign at a cross-party event, describing exit as a 'leap into the dark'. He stressed the economic dangers by raising fears about 'the shock impact, the uncertainty impact, the trade impact' and the worry that to leave would 'put a bomb under our economy' (quoted in Mason and Asthana, 2016). The leap into the dark analogy implies that Brexit was a huge gamble; indeed, Cameron used the metaphor of a bomb to convey the huge sense of danger. Twice in the speech Cameron employed the word 'reckless'. By articulating such a message in a cross-party setting, standing alongside Harriet Harman (Labour), Natalie Bennett (Green) and Tim Farron (Liberal Democrat), Cameron was conveying to his audience that unlike his opponents on Brexit he was articulating a non-partisan, rational and reliable message (contextualization).

Cameron's comments were part of an offensive crafted by his chancellor, George Osborne, centred on the topoi of danger/finance. The Treasury released a series of reports and predictions prophesizing severe economic consequences in the event of Britain leaving the EU and sought to set the terms of debate at the onset in a carefully orchestrated and choreographed blitz of forecasts focusing on the economic risks of Brexit. Osborne (2016) announced in an article in *The Times* that in the event of a Leave vote there would need to be an increase in tax and cuts to NHS spending. At the launch of a key 200-page Treasury report on the economic impact of Brexit, Osborne was pictured with the key figure of £4300 starkly visible in the background (expressive structure). Osborne claimed that every British family would be £4300 worse off if the UK left the EU, nearly a quarter of an average earner's disposable income. Marketing experts know that numerical figures are more likely to stay in the mind of an audience than a complex argument. Another claim was thus that the economy would shrink by 6 per cent by 2030. The focus on the simple headline of a monetary value was designed to make people associate Brexit with personal financial costs; the message of alarm was bolstered by Osborne's staging of an emergency budget to take measures in readiness in the event of the public voting to leave, a performative act designed to heighten pathos. In his *Times* article, Osborne contended that families would be 'permanently poorer' after Brexit and played upon the theme of recklessness highlighted by Cameron by claiming exit from the EU would be the 'most extraordinary self-inflicted wound'.

Critics argued Osborne was engaged in a deception by translating a possible reduction in potential GDP by 2030 if Britain left the EU to a direct effect on household income. The Treasury does not normally convert GDP into a per-household cash figure because (unlike debt, tax etc) it is meaningless to do so. GDP contains measures such as the operating surplus of corporations and many other metrics. If GDP were to be divided by households, it would be £68,000 – nothing like the average disposable income (£18,600 per head, or £45,400 per household circa 2016). In addition, to arrive at the £4300 figure, the Treasury divided

GDP in 2030 by the number of households in 2016, but of course the population is likely to be larger by 2030 (Nelson, 2016). The beauty of monetary figures is people are prone to accept them without trying to decipher the complex formulations behind them, but on this occasion the figures paraded were met with derision. Trevor Kavanagh (2016) of *The Sun* referred to all the numbers as a 'Hitler-style Big Lie'. The Treasury's forecast and the emergency budget Osborne had made on the basis of it were seriously undermined by a letter from fifty-eight Conservative MPs, refusing to support what they derided as the 'punishment budget' (Mason et al, 2016). The announcements by Osborne were followed up with what appeared to be orchestrated statements from organizations such as the International Monetary Fund, voicing similar concerns.

The referendum debate also had a strong cultural strand that was tied to notions of liberal elites. Boris Johnson (2016b), just prior to US President Obama's visit to Britain and anticipating the latter's support for Remain, aroused great controversy by claiming that Obama had an 'ancestral dislike' of Britain and its former empire. As predicted, Obama sought to bolster Remain by declaring Britain would be at the back of the line in securing a trade deal. This and other such interventions actually had a negative poll reaction. Some were annoyed at foreigners interfering in a British question and for some it was confirmation that distant elites had a vested interest in keeping Britain within the EU (Taylor, 2016). In a speech Gove (2016b) made at the Leave headquarters and targeted at the press, he complained that 'The Remain campaign treats people like mere children, capable of being frightened into obedience by conjuring up new bogeymen every night.' This line insinuated Remain was paternalistic and hierarchical, like an authoritarian parent who intimidates their children into submission. Twice in the speech, Gove used the metaphor of the EU treating Britain like a child (topos of hierarchy).

A major theme promoted by Gove and Leavers was centred on sovereignty, to 'take back control' and be liberated from the stifling bureaucracy of Brussels. As Gove (2016b) argued:

> If we vote to stay, the EU's bosses and bureaucrats will take that as carte blanche to continue taking more power and money away from Britain. They will say we have voted for 'more Europe'. Any protests on our part will be met with a complacent shrug and a reminder that we were given our own very special negotiation and our own bespoke referendum and now we've agreed to stay and that's that. Britain has spoken, it's said 'oui' and now it had better shut up and suck it up. In truth, if we vote to stay we are hostages to their agenda.

References to 'bosses' and 'bureaucrats' give the speech a hint of insurgency and of speaking up for those who are oppressed, a classic populist trait (topos of elitist and hierarchical manipulation). Reference to being 'hostages' implies that the EU is undemocratic and authoritarian. In fact, over a dozen references were made in this one speech to the implied undemocratic nature of the EU. The day of the referendum was referred to as 'independence day', implying the act of leaving would be a day of national salvation and liberation. The modal verb 'will' is used three times in the Gove extract and implies a strong sense of certainty and authority that Gove accords to his thinking.

Gove's entreaty to leave plays on nostalgic and an outdated idea of sovereignty, which fails to acknowledge that by pooling sovereignty you can prevent a greater loss of sovereignty in the face of, say, economic decline or challenge through trade wars and so forth (Heywood, 2015). Gove prefers to paint a stark and binary picture of the choice the country is being presented with and is rather masculinized, with voting Leave depicted as an act of bravery but Remain as an act of timid compliance. The speech also highlights another important theme of Leavers by promising, in contrast, to risk a vision of Britain being free to utilize its 'tremendous untapped potential' and enhance its growth rate over an unproductive EU – but only if it is 'unshackled' from its past. Such language evokes something of a renaissance, a rebirth of greatness and prestige. Restoring Britain to a state of prestige was a central theme of Leave, playing upon a nostalgia for past greatness (see Chapter 1).

Both sides made accusations of lying (552 articles), of misleading (464 articles) and of dishonesty (234 articles). Each side said the other was guilty of trying to scare voters, though it appears the label 'Project Fear' was most successfully attached to the approach of the Remain campaign, referenced in articles 739 times, weakening a central part of the Remain campaign, namely the fear of economic consequences (Moore and Ramsey, 2017).

A central feature of Vote Leave was the promise to divert a saving of £350 million a week to the NHS, thanks to departure from the EU and no longer contributing to its budget. This pledge did not acknowledge the rebate or the probable need to continue paying into the EU to secure market access. Use of this figure was castigated by the UK Statistics Authority (2016) for undermining faith in statistical data. Technical and expert warnings, which sought to deflate claims by the Leave campaign, were dismissed as an irrelevance. Gove declared people had had enough of experts (Sky News, 2016). Tellingly, Arron Banks (2017, 279) felt Gove had lifted this line from the more populist Leave.EU playbook. Craig Oliver (2016, 280) described it as 'perhaps one of the most cynical things I've heard a politician say'. He concluded, before the close of the campaign, 'I am worried by the extent to which Gove and Leave are running an anti-expert, anti-establishment, anti-sense strategy that is gaining traction' (Oliver, 2016, 327). As already noted, though, lead Conservatives were hesitant to publicly reveal such concerns.

Both Vote Leave and Leave.EU became increasing emotive in their core message on migration. During the campaign, the immigration figures released for 2015 revealed 330,000 migrants had entered the UK. Cameron had promised to bring the number down into the tens of thousands, so the announcement added to tensions and the timing was far from ideal for Remainers. Initially, Vote Leave was hesitant on the topic of immigration but later in the campaign appeared to match the xenophobia of Leave.EU.

For instance, a Vote Leave poster featured a passport depicted as an open door with a trail of footprints going through it, alongside the slogan 'Turkey (population 76 million) is joining the EU [expressive structure]. Vote Leave, take back control.' Turkey being a Muslim and non-European country stirred longstanding and deep-seated fears of the Orient, with insinuations that these perceived 'outsiders' might be set to invade Britain, which could be conceived as weak and defenceless – as symbolized with the open door (topos of danger and threat). The implied wave of migrants would seize British rights, as was implied by the image of a passport. 'Orientalism' exaggerates and distorts the differences of Eastern peoples and cultures as compared to those of Europe. It perceives the East as backward, uncivilized and dangerous (Said, 1978). Such tropes were to play a prominent role in the referendum campaign on a number of occasions.

Thus, Vote Leave stated: 'Since the birth-rate in Turkey is so high, we can expect to see an additional million people added to the UK population from Turkey alone within eight years. This will not only increase the strain on Britain's public services, but it will also create a number of threats to UK security. Crime is far higher in Turkey than the UK. Gun ownership is also more widespread. Because of the EU's free movement laws, the government will not be able to exclude Turkish criminals from entering the UK' (Boffey and Helm, 2016). In addition, it was claimed by Vote Leave that a growing Turkish population in the UK would cost NHS maternity services an extra £400 million within ten years of the country joining the EU. Insinuations of a tsunami of Turks flooding into Britain with an alleged greater propensity for crime (reification) was an explosive cocktail of invective designed to maximize fear and apprehension. Chilton and Schäffner (1997) have explained that a central feature of racism in political speech acts is to make assumptions about birth rates, criminality and the aggressiveness of migrants. Such othering is a classic trait of elite discourse centred on othering and stressing the moral, biological and intellectual inferiority of the 'other', which stretches back to the age of discovery (Van Dijk, 1998).

The whole controversy was somewhat contrived anyway, as the prospect of Turkey's associate membership progressing to full membership is a very distant dream. Despite this fact, the pro-leave Conservative minister Penny Mordaunt categorically denied to the BBC's Andrew Marr that Britain had the right to veto Turkey's membership (Marr 2016). Mordaunt's fellow Leave campaigners Boris Johnson, Michael Gove and Gisela Stuart signed a joint letter to Cameron on 16 June 2016, calling on him to veto Turkish accession to the EU. In 2019 Boris Johnson claimed he had never mentioned Turkey in the referendum campaign (Sabbagh and Rankin, 2019).

Almost as if the two Leave campaigns were vying with each other, in an interview with *The Telegraph* Farage played upon fears of sexual attacks by talking about the dangers of sexual assault posed by migration with reference to the Cologne and other German cities where mainly Muslim migrants were alleged to have sexually assaulted women during New Year's Eve celebrations (Ross, 2016). The notion of the Muslim male as an illiberal and dangerous sexual predator is another facet of Orientalism. A *Daily Mail* article entitled 'Nigel Farage says British women will be at risk of mass sex attacks by gangs of migrants if we vote to stay in the EU' (Hawken and Matthews, 2016) received 1,756 comments in the online version – in the first 100 comments 91 were in support of Farage with only nine dissenting. Comments from the public included:

> Farage has just come out with pure common sense for years. And finally politics has caught up to his way of thinking. The left label him racist and xenophobe, as they always do with anyone who dares disagree with their multi-kulti utopia. In reality he wants to simply keep Britain safe and control our borders sensibly like Australia or Japan. I think in time, he'll be seen as a bit of a hero.

The highpoint in nativist campaigning was felt by some to be in the final week before the referendum, when Farage unveiled the Leave.EU 'breaking point' poster. This poster contained the caption 'Breaking Point: the EU has failed us' and 'we must take back control of our borders'. The modal 'must' implies the sense of urgency needed for action and reveals a central trait of populism: an emergency politics where strong and rapid action is required in a moment of crisis. Below the caption was a picture of mainly male Syrian refugees lining up at the Slovenian border during the migration crisis of 2015 as they hoped to gain entry. The choice of a picture of dark-skinned men, who were in fact Muslim, was no doubt intended to pander to racist sentiments. The choice of this image was also designed to evoke the episodic memory of the audience, for whom the 2015 migration crisis was a vivid memory based on extensive news coverage of events at borders on the Continent (pathos). The caption of 'breaking point' and exhortation to take back control implied the system was irretrievably broken and the country was now susceptible to a wave of migration. The technical fact, though, that with Britain being outside the Schengen area it was thus unlikely to see such border pressures was conveniently sidelined.

Farage was widely condemned for this poster, which was derided as racist, but the incident perhaps serves to illustrate an aspect of the populist playbook where the demagogue shocks the liberal establishment and attracts their condemnation, then appears and poses as a brave champion willing to stand up to the tyranny of political correctness (Wodak, 2015). This is a tripolar stratagem where the populist leader implies they are voicing the concern of the masses; the condemnation heaped upon them for controversial statements symbolizes the contempt elites have for those masses. Revealing a sense of victimhood after the release of the poster, Farage stated: 'I think I have been a politician who has been a victim of it, to be honest with you. When you challenge the establishment in this country, they come after you, they call you all sorts of things' (Sculthorpe, 2016).

On the same day as the poster was unveiled, Labour MP Jo Cox was killed by one of her constituents, Thomas Mair, who had links with radical right groups. Mair shouted in court, 'Britain first, death to traitors.' Johnson and Cummings are reported to have thought this would cause serious problems for Leave, in that voters would link the xenophobic campaigning with the attack and recoil from the Leave campaign in disgust. The murder shocked the country and campaigning was suspended by the various groups. However, the death of Jo Cox may actually have been a disaster for the Remain campaign as due to this other news the weekend papers did not splash on the lead that Leave was now enjoying in the polls – this had happened in Scotland, where in the run up to the poll the nationalists seemed to enjoy a slight lead. The focused coverage on Leave's lead could have galvanized opposition and helped Remain bounce back, but this did not happen (Shipman, 2016).

The result of the referendum was 52 to 48 per cent in favour of leaving. England and Wales were in favour of leaving but Scotland, Northern Ireland and London preferred to remain. Farage commented that the vote was a 'victory for ordinary decent people' and with some irony and little sensitivity given the tragic event preceding the poll, he declared we did it 'without a shot being fired'. Cameron immediately tended his resignation and shortly afterwards a no-confidence motion against Jeremy Corbyn was put down by Labour MPs Margaret Hodge and Ann Coffey. There were 172 MPs that supported the motion, that is, 80 per cent of the parliamentary Labour Party.

Following the result there was an estimated 500 per cent increase in hate crimes; some seemed to have thought the referendum result was a sanction to the worst forms of racism (Seidler, 2018). Many found themselves in a deep sense of shock, with Leave campaigners surprised that they had won and Remain supporters now pondering what the result meant for the economic, social and cultural fabric of the nation, fearing the event would be cataclysmic. The sense of foreboding was accentuated by the momentary free fall of financial markets. Post-referendum, the largest indicator of political failure stemmed from the fact people were not sure what they had voted for, such had been the volume of misinformation and lack of clarity in the debate – a fact that raises serious questions about the state of British democracy.

Inquest: the state of British democracy

A sense of surprise at the events that transpired and the strategy of Leave is evident in comments by Craig Oliver, when in the closing stages of the campaign he concluded that Gove and Johnson were setting out an alternative government: 'The words attempted coup spring to my mind. They seem strange on my lips as I later test them out on other people' (Oliver, 2016, 264). Oliver (2016, 332) also wonders: 'What kind of country do we live in? This has gone way beyond winning and losing on the EU – it feels like a Battle for Britain.' What Oliver detected was an important shift in British politics, in which mainstream politicians such as Gove and Johnson assumed a populist mantle in their approach in terms of pursued aims and rhetoric, and were thus able to accrue political success. Populist figures had appeared in British politics before but the likes of Oswald Mosley and Enoch Powell had been at the periphery of the political system and had enjoyed little success. Things were different now, which raises questions about the strength and value of British democracy and its ability to safeguard the country from extremes. This observation also raises questions as to the cohesiveness of the British elite, a fissure appearing where one section was prepared to embrace and promote populist radicalism and ignore the concerns of mainstream business interests.

A lack of education and/or political comprehension, in the opinion of some, allowed the political class to resort to forms of rhetoric where emotion seemed to count more than fact. Indeed, facts seemed to be discounted by both sides, but some would say in particular by Leave, in a manner that lends some credence to what is termed 'post-truth' politics. In relation to President Trump, *The Economist* (2016) defined post-truth politics – in a definition that has relevance to Brexit campaigners – as a reliance on assertions that 'feel true' but have no basis in fact: 'His [Trump's] brazenness is not punished but taken as evidence of his willingness to stand up to elite power.'

Post-truth politics can be seen as an extension of 'dog whistle politics' that had been a feature of British politics for over a decade (see Introduction). It also has some connection to the sharp media and advertising-orientated campaign management that had become the political vogue since advertising agency Saatchi & Saatchi helped bring Thatcher to power in 1979. Campaign strategies have increasingly utilized emotive speech acts, often condensed into short soundbites that can dominate the news cycle but also transmit and evoke important signals and codes based on identity or fear, which then galvanize and mobilize. MacShane (2017) argued that the political class had created narrow limits on the parameters of reasonable debate through decades of incessant carping about Europe and had set the terms for sensationalist media coverage, while others blame the media for creating controversies related to the EU which politicians have followed rather than challenged. Perhaps the two groups were mutually reinforcing. The negativity and division accentuated an already great sense of disillusionment with the political class among the public and weakened the fabric of British democracy through increased cynicism and intemperate rhetoric becoming the norm.

During the referendum, newspapers enthusiastically promoted and amplified the campaign messages of Leave, building upon three decades of Eurosceptic reporting. One study found that of the 1,558 articles published by nine national papers over a three-month period which focused on the referendum, 41 per cent were in favour of leaving, with only 27 per cent in favour of staying in the EU, while 23 per cent were categorized as 'mixed or undecided' and 9 per cent as adopting no position (Levy et al, 2016). Another study into media coverage of the referendum campaign noted the economy was the most covered campaign issue but was highly contested. Warnings about the repercussions of Brexit were routinely dismissed as deliberate Remain 'scaremongering' (a term used 737 times). Immigration was the most prominent referendum issue, based on the number of times it led newspaper front pages (there were 99 front pages about immigration, 82 about the economy). Coverage of the effects of immigration was overwhelmingly negative. Migrants were blamed for many of Britain's economic and social problems. The study also found sovereignty was a major issue, often linked to migration and economic performance (Moore and Ramsey, 2017). The BBC was criticized for failing to shift the bias of the Leave press by creating a stance on balanced reporting that meant it was hesitant to challenge directly the lies of Leave, in part because it wanted to appear impartial and not be accused of interference (Zelizer, 2018). It could be argued, though, that if Remain had also been more factual and grounded in truth it would have been easier for the BBC to challenge the falsehoods of Leave.

The print media is in decline and the growth of social media has been seen as a tool that could become a counter-public sphere, offering challenges to the mainstream media and longstanding Eurosceptic tropes. However, in the referendum social media may have had a more malign influence. Arron Banks realized the value of social media and spent heavily on it (Shipman, 2016). Banks (2017) claimed to have twice the social media reach of the two official campaigns. The mastery of Leave in the sphere of social media and their ability to impassion users is reflected by the dominance they enjoyed for most of the campaign on Twitter, where sentiment was on average for much of the campaign two thirds in support of Leave (Llewellyn and Cram, 2016). Perhaps most importantly, Banks hired US pollster and referendum expert Gerry Gunster as a consultant. According to Banks (2017), an important aspect of the campaign was raising the profile of Leave.EU's social media – providing a platform bigger than those built up by either the Remain campaign or the official Vote Leave group. This provided a tool for direct outreach but also a database to mine, allowing for in-depth demographic polling and consequently precision targeted messaging. Targeting involved the transmission of sharp messages likely to invoke emotive feelings and anxieties.

Leave.EU and UKIP had some interactions with Cambridge Analytica, the controversial company partly established by Steve Bannon and used to assist the Trump election campaign. It used big data and social media to deploy the military methodology of 'information operations', basically propaganda and disinformation, in an election rather than a war. The degree of involvement of Cambridge Analytica is at present unclear and contested, with some claiming it was significant. Brittany Kaiser, former head of business development at Cambridge Analytica, claims that Leave.EU used datasets created by Cambridge Analytica to target voters with online political messages (Lewis and Hilder, 2018). For Vote Leave, Cummings employed Henry de Zoete as digital director. De Zoete hired AggregateIQ, a software data firm with connections to Cambridge Analytica. AggregateIQ was able to build up a core audience and use a Facebook tool called lookalike – an audience builder which helped find similar people (Shipman, 2016). Concerns have been raised about this almost Orwellian use of social media and messaging to influence voting intentions, especially where emotive and non-factual communications were relied upon.

A number of investigations and allegations related to Brexit have raised further serious concerns. The Labour MP Ben Bradshaw raised concerns about the influence of dark money in the Brexit campaign; these funds came from foreign sources, some of which may have been Russian (Harding, 2017). Questions were raised as to how Banks could afford to support Leave to the extent he did, given the alleged financial difficulties of his business (Leroux and Baldwin, 2018). Serious allegations also emerged after a whistleblower from within Vote Leave charged that the campaign had illegally exceeded the agreed electoral expenses for the referendum by syphoning money to pay for AggregateIQ, so that it did not appear in the official records of expenses for Vote Leave (Buchan, 2018). An investigation by the Electoral Commission concluded that Leave.EU broke the spending limit by at least £70,000 and possibly substantially more, and referred the matter to the National Crime Agency (NCA) (Weaver and Waterson, 2018). However, the NCA reported in 2019 that it found no evidence of criminality after investigating a series of claims against Leave.EU and Arron Banks (Ramsey, 2019).

Despite the Leave campaigns displaying the traits of an insurgency, the campaigns relied heavily on rich philanthropists like Banks and other establishment figures such as media barons, editors and hedge fund managers. Such individuals were united in a shared vision of Britain as a low tax, low regulation – 'Singapore on stilts' cast adrift from Europe (Clegg, 2017). There is thus some irony to Farage's victory speech and its tone of insurgency – 'We have fought against the multinationals, we have fought against big merchant banks, we have fought against big politics.' (Press Association, 2016) Some of the most powerful supporters of the Brexit campaign appeared in the Paradise Papers, leaked documents with the offshore financial details of some of the richest companies and individuals in the world (Garside et al, 2017). With the EU starting to crack down on tax havens, was this part of the rationale for some sections of the financial elite in supporting Brexit (Morphet, 2017)?

So, a number of issues raise serious questions as to the legitimacy of the referendum and whether there was a free, honest and open debate and, in that sense, gives some insight into the health of British democracy. Liberal representative democracy has been defined as a means by which experts, that is, the professional political class, might take decisions which are rational and formed in the interests of the greater good. It is also a conception of democracy that asserts the importance of assisting minorities, which majoritarian society may not be kindly disposed to and if empowered through more direct forms of democracy may choose to discriminate against. The Brexit referendum seemed to cast these conventions aside and constituted a populist turn, where fact and informed opinion were discarded and discourse was a proxy for anxieties and insecurities centred on race and migration (Bhambra, 2017). In the next section, I chart the period that followed the referendum to assess the degree to which these trends remained evident.

The first year of the May premiership

As Oliver (2016, 10) noted with reference to the period following the decision to leave the EU, 'What now is crucial is that we proceed with care and respect understanding that all of us want what is best for this country. That means listening to the legitimate concerns of both sides and not stifling debate with contemptuous rhetoric and headlines or the demons will remain unleashed.' A review of the period following the referendum casts some doubts on whether Oliver's hopes were achieved, given the unprecedented level of intrigue and invective injected into the body politic. Johnson, who seemed somewhat bemused by the victory (according to some he had only intended to raise his profile for a future leadership bid and not actually to win), announced his candidacy for Conservative leader but then withdrew it after onetime ally Gove announced that he believed Johnson lacked the skills of leadership and decided to stand himself. At the end of the process, though, it was former Home Secretary Theresa May who was chosen as leader, following the withdrawal of the other last remaining MP Andrea Leadsom in the parliamentary selection process. Hence, May did not need to face a membership poll where opinion polls suggested she was the clear favourite to win anyway.

May had been at the Home Office for six years and had developed a reputation for being tough on migration. Some felt May would be a formidable opponent in Britain's exit negotiations with the EU. At the outset, May sought to placate Brexiteers by stating 'Brexit means Brexit' – basically a signal that there would be no U-turns or dilution; despite having been a low-profile Remainer under Cameron, she was now committed to Brexit. This was affirmed through her appointment of Brexiteers to leading cabinet positions on Brexit: David Davis (Secretary of State for Exiting the European Union), Liam Fox (Secretary of State for International Trade and President of the Board of Trade) and, to the surprise of some, Boris Johnson became Foreign Secretary.

In her Mansion House speech of January 2017, May set out her vision for Brexit, where she confirmed she wanted Britain to leave the single market and customs union and would, if necessary, walk away from negotiations – declaring no deal would be better than a bad deal. At the same time, May stated that Britain could retain access to the single market. Her first important act in the Brexit process was to initiate Article 50, the notification sent to the EU informing them of Britain's formal intention to leave, which would trigger a two-year negotiation period to resolve the departure details. May had initially felt that she could rely on the Royal Prerogative, the powers invested in the government by the monarchy, rather than seek a mandate from parliament because in her opinion the referendum had given her the authority to do so. It appeared she had decided to espouse the ideals of the populist turn. The rationale and rhetoric of May are explored in more depth in Chapter 3.

Failure to hold a vote in parliament about whether to leave the EU led to a legal challenge, with the plaintiffs including the anti-Brexit campaigner Gina Miller arguing that May was acting unconstitutionally. Judges supported the appeal. The *Daily Mail* declared the judges were 'enemies of the people' (Slack, 2016). Miller received death threats. The Supreme Court proceeded to issue a ruling that to trigger Article 50 without a parliamentary vote would be a breach of settled constitutional principles stretching back centuries (Morphet, 2017). Article 50 was thus debated and eventually endorsed by parliament in February 2017. Labour issued a three-line whip in support, in part because of fear of an election and due to the argument that the referendum result had to be respected. However, with some irony Cummings noted that triggering Article 50 before a Brexit blueprint was ready was like putting a gun in your mouth and pulling the trigger (Bush, 2017). May's eventual difficulties in the negotiations may have confirmed this prognosis.

With a majority of thirty seats and around a dozen Europhile backbench MPs, May had a difficult task ahead of her to pass the European Union Withdrawal Bill to repeal the European Communities Act 1972. A decision was made to hold an early General Election, in the hope of gaining an increased majority to ease the passage of Brexit legislation. There was also a perception that the weak state of the Labour Party would allow May to achieve a landslide majority. Although Corbyn had decisively won the 2016 leadership contest with 60 per cent of the Labour membership vote, this contest had been deeply acrimonious. Labour was now badly split. Despite the adulation Corbyn achieved among a significant section of the membership for his conviction politics and for returning Labour to a more radical conception of socialism, for some people he was an extremist and an incompetent politician. Conservatives such as David Davis reasoned that a contest with Corbyn presented an ideal opportunity, in which May could be bolstered by a large majority, endorsing her vision of Brexit and giving her a mandate that might strengthen her hand in negotiations with the EU (Mairs, 2017).

This was to be the Brexit election – a chance for the country to return to the greatest issue of the day. The front page of the *Daily Mail* proclaimed 'crush the saboteurs' and *The Sun* headline was 'Blue Murder'. In the view of these tabloids, the election would present May with an opportunity to triumph once and for all over those who resisted Brexit. On an official visit to meet May by Jean-Claude Juncker, President of the European Commission, it was reported in the media that Juncker thought the British government's position was delusional. In a press statement, May responded by claiming '[t]hreats against Britain have been issued by European politicians and officials. All of these acts have been deliberately timed to affect the result of the general election which will take place on 8 June.' *The Telegraph* reporting May's statement heralded her as the new 'iron lady' (Rayner and Swinford, 2017). Some felt such bellicose rhetoric might set the tone for the election, but overall little attention was spent debating the details of Brexit.

The Conservative campaign proved to be a disaster. There was confusion as to whether Lynton Crosby or Nick Timothy (chief of staff to May) was in charge and they had diverging visions on strategy, which created a confused campaign (Shipman, 2017). Crosby wanted a focus on May and to reinforce and articulate a perception of her as an experienced and strong leader, best placed to negotiate a good deal in the Brexit negotiations. His vision of the campaign was encapsulated in the infamous 'strong and stable' slogan. On the other hand, Timothy saw May as an agent of change and devised a manifesto with some radical and hard decisions, not least on social care, which involved asking people to pay more of the costs of themselves; this proved to be hugely unpopular and was branded a 'dementia tax'. May was forced into an embarrassing U-turn, which severely damaged her reputation for competence and assertiveness; she also seemed robotic and uncomfortable in the campaign and her repetition of 'strong and stable' led to her being lampooned as the 'Maybot'. Meanwhile, her unwillingness to participate in television debates with Corbyn made her appear evasive. Terrorist attacks during the election campaign also brought into question the cuts she had imposed while Home Secretary and this raised questions about whether British security had been compromised by austerity (Cowley and Kavanagh, 2018). All of these events made May look extremely weak.

Labour had a much better campaign than expected, with a strong manifesto and a leader who was energetic and relished canvassing. The Labour manifesto was also well received but vague on Brexit. Labour stated the referendum result must be honoured and was aiming for a 'close new relationship with the EU' with workers' rights protected, but as with the Conservatives, little detail was provided. However, the vagueness of Labour's position allowed voters to project their aspirations onto the party, thus Labour secured support from Remainers and Leavers.

The result was a huge surprise. The Conservative Party gained 42.4 per cent of the national vote – its highest share since 1979 but gained only 318 seats, winning thirteen fewer than in 2015 and coming in eight short of a majority. This forced May to seek support from the Democratic Unionist Party (DUP) in order to form a government with a slight majority. The Labour Party polled 40 per cent of the national vote – its highest share since 2001 and a 9.5 point increase since 2015. It achieved 262 seats, thirty more than in 2015. The result and the new parliamentary arithmetic raised a whole series of questions and doubts over the feasibility of the government being able to deliver Brexit.

Negotiations

Joschka Fischer (2017), the former German foreign minister, felt that this election result revealed that there was no support in Britain for a hard Brexit, but any softening was not evident in May's approach. May's threats to leave the talks, in effect indicating that Britain was willing to adopt a completely different economic model, which would be a threat to EU interests. In the wake of the General Election, May was still wedded to 'red lines' she had set out before the election which stated there should be no more free movement for EU citizens, full autonomy over British laws, autonomy to conclude trade agreements (no customs union with the EU) and no role for the European Court of Justice (see Chapter 3).

If Britain left the EU without a customs union there could be a return to a hard border in Northern Ireland, with checkpoints and possibly a renewal of tensions. On this question May faced a difficult dilemma of either accepting an EU proposal, thereby keeping Northern Ireland within the customs union and losing the support of the DUP who were against any arrangements which set them apart from the rest of the UK, or to accept that the whole of the UK remain in the customs union. The latter option would have led to a loss of support from the sixty or so backbench Conservatives supporting hard Brexit, as being in a customs union would mean Britain could not negotiate independent trade deals (Powell, 2018). Both groups had the potential to end May's premiership and created gridlock in the Brexit process and serious delays as the government scrambled to find a solution acceptable to all parties.

Charges of authoritarianism and poor communication were also levelled at May, with reference to the parliamentary agenda to facilitate Brexit through the European Union Withdrawal Bill, a bill to repeal the European Communities Act 1972 and make other provision in connection with the withdrawal of the United Kingdom from the EU. A key aim was to transpose forty-four years of EU legislation, including 19,000 regulations, directives and other rules, into UK law. Early political skirmishes centred on the streamlined procedure proposed by ministers to make this huge task manageable. The government assumed 'Henry VIII powers', named after the monarch who ruled by proclamation, allowing some decisions on EU rules to be taken without the full parliamentary scrutiny given to bills. Critics argued that with such measures far from 'taking back control', the raison d'être of Brexit, such measures gave the executive greater arbitrary powers to rewrite rules in ways which undermined important basic rights (Thompson and Pickard, 2017). During the passage of the bill, the government suffered a series of defeats and amendments in the House of Lords which was emboldened by May's weak mandate and lack of effort to build consensus. Many of the amendments sought to strengthen parliamentary say and curb executive authority in the Brexit process.

In a review of May's strategy to navigate Brexit through parliament, it is perhaps telling that in the twenty-four months given to negotiate under Article 50, five of them were used for a General Election and another sixteen were run down before the government came forward with the Chequers plan, a blueprint for departure. It was left until twenty-two months had passed before parliament was able to vote on the withdrawal agreement.

Conclusion

Those who sought to inject caution, scrutiny or moderation into the Brexit process were subject to sharp and personal attacks by the supporters of Brexit, which demonstrated a lack of understanding and respect for the British constitution and a tradition of facilitating scrutiny and open debate (Morphet, 2017). One of the trumpeted assets of Britain's parliamentary system is that although the government is invested with strong executive powers, through deliberation and scrutiny parliament is able to offer some balance to that power and often is able to strengthen and improve legislative outcomes. In efforts to ignore this tradition, there was a danger of parliamentary democracy being undermined. In a similar vein as noted through the terms of the EU Withdrawal Bill and avoidance, where possible, of debate or accountability, on central tenets of Brexit it was evident that far from taking back control it seemed to be leading to the executive assuming greater arbitrary powers.

The degree to which political rhetoric was securitized is also a serious point of concern, with mainstream politicians resorting to nativism or binary arguments in which opponents were cast as a threat, motivated by privilege or as being self-interested elites who were undermining the 'will of the people'. Journalist Matthew Parris (2016) raised concerns as to the intemperate rhetoric of Gove – 'but when he grows eloquent I cannot quite banish the smell from my nostrils the smell of burning witches'. These concerns go to the heart of the apprehension held apropos Brexit nationalism in that it represented a populist turn, a radical change in not only the language of politics but how it has been conducted.

This was part of the dilemma for Britain and was crystallized in the predicament May found herself in. In 2017 her key advisors sought to stage a campaign centred on May as a determined and dynamic politician, a role she signally failed to fulfil. Taggart (2000) notes that populism requires the most extraordinary individuals to lead the most ordinary of people. May was probably not made in the mould of such a leader – one who might have been better suited to the mood of the times and the Brexit agenda (Johnson may have been a better fit for the Weberian role of 'charismatic leader'). Nevertheless, Brexit presents a further dilemma in the sense that a populist goal achieved through populist tactics needed a political system based on representative democracy to achieve its ends. This mismatch may have hindered efforts to achieve Brexit and is a point of tension detailed in the following chapters.

It was clear that Brexit and the referendum debate had created a major paradigm shift, bolstering the place of Euroscepticism in political discourse and setting the course for a sharp departure from the policies that had steered British relations with Europe for nearly fifty years. Public support for that position was to remain strong over the coming three years.

Having provided a broad overview of the referendum, the negotiations and attempts to prepare for Brexit, this book drills down into the issues raised in this chapter – primarily by seeking to assess whether Britain is following a populist trajectory and fundamental shift from representative democracy. Chapters 3, 4, 5, 6 and 7 explore the stances adopted by the political parties and the EU, dissecting their speech acts and the ideas and values behind them.

3

Politics in Focus: The Conservatives

The Conservative Party is the oldest and most successful political party in Britain, if not in Europe, in terms of electoral success. However, modern conservativism has been riven by the issue of Europe to the same degree that free trade divided the Conservatives in the early nineteenth century (Gambles, 1998). The repeal of the Corns Laws in 1846 ruptured the party and led to a long period out of office; the chance that the same outcome might occur for the Conservatives seemed to be a constant feature of Brexit.

The Conservative debate on Brexit reflected a sense of soul-searching within conservatism as it sought, influenced by its history and tradition, to preserve or recast what some consider to be its core values. Thus, it was with great pertinence in the debate on Article 50 that Prime Minister Theresa May (2017a) declared: 'At moments such as these – great turning points in our national story – the choices that we make define the character of our nation.' This chapter seeks to navigate, through a study of speech acts, the shifts and flows of that debate and posits that at the centre of this discussion is a redefinition of conservatism, which may have decisively reframed the party. The discussion covers the period up to the summer of 2019.

The historical context

The Conservative Party has, as with all parties, never been a homogeneous political grouping but consists of a broad array of traditions and interpretations of conservative ideals. The Conservative Party, Blake (2011) has argued, is a pragmatic rather than ideological party where traditionally ideology has been subordinated to the practicalities of governance and statecraft; some would posit that the fragmentation of that code during the final years of the Thatcher premiership explains the mixed fortunes of conservativism since the late 1980s. The ideological stance of the Conservative Party in the postwar period is often characterized as one where, from 1945 to 1975, one nation conservatism was in the ascendancy, where the party supported the welfare state, full employment and forms of statism in a mixed economy. In 1975, prompted in part by inflation and economic crisis, Thatcher advocated a more limited role for the state, with curbs on trade unionism, to unfetter the free market and individualism. Coupled with this was social conservatism, there was an emphasis on traditional moral values and a reassertion of British identity and corresponding desire to protect British sovereignty from perceived threats (Bale, 2016). Here, though, there was an element of contradiction. Thatcher and her followers welcomed the single market as a key instrument in promoting free trade, but membership also entailed the pooling of elements of sovereignty where Britain surrendered some power, so it was collectively stronger by being able to negotiate as part of a wider European economic bloc. However, this obviously compromised traditional notions of conservativism, which cherished national autonomy and have been at the heart of the party's difficulties with Europe – a state of affairs that culminated in Brexit.

Depiction of postwar conservatism as a tension between pragmatism, as represented by the one nation tradition, and ideological fervour, as represented by neoliberalism, may be an oversimplification (Heppell and Hill, 2005). A more nuanced outline of conservatism in the Thatcher period is presented in a typology devised by Dunleavy (1993), which outlines four broad categories: (i) Tory paternalists who represented the one nation tradition; (ii) Tory technocrats committed to Europe and an interventionist government strategy; (iii) the traditional right, who believed in strong government and the maintenance of hierarchy and tradition; (iv) the market liberals, part of the new right who believed in the centrality of the free market. The market liberals or Thatcherites, as with Thatcher herself in the closing years of her premiership, saw the EU as a threat to sovereignty and the market through the promotion of federalism and social protection. However, some neoliberals were strongly in support of the free market ushered in through the Single Market Act and thus willing, like the remnants of the one nation tradition, to accept monetary union and, for technocratic reasons, the general direction of the EU.

John Major's premiership was deeply divided by the issue of Europe, with a number of rebellions by the Eurosceptic market liberals against Major's support for the Maastricht Treaty to further European integration (Wall, 2008). This division was a contributory factor in the Conservative election defeat in 1997. The influence of the Eurosceptic market liberals grew under the leadership of William Hague (1997–2001), Iain Duncan Smith (2001–03) and Michael Howard (2003–05). To a degree, the growing Euroscepticism of the Conservatives in opposition was an attempt to shore up the Tory core vote – for much of New Labour's time in office, their party was seriously lagging behind the government under Blair in the polls. In 1997 the Conservatives polled 30.7 per cent of the vote, their lowest representation in parliament since 1906; the following two elections showed little improvement in terms of percentage share. The Euroscepticism of this period also reflected a shift to the right and a more populist interpretation of conservatism, accentuated by the growing influence of the Conservative grassroots through new reforms in the leadership and candidate selection which empowered the predominantly white, elderly, male and Eurosceptic membership of the party. Thus, under the leadership of Hague, Duncan Smith and Howard, who were all Thatcherite with a predilection to populist campaign themes, Euroscepticism gained further ground (Bale, 2016). A populist strategy led to the Conservatives becoming more vocal, not just on perceived threats to British sovereignty but also evoking rhetoric that was hostile towards asylum seekers and migrants.

Cameron's assumption of the leadership in 2005 marked, despite his mild Euroscepticism, a more one nation approach, which alongside the impact of a recession and Gordon Brown's unpopularity enabled the Conservatives electorally to recover and to return to power in 2010. However, this recovery was limited as the absence of a parliamentary majority compelled the Conservatives to enter into a coalition with the Liberal Democrats. The Eurosceptic right were not impressed by this progress and some deemed Cameron's failure to secure a majority to be a reflection of his inability to fully resonate with the public by seeming to abandon traits of Thatcherism (Oborne, 2012). Although Cameron purported to represent the mainstream or a form of more socially orientated conservatism, much of his party still subscribed to forms of inflexible Euroscepticism and neoliberalism. It was pressure from this wing of the party that ultimately compelled Cameron to promise a referendum on EU membership in his Bloomsberg speech in 2013 (see Chapter 2).

This chapter gives an overview of Conservative positions on Brexit since the referendum. As will become apparent, there has, in some respects, been a return and rejuvenation of the populist traits evident in the party before Cameron. Such traits are evident not just in a desire for a hard form of Brexit but also conceptions of the relationship between parliament and the public, the type of economic system Britain aspires to in the twenty-first century but also profound questions on identity.

It is with reference to parliament that one of the greatest junctures is evident. A central tenet of conservativism has been the defence of executive autonomy as articulated through parliamentary sovereignty. A long-established notion in British politics is that parliament is invested with a degree of power where the electorate abdicate some of their freedom for the greater good, expecting in turn for the political class to make informed and expert decisions in a deliberative manner, where scrutiny and revision are encouraged. As will become evident, Brexit presents a direct challenge to this form of governance and this aspect of the Brexit phenomenon is a central thread of discussion in this chapter. As noted, Brexit also touched upon profound questions related to the economic, social and cultural direction of Britain.

In seeking to understand the diverse strands of Conservative thinking on Brexit, the chapter places Conservatives into three distinct groups. The *Hardheaded Brexiteers*: a group who wished to leave the single market and customs union but who desired the closest possible relationship with the EU; although they were certain and resolute in seeking departure from the EU, they were pragmatic and willing to compromise to some degree on their goals or achieve their aims through incremental steps. The second group were the *Clean Break Brexiteers* who, while seeking an exit from the single market and customs union, were less willing to seek alignment with the EU and or offer concessions. The final group, termed *One Nation Europhiles*, were Conservatives who were more wedded to the EU and hoped Brexit could be interpreted as a decision to remain in the single market and/or the customs union; they had reservations about the process used to achieve Brexit and the impact it had on parliamentary sovereignty.

Hardheaded Brexiteers

Theresa May and many in her cabinet could be placed in this category. Many were originally Remainers, albeit critical in their perception of the EU, they came to recognize the need and merits of leaving and rapidly became aligned with more longstanding Leavers. May appeared unwilling to appease the 48 per cent who had voted to remain with substantive compromises; she and her supporters though were more willing than the most ideologically driven Conservatives to offer some concessions to the EU to secure a form of Brexit that might minimize some of the inevitable disruption and offer a staged route to a desired final destination. Such pragmatism was not always evident, especially in May's keynote speeches at Lancaster House (May, 2017b) and Mansion House (2018) which set out her broad principles for Brexit. The overriding objective of this group was to secure sovereignty, which in their opinion was under threat through a creeping federalism. This theme was a central part of May's repertoire for the justification for Brexit.

In May's speech at Lancaster House in January 2017 that followed the genre of a formal leader's speech, in a carefully drafted and choreographed formal speech, designed to instil confidence in the audience and establish the authority of the leader, May sought to add greater context to her Brexit aims. She clearly reflected the 'take back control' message:

> Our political traditions are different. Unlike other European countries, we have no written constitution, but the principle of parliamentary sovereignty is the basis of our unwritten constitutional settlement ... The public expect to be able to hold their governments to account very directly, and as a result supranational institutions as strong as those created by the European Union sit very uneasily in relation to our political history and way of life ...That means taking control of our own affairs, as those who voted in their millions to leave the European Union demanded we must [topoi of history, custom and uniqueness].

Here, May stresses how the different political traditions of the EU versus the Westminster system are at the centre of her government's desire to seek an exit from the EU, which is portrayed as an effort to respect the strong demands of the public to protect and preserve the British 'way of life', thus Brexit is shaped in part by nostalgia and tradition (topos of custom and tradition). Critics would argue, though, that the notion of the Westminster model and representative democracy providing deliberative, informed and autonomous government is rather an outdated fallacy which disguises the reality of a political system that has always been remote from the public. The Westminster model places an emphasis on the informed opinions of expert politicians guiding decision-making, rather than the direct empowerment of the public.

Brexit in fact was in itself a threat and challenge to representative democracy and judgement. In her defence of Brexit, May continuously stressed that it was 'the will of the British people', and that the government, therefore, had a 'duty to deliver' (topos of direct democracy). Such language evokes an image May was keen to cultivate of her acting with a sense of duty, like a loyal and trustworthy servant of public opinion. The flaw with such reasoning was that the referendum was under British law merely advisory, but May was choosing to ignore the topos of representative judgement, that is, the independent and deliberative decision-making which has been a prized facet of the British representative democracy (Chalmers, 2017). Thus, for May, politicians could not ignore a fractious and poorly managed referendum, despite British political traditions having the propensity to enable such an act. Furthermore, the margin of victory had been slight and some argued this warranted a softer interpretation of Brexit. But despite the small majority in favour of Brexit and the fact a detailed vision of Brexit had not been approved in the referendum, May chose to interpret the result in a way that would lead to a hard form of Brexit with Britain leaving the customs union and single market. By brandishing the 'will of the people', May implied that the referendum result had given her government a premium mandate which surpassed parliamentary sovereignty and could discard representative judgement. By failing to find compromise, May was in fact undermining representative government and fuelling a reconfiguration of British democracy by allowing fundamental areas of policy to be directed by one single and direct form of decision-making in the form of a referendum that was in fact counter to British political tradition.

May was scathing of the notion of holding a second referendum. She asserted such a measure would be a 'breach of trust' and declared that a referendum 'would do irreparable damage to the integrity of our politics, because it would say to millions who trusted in democracy, that our democracy does not deliver' (quoted in Stewart, 2018). Such a view was working within the frame that the liberal establishment was seeking to frustrate Brexit and that the duty of politicians was to obey the referendum mandate – an argument undermined by the fact that after a referendum endorsed a Welsh Assembly in 1997, Conservative MPs including Theresa May voted against the requisite legislation in parliament and the Conservatives in 2005 had a manifesto pledge to hold another referendum (Walker, 2019). The logic of the Conservative argument seemed to imply that the referendum result provided a super-mandate which transcended the fact that people might change their minds after three years of deadlock or that a referendum might be the only means to break the aforementioned impasse.

Although May had been a subdued Remainer during the referendum campaign, she displayed an ideological interpretation and commitment to Brexit centred on hyperglobalism. Brexit constituted a major re-evaluation of Britain's economic model in a rapidly changing globalized world. We now occupy such a highly interconnected world economy where national governments have limited discretionary powers to protect and subsidize economies, policies that in effect no longer work because of the sheer pressure of competition aggravated by the threat and danger of capital and investment flow. In the view of those who can be termed hyperglobalists, the role of government should be to control inflation and the deficit and resist excessive interference in the market. However, hyperglobalists believe the EU is a Franco-German (and now increasingly) German-dominated project to create a European federal state that will augur excessive regulation and taxation, leading to economic decline. For the hyperglobalists, the solution lies in regaining British sovereignty and returning to a more neoliberal agenda which emphasizes deregulation and a minimal role for the state and develops new trading partnerships with North America and Asia. Yet such an ideal it could be said is tinted with a degree of nostalgia for Britain's imperial past where it became a global superpower through free trade, innovation and a pioneering spirit (Baker et al, 2002).

May's use of the topos of hyperglobalism led to her calling for Britain to reassert its economic greatness. It was a prominent feature of keynote addresses on Brexit, with a rallying call for a 'global Britain'. Such sentiments reflect a longstanding trope in British economic chauvinism, which has its antecedents in the age of exploration and summons up references to Sir Walter Raleigh, the Industrial Revolution and Britain as a global trading superpower. Brexit could thus be construed as an act of rebirth and was aligned with the nostalgic hankering for a return to greatness which was a prominent feature of a revived and rampant English nationalism and of a section of the economic elite keen to see Britain emulate economies like Singapore (Dorling and Tomlinson, 2019). In her Lancaster House speech, May envisioned Britain as 'a magnet for international talent and a home to the pioneers and innovators who will shape the world ahead. I want us to be a truly Global Britain.'

The importance of these sentiments is evidenced by the fact that the theme of Global Britain appears to be such a central one in the Lancaster House speech, appearing eleven times alongside ten references to free trade. What was unclear in May's rhetoric was the scale and significance of change that these reforms would entail – changes that would fundamentally change the economic and social model of Britain, bringing it closer to the United States as it moved away from Europe. May's Mansion House speech on Brexit in March 2018, through antithesis, echoed some of Trump's repertoire of attacks on privileged elites:

> The government I lead will be driven not by the interests of the privileged few, but by yours. We will do everything we can to give you more control over your lives. When we take the big calls, we'll think not of the powerful, but you. When we pass new laws, we'll listen not to the mighty but to you. When it comes to taxes, we'll prioritise not the wealthy, but you.

In her vision of Britain's economic future, May appealed for a more interventionist role for the state. For example, there were May's commitments to the greater regulation of utility companies and the fees they charge and claims to be the party of the working class. But these relatively minor interventions should be placed in the context of May's hypoglobalist sentiments, espousing a predisposition to deregulation and competitive pressures on social protections. May also claimed that the Conservatives would promote a more aspirational society, as reflected in her commitment to grammar school education and the opportunities this could provide for working-class pupils, and as part of her 'shared society' emphasized 'social mobility for all' (Williams, 2017). Again, though meritocracy is a notion that can sit comfortably within the framework of hyperglobalism, such meritocratic sentiments reflected in part the ideological vision of May's former advisor Nick Timothy, who sought to recast Conservatism in a more Disraelian form, in the sense of appealing to non-elite sections of society (Shipman, 2017). In another sense, though, May was also acting within the tradition of Disraeli by trying to couple conservatism with strong conceptions of national identity.

A sharp departure in convention was evident in May's (2016a) conference speech shortly after the referendum result, when she argued: 'If you believe you are a citizen of the world, you're a citizen of nowhere.' Although the line was directed at elites, it was perceived to be an attack on liberal multiculturalism and cosmopolitanism but also groups like migrants, with their multiple identities (orientation to difference − accentuation of difference). The Liberal Democrat MP Vince Cable was moved to proclaim the statement to be quite evil and stated it 'could have been taken out of Mein Kampf' (Chakelian, 2017). The then Home Secretary Amber Rudd caused similar controversy at the 2016 Conservative conference by unveiling proposals where firms could be forced to disclose what percentage of their workforce is non-British, as a way to encourage them to hire more locals. These acts by May and Rudd were seen as reflections of a new Brexit nationalism which was nativist and insular.

May also sought to highlight the value of her deal over other touted options such as Norway Plus, which she argued − unlike the proposal she supported − would not end free movement. To draw attention to this point, May pledged her proposal would stop people from within the EU 'jumping the queue' in terms of coming to the UK to secure work (Block, 2018). This was employment of an everyday idiom to signal abuse, which critics denounced as manipulating xenophobia, for which May later apologized for in parliament.

May's position on Brexit can be construed as an effort to project a more monocultural conception of national identity, which could also be characterized as nativistic in its approach to migrants. The importance of migration is reflected by the following statement (May, 2016b):

> I have said all along that I believe that underlying part of the vote to leave the European Union was the desire of the British people to have control over immigration, and for decisions on immigration to be made by the Government here in the United Kingdom. We should deliver on that. I look at these issues in terms of the deal we want to negotiate and the outcome we want, which is the best possible deal for trading with, and operating within, the single European market, but that should be commensurate with the other requirements we have: British laws made here in Britain and control on immigration.

The logic of this statement meant that despite the economic costs of leaving the single market, a soft Brexit was to be avoided as this would entail the continuation of free movement – an argument that some said placed an element of irrationalism at the heart of government thinking, thereby weakening economic pragmatism.

Despite her hyperglobalist and nativist stances, May failed to command the full support of the Conservative Party, with most challenges emanating from the section of her party agitating for a hard Brexit, namely the Clean Break Brexiteers.

Clean Break Brexiteers

The Clean Break Brexiteers aspired to what has been termed a hard Brexit: leaving the single market and customs union potentially without an agreement with the EU. Brexiteers held key cabinet positions related to Brexit (David Davis – Exiting EU; Boris Johnson – Foreign Office; Liam Fox – trade). An estimated sixty MPs could be categorized as ultra-Brexiteers belonging to the European Research Group, chaired by hardline supporters of Brexit such as Steve Baker, who in 2017 became a minister in the Department for Exiting the European Union and was replaced as chair of the group by Jacob Rees-Mogg (Baker resigned as a minister in 2018).

The use of strong language and their media prominence also accentuated another populist feature of the Clean Break Brexiteers as celebrity politicians, in particular Boris Johnson and Jacob Rees-Mogg, utilizing a post-democracy public obsession with entertainment and taking on the guise of the anti-politician – saying and doing the unthinkable and challenging established elites (Wood et al, 2016). In an address to a closed meeting, Johnson (2018) gave some indication as to the purpose of his use of colourful invective. He expressed admiration for Trump by quipping that he thought Trump might be a good person to lead Brexit negotiations: 'I have become more and more convinced that there is method in his madness ... imagine Trump doing Brexit ... He'd go in bloody hard ... There'd be all sorts of breakdowns, all sorts of chaos. Everyone would think he'd gone mad. But actually you might get somewhere. It's a very, very good thought.' In other words, emotive and securitized rhetoric designed to cause discord and controversy and provide media headlines was now considered a valid strategy.

As well as being composed of younger more showman-like politicians like Johnson, the Clean Break Brexiteers included veteran Eurosceptics such as MP Sir William Cash. In a parliamentary debate, Cash (2017) declared his support for the EU Withdrawal Bill:

> For me, the referendum was a massive peaceful revolution by consent, of historic proportions. This Bill at last endorses that revolution. From the seventeenth century right the way through our history – through the Corn Laws, the parliamentary reform Act that gave the vote to the working class, the suffragettes who got the vote in 1928, and then again in the period of appeasement – there have been great benchmarks of British history and they have all ultimately been determined by the decisions taken in this House, and, if I may be permitted to say so, by Back Benchers. That is where the decisions have so often been taken. The fact is that the fundamental question on which we have fought not only this referendum but all the battles back to the 1980s has been that of who governs this country. This Bill answers that question.

Cash was implying that, although a revolutionary act, Brexit is part of a long and noble tradition which he is closely aligned to (face work) that follows a trajectory dating back to the seventeenth century, where the British have fought for important political and social rights (topoi of history and custom). Thus, in his view Brexit should be seen as a progressive and emancipatory act. Priti Patel (2016) made a similar argument, comparing Brexiteers to the suffragettes, while Iain Duncan Smith (2019) made reference to the reformation. Like Cash, many of the Brexiteers exhibited a revolutionary fervour, invariably based on tradition and conservative values and a sense of nostalgia. But they were also revolutionary in the sense they embraced a populist approach to politics.

The Clean Break Brexiteers were greatly influenced by populism. Populism supports an extreme majoritarian model of democracy, opposing any group or institution that stands in its way. This approach has a long tradition in the United States but is new to Britain. In accordance with populist positions on governance, the Clean Break Brexiteers placed a strong emphasis, in the sense of Rousseau (1762), on the 'will of the people', at times criticizing representative democracy as seeking to hijack and subvert the 'revolution'. Boris Johnson had proclaimed during the referendum campaign that the country should 'take back control', with 'Vote Leave, Let's Take Back Control' becoming a key slogan. In a speech on Brexit, though, Johnson (2018) warned of a counterrevolution: 'I fear that some people are becoming ever more determined to stop Brexit, to reverse the referendum vote of June 23rd, 2016, and to frustrate the will of the people. I believe that would be a disastrous mistake that would lead to permanent and ineradicable feelings of betrayal. We cannot and will not let it happen.' Another feature of the populist tradition reflected in the Clean Break Brexiteers was to portray themselves as standing in defiance to established elites and external threats. Liam Fox's position provides insights into their perceived radicalism here. In his view, '[t]he Out campaign is "something of a peasants' revolt" while their rivals who want to remain in the EU look "like the elite, the establishment"' (Groves, 2017).

Opposition to a soft Brexit was intense. Interviewed by *The Telegraph*, Rees-Mogg warned the government against delivering 'Brino' – Brexit in name only – and declared: 'If you get a good, clean Brexit and get the advantages from it then the chances of getting Jeremy Corbyn are much diminished' (Singh, 2018). The risk and danger of division and a poorly negotiated deal enabling Corbyn to assume power and unleash a supposedly 'hard left' government agenda was a threat utilized not just by ultra-Brexiteers but also core government figures, as part of a stratagem to try and enforce their interpretation of Brexit. In defiance of such strictures, Johnson warned that too close alignment with the EU would defeat the purpose of Brexit and represent a form of subjugation. In *The Times* newspaper, Johnson said in the event of such alignment people 'would say, "What is the point of what you have achieved?" because we would have gone from a member state to a vassal state' (quoted in Watts, 2017a). Rees-Mogg condemned the government's withdrawal strategy as being 'timid and cowering and terrified of the future' (Merrick, 2018).

Aside from the 'take back control' argument revolving around the question of sovereignty, the Clean Break Brexiteers were deeply influenced by a hyperglobalist desire to promote free trade. A longstanding supporter of the Atlantic partnership (close ties with North America) and the 'American model' of laissez-faire capitalism, who had with bravado proclaimed Brexit and the securing of free trade deals would be 'one of the easiest in human history' (BBC, 2017), Fox saw free trade as a great agent for equalization that had brought prosperity to poorer parts of the world. In almost evangelical language Fox (2017) declared:

> As we regain our independent membership, we will use our position to resist attempts to put up barriers to business, including by G7 and G20 countries that are turning their backs on the principles that made them rich and powerful. The economic and moral reasons for doing so are compelling. Britain has long been on the frontline of free trade. Now, as we prepare to leave the EU, we can move forward with more purpose, for the good of Britain, and the world.

For ardent hyperglobalists like Fox, Brexit was an attempt to reverse the vested interests of economic elites who were undermining free trade through forms of protectionism and other interventions that unbalanced the market. As Fox (2017) asserted, 'One of the great constants of the postwar era has been the growth in global trade. This development has lifted entire nations out of abject poverty, while providing jobs, security, better health and longer lives for billions of people around the world' (topos of resources – redistribution centred on free trade). In making the last point, Fox clearly discards the argument that free trade and the Washington Consensus has been a significant catalyst for developing world poverty and was instead an agent for equality, a point that might explain the decision to publish the article in the *Guardian* (contextualization). Fox was thus making a pitch to progressives through a topos of justice.

Clean Break Brexiteers gave indications of the implications of their ultra-neoliberal vision for a post-Brexit Britain. Priti Patel spoke of 'halving' the 'burden' of regulation (cited by Umunna, 2017). Fox called workplace rights 'intellectually unsustainable', while Johnson demanded scrapping of the social chapter. One of the most prominent broadsheet supporters of Brexit, *The Telegraph* (2017) exclaimed, 'the ultimate goal of this whole process should be to … set the wealth creators free'.

The revolutionary fervour of the Clean Break Brexiteers was a major cause of their rift with May, and despite their alignment with some of the central aims of May regarding Brexit they were suspicious of what they considered was her inclination to compromise and thus disadvantage Britain's effort to leave the EU. This perception explains the level of vitriol and anger expressed by these Conservatives towards the EU, blaming obstructionism as an obstacle in reaching a final deal. Redolent of such hostility was the assertion by Fox that the EU wanted to deter further departures by other member states by ensuring Britain paid what to many, like Fox, would be a prohibitive price for exit: 'The idea of punishing Britain is not the language of a club, it's the language of a gang.' *The Sun* coupled this quote with the headline 'FOX ON THE HUNT: Liam Fox accuses EU of behaving like gangsters in its threat to punish Britain for Brexit' (Dathan and Clark, 2018).

One nation Conservatives

This group included former ministers such as Anna Soubry, Dominic Grieve and Nicky Morgan who had held office during Cameron's premiership but also ex-ministers and party grandees from the Thatcher and Major years, such as Kenneth Clarke and Michael Heseltine. These conservatives can be characterized as centrists, sympathetic to what they considered the EU to be, namely a pragmatic project that allowed states to achieve political, economic and social stability (Susen, 2017). It was the threat to these ideals that motivated one nation Conservatives' opposition to hard Brexit. In the Commons they numbered only around a dozen in terms of defying the government whip, but their numbers overall were greater with some being cowed by the displeasure of government whips or the potential anger of their local Conservative Party associations. However, given May's slight majority, a mere dozen or so rebellious Conservative MPs posed serious problems for the government agenda, while the size of the Conservative rebellions in the Lords was much greater. Of the various amendments that rebels promoted, the most serious were perhaps those which sought to secure a 'meaningful vote' for parliament on the final negotiated deal and on remaining in the customs union.

For one nation Conservatives, the significance of Brexit and the danger to the country's status and wellbeing was articulated by Lord Patten, a former minister under Major who warned that the Brexit deadlock represented one of the bleakest moments in British postwar history. Patten stated in a television interview: 'I think it's the worst time since Suez, though maybe even worse than that because Suez was the end of an era, the end of our colonial aspirations … The European Union was our replacement for that colonial role, and thanks to the calamitous errors of two Conservative prime ministers in a row, who thought they could manage the unmanageable – the English nationalist right wing of the Conservative Party – we're in this hell of a mess' (quoted in Peston, 2017). The Suez Crisis (see Chapter 1) was a serious disaster in British diplomacy, being a clear turning point where Britain's loss of influence as a consequence of the break-up of its empire and decline in industrial might became glaringly apparent. Here, Patten is hankering for the topoi of modernization and Europe as a future direction. For Patten and likeminded Conservatives, Britain was in a comparable crisis caused by the excesses of political zealots within the Conservative Party driven by their obsession with a narrow and insular form of national identity. Patten's alarm at the dangers of political extremism was highlighted in the interview, when he noted that there was a risk of the Conservatives becoming the 'nasty party' of British politics. With this Patten injects irony into his comments, as May had used the same term herself to help guide the party into a more conciliatory approach to politics when she was party chair in 2002.

Writing in *The Independent*, Lord Heseltine argued that '[t]hose who are now pushing for a harder Brexit were on the margins of our party. They were always there, but they are the ones who have betrayed the achievements of Conservative governments from the 1950s onwards' (quoted in Watts, 2017b). In other words, the Clean Break Brexiteers had undermined the one nation traditions that had sought to cast conservatism as a mainstream consensual political force working in close alignment with its European partners. Heseltine uses language to depict these Conservatives as interlopers who at best belonged to the fringes of the party.

For rebels such as Anna Soubry, the Conservative Party had become overridden by hard Brexit ideologues and such was their fervour that reaching a consensus and taking note of the 48 per cent against Brexit was discounted. Soubry (2018) declared: 'They have got rid of leaders and anybody and anything that stood in their way, and they will continue so to do. Even if they are supported by Russian bots and their dirty money, they will do what they have had a lifetime's ambition to do, which is to take us over the cliff into the hard Brexit that my constituents did not vote for. I will continue to represent my constituents.' Clearly, for Conservatives like Soubry the Clean Break Brexiteers had little moral fortitude (ad hominem) possibly being funded and supported by Russia and dirty money (topos of Orwellian manipulation). Soubry also makes reference to a 'cliff edge' – a popular metaphor in Brexit discourse that implied the Brexiteers were fanatical and that their brinkmanship and bravado could lead to Britain crashing out of the EU without a deal, leading to turmoil and dislocation (pathos).

Kenneth Clarke was a prominent one nation Conservative MP who, along with around a dozen other Conservatives, frequently voted against the government line on Brexit. In justifying such action, Clarke (2017) invoked the topos of representative judgement and democracy by recounting Burke's address to the electors of Bristol: 'If I no longer give you the benefit of my judgment and simply follow your orders, I am not serving you; I am betraying you.' Clarke declared he would vote with his conscience and was the sole Conservative to oppose Article 50, also supporting numerous amendments to curb Brexit in defiance of government policy. His statement was a reminder that for Conservatives like him a referendum and the resulting argument that the 'will of the people' must be respected undermined traditional notions of representative democracy, where parliamentarians as custodians should act in the interests of the country and use their judgement to reach informed and reasoned decisions that safeguarded the interests of the nation.

The *Daily Telegraph* branded one nation rebels 'The Brexit mutineers' on a front page featuring the profiles of the fifteen MPs who had voted against the government on the question of the date of Britain's EU departure (Swinford, 2017). In the wake of the government's defeat on the Grieve amendment for a meaningful vote in parliament on the negotiated deal, the *Daily Mail* profiled the images of the eleven Conservatives who voted in support of the amendment on the front page with the caption 'Proud of yourselves?' and denounced them as 'self-consumed malcontents' who had decided to 'betray their leader, party and 17.4 million Brexit voters' (Groves, 2017). In the wake of *The Telegraph* report, Soubry was compelled to report a number of tweets and messages to the police – one of which called for her to be hanged in public – and appealed to the speaker to try and encourage the media to report responsibly on Brexit (Buchan, 2017). Dominic Grieve who was also targeted by the media argued 'the atmosphere is so febrile that it leads firstly to people not listening to what the debate is about, secondly suggests that any questions around Brexit amount to an intention to sabotage and, thirdly, results in some people expressing themselves in terms that at times include death threats' (quoted in Asthana and Stewart, 2017).

Nicky Morgan used these examples of intemperate reporting to highlight a crisis in British democracy by declaring 'something is going badly wrong in our democracy'. Morgan accused politicians and the media of inciting a furore, 'playing with a fire which will eventually consume them as well … Whether it was Momentum targeting Conservative candidates during the general election, the routine trolling on social media, the "mutineer" *Daily Telegraph* headline or the calls for de-selection, death to Brexit traitors and compulsory loyalty tests, something is going badly wrong in our democracy at the moment' (Watts, 2017c).

It is evident that Brexit constituted a huge shift in the Conservative Party, with mainstream Conservatives gravitating towards the right with support for harder forms of Brexit centred on free trade and national sovereignty, with a further shift towards radicalism by the right of the party who seemed to be even more enthralled by the populist turn. Both developments appeared to leave the one nation Conservatives marginalized. These tensions between the different factions had a huge impact on the success of May's Brexit strategy.

The Chequers proposal and withdrawal agreement

The diverging views on Brexit within the Conservative Party were highlighted by the reactions to the 'Chequer's proposal'. Prior to the Chequers proposal being devised, the EU was becoming increasingly frustrated by the British Government's procrastination, a state of affairs accentuated by the deep divisions in the cabinet and challenges to May's authority. The most prominent and recalcitrant minister was Johnson, as characterized by his frequent displays of concern about the direction of the negotiations. In the opinion of some, Johnson was brandishing his hard Brexit credentials ready for a leadership challenge. May's former deputy Damian Green (2018) was scathing about cabinet disunity and insubordination: 'It has been an unedifying spectacle of oversized egos showing they are not fit to be officers.' The line about being 'fit to be officers' implied that some of the Clean Break Brexiteers lacked the sense of duty and integrity that was expected of frontline politicians.

Just over two years after the referendum in July 2018, May was able and willing to unveil in a special cabinet meeting at Chequers, the Prime Minister's country home, a clear outline of a post-Brexit vision (Chequers proposal). The proposal advocated a UK/EU free trade area with a common rulebook for industrial goods and agricultural products but ensuring no new changes in the future would take place without the approval of parliament. However, the proposal was unacceptable to Clean Break Brexiteers, who envisaged a sharper exit from the EU, and it prompted the resignation of David Davis and Boris Johnson.

Polling by the website Conservative Home found party members bitterly opposed to the Chequers proposal, with three in five calling it a bad deal (Elgot, 2018). A YouGov poll in July found only 12 per cent of the respondents saying the Chequers proposal would be good for Britain. More than 40 per cent said it would be bad for Britain, and roughly the same amount said they did not know. In the same month, Deltapoll found 7 per cent thought Chequers was the 'best possible Brexit solution', and another 13 per cent saying it was 'a good compromise', against more than 50 per cent opposed to it. Apparently this meant that the Chequers proposal was more unpopular than the poll tax was prior to implementation (Wright and Coates, 2018).

May continued to promote the Chequers proposal until the autumn of 2018, despite limited domestic and EU support. The stubborn intransigence on the part of the British Government to adapt in the face of criticism culminated in what was widely regarded as the humiliation of the Salzburg Summit in September 2018, where EU leaders rejected the Chequers proposal as unworkable. In the wake of the Salzburg humiliation, former advisor Nick Timothy (2018), who had left his post after the poor electoral performance of the Conservatives in 2017, counselled May to make a stand and find her 'Boudicca moment'. He declared: 'It is time for Theresa May to call on her deepest reserves of defiance and stand up to the European Union. Brussels has rejected her Brexit proposals, insulted us at the recent Salzburg summit and wants to dismember the United Kingdom by effectively annexing Northern Ireland for itself.' With this, Timothy appeals for May to strike a chord of defiance in the spirit of Boudicca, who had staged a rebellion against the cruelty of Roman imperial rule – but in this case a stand should be made against the arrogance of the EU. Supporters of May's approach, such as Foreign Secretary David Hunt, were left to use Dunkirk fighting spirit rhetoric to try and secure concessions. In a speech to the Conservative Party Conference in 2018 and in the wake of the Salzburg humiliation, Hunt (2018) suggested that the perceived intransigence of the EU was equivalent to Britain being held 'prisoner' and was reminiscent of the Soviet Union: 'Let me say one more thing about these talks. Never mistake British politeness for British weakness because, if you put a country like Britain in a corner, we don't crumble – we fight.'

Such a speech was designed to appeal to the party faithful who gather at the conference and are in general the more radical elements of the party. Fighting talk centred on the topos of EU hierarchy was designed to bolster Hunt's personal support, which might be needed in any leadership contest. This having an eye to possible future leadership was an added problem in the Brexit negotiations more broadly, with statements by political figures – although ostensibly directed at the negotiations – in reality being aimed at a domestic political audience and designed to bolster or accrue support at home. Conversely, such comments often damaged negotiations by undermining trust and stoking nationalist hostilities.

Despite such bellicose language and exhortations, May was reluctant to initiate the only act of real defiance to the EU in negotiations – to leave without a deal. Although this course of action had been hinted at by May and urged on her by the likes of Timothy, it was in fact nothing more than a negotiation stratagem. Much to the chagrin of the Clean Break Brexiteers, May had limited appetite for the potential chaos of a no-deal scenario.

In November 2018, May had to accept the weakness of her position and reach agreement with the EU on a proposal that contained marked differences to the Chequers proposal. The Brexit withdrawal agreement contained the following core proposals:

(i) A transition period from 29 March 2019 lasting until 31 December 2020, where Britain would leave EU institutions but continues to abide by EU rules.
(ii) A financial settlement expected to be £39 billion.
(iii) UK citizens in the EU, and EU citizens in the UK, would retain their residency and social security rights after Brexit.
(iv) An expressed hope that a trade deal could be negotiated by December 2020, but this would not be the frictionless trade agreement the Chequers proposal had promised.
(v) The backstop was an arrangement for the Irish border that would come into effect if no other solutions to maintain the current open border could be agreed once Britain left the EU.

The last point was designed to protect the Good Friday Agreement and keep an open border between Northern Ireland and Ireland after Brexit. Once Britain left the EU single market and customs union, it would become a 'third country' to the EU. This would create, for the first time, a land border between the UK and the EU – the border between Ireland and Northern Ireland – and if no special arrangements could be found for the Irish border then the EU would impose the standard checks it has at its border with any third country. As part of the draft Withdrawal Agreement, a protocol on Northern Ireland was included setting out the backstop. The EU made a significant concession in granting a UK-wide 'single customs territory', avoiding the need for customs checks between Great Britain and Northern Ireland, while the requirement for regulatory alignment was limited to Northern Ireland.

The agreement also contained 'level playing field' commitments – a set of common rules and standards that are used primarily to prevent businesses in one country undercutting their rivals in other countries in areas such as workers' rights and environmental protections. These were put in by the EU to limit the UK's capacity to gain an unfair advantage by lowering standards. These commitments were a major source of frustration for the more ardent Clean Break Brexiteers and their hyperglobalist aspirations. May, though, was able to use such level playing field commitments as a means to try and entice support from Labour MPs representing Leave constituencies, but as she did so in order to gain a parliamentary majority for her agreement she further alienated the Clean Break Brexiteers.

From winter 2018, May attempted to navigate the withdrawal agreement through a hostile and belligerent parliament. Once unveiled, the EU withdrawal agreement was met with widespread opposition from within the Conservative Party, including from members of the cabinet – leading to the resignation of ministers sympathetic to a Clean Break Brexit such as Dominic Raab (Brexit Secretary) and Esther McVey (Work and Pensions) in November 2018.

Opposition from Clean Break Brexiteer backbenchers was vociferous and predictable. It was asserted that, as with the Chequers proposal, the withdrawal agreement crossed the red lines of May's Lancaster House speech. For Boris Johnson, the agreement consigned Britain to the status of a 'colony'. David Davis, former Brexit Secretary, argued that the deal was an affront to Britain's constitution, as the EU would continue to influence British affairs as a consequence of the backstop solution to the Irish border, declaring that 'the authority of our constitution is on the line' (quoted in Syal and O'Carroll, 2018). In the mind of these Brexiteers, May had capitulated to EU pressure, with Rees-Mogg describing the EU as a 'mafia'. Brexiteers like Davis claimed that the fears of a no-deal were being greatly exaggerated and that this should remain the destination for Britain's departure. May also sought to attract opposition support by guaranteeing that workers' rights would keep pace with the rest of Europe, but such pledges in the final stage of her premiership did little to attract new support and further alienated the Clean Break Brexiteers (Elgot and Sabbagh, 2019).

In an article for the *Mail on Sunday*, Johnson used metaphor and a topos of danger which generated huge controversy by denouncing the backstop plan to ensure no hard Irish border, which would see Northern Ireland effectively remain part of the single market if no other workable solution was found. Johnson (2018) wrote: 'We have opened ourselves to perpetual political blackmail. We have wrapped a suicide vest around the British constitution – and handed the detonator to Michel Barnier.' The Irish backstop proposal in the agreement was a significant point of contention, with the Democratic Unionist Party (DUP) believing that if this came into operation it would compromise the integrity of the United Kingdom as a consequence of Northern Ireland being governed by different regulations to the rest of the UK. For the Clean Break Brexiteers, the backstop was a ruse by the EU to keep Britain perpetually within its orbit, as the backstop agreement could only be terminated by mutual agreement, hence the use of terms like 'vassalage' or 'blackmail' to denounce the intentions behind it. The metaphor of the suicide vest, which Johnson must have realized would stoke great controversy given the number of such suicide attacks that have been directed at British armed forces and the public, was intended to convey pathos, the danger the backstop presented. The metaphor also implies the bullying and power that figures like EU chief negotiator Barnier were seeking to employ against Britain. The Clean Break Brexiteers agitated for a time limit on the backstop or for power to unilaterally end the agreement. May's failure to align with this stance was a major point of tension between her and Clean Break Brexiteers. She gave an assurance that the government and EU hoped to avoid a backstop by prioritizing the drafting of a new trade deal. Despite such assurances, May failed to assuage the critics of the backstop. Given May's reliance on DUP parliamentary, votes this was a critical issue, with the DUP signalling that if the proposal was accepted it would withdraw its support from May's minority government.

The counternarrative was that the Clean Break Brexiteers were dangerous ideologues. In the wake of criticism around the withdrawal agreement even the conservative *Daily Mail* newspaper (2018), now under new editorship which was more sympathetic to May, derided the critics of the agreement. In a frontpage editorial the *Daily Mail* called May's Brexiteer critics 'peacocking saboteurs', 'low-grade assassins' and 'preening Tory saboteurs' who would 'undermine the PM, their party, Brexit and Britain's future', who did not have a 'grand plan' but only an 'economic suicide note'. The May loyalist minister Alistair Burt quipped in a tweet directed at the Brexiteer parliamentary caucus the European Research Group (ERG): 'They [Clean Break Brexiteers] never, ever stop. Votes against them, letters going in late – nothing matters to ERG. After the apocalypse, all that will be left will be ants and Tory MPs complaining about Europe and their leader.' The perception of extremism thus seemed to have taken root among a large section of the public, with numerous cartoons and jokes emphasizing buffoonery, elitism and fanaticism as being redolent of lead Brexiteers.

The end of the May premiership

In order to further the new withdrawal agreement and in response to backbench pressure to see parliament be given a more proactive role, the government staged a series of parliamentary debates consisting of 'meaningful votes' to approve a deal with the EU, and 'next steps' allowing MPs to vote on amendments about what should happen next. The first meaningful vote was to have taken place in December 2018 but was postponed. Shortly after the postponement, Sir Graham Brady, chair of the 1922 Committee, which represented Conservative backbenchers, announced that he had received the requisite forty-eight letters from

Conservative MPs to trigger a vote of confidence in May. Such a vote had been anticipated for months and relations between some backbenchers and the prime minister had become highly acrimonious.

In the leadership contest, May secured the support of 200 of her MPs but 117 voted against her. The contest appeared to further weaken a prime minister who appeared increasingly beleaguered and cornered. May suffered a series of parliamentary defeats, lacking support in key votes from one nation Conservatives and Clean Break Brexiteers. In 2019 a series of meaningful votes (MV) and next steps (NS) were staged in parliament (see Table 3.1).

The meaningful vote in parliament on 15 January 2019 saw 202 MPs vote in favour of May's deal, with 432 against. The previous biggest

Table 3.1: Meaningful votes and next steps

MV1	**15 January 2019:** MPs voted down May's Brexit deal for the first time, by a majority of 230. Some 118 Conservatives voted against.
NS1	**29 January 2019:** May won the vote, but only by getting Tory MPs to unite behind the Brady amendment, which said her deal would only be acceptable if the backstop were 'replaced' by 'alternative arrangements'. May was defeated when MPs passed the Spelman amendment, ruling out no deal. Some 17 Tories defied the whip to back it.
NS2	**14 February 2019:** May suffered a defeat when a motion restating the NS1 result got voted down, by a majority of 45, because hardline Brexiteers did not want to be seen to be endorsing the Spelman result.
NS3	**27 February 2019:** Tory and Labour MPs united to support a backbench amendment, committing the government to allowing a vote on extending article 50 if it lost MV2. Motion defeated.
MV2	**12 March 2019:** This was the second vote on the deal, taking place after a late-night trip by May to Strasbourg to clarify new assurances with Juncker, European Commission president. But legal advice from Geoffrey Cox, the attorney general, saying the legal risk of being stuck in the backstop remained 'unchanged', led to the motion being voted down by a majority of 149, with 75 Tory MPs voting against.
NS4	**13 March 2019:** This was the debate on ruling out a no-deal Brexit. But the government motion only ruled out no deal on 29 March, and May was defeated twice as MPs voted to rule out a no-deal Brexit for good. Some 17 Tories defied the whip and voted against any no deal in the final vote, with another 29 Tories abstaining, including four cabinet ministers.
NS5	**14 March 2019:** MPs approved, by a majority of 211, a government motion approving an Article 50 extension until 30 June if MPs backed May's deal. The Benn amendment stating parliament should take control was defeated by a majority of two.
NS6	**25 March 2019:** The Commons approved the Letwin amendment allowing for indicative votes to enable parliament to express its preference on Brexit. Three ministers resigned to join the 30 Tories who defied the whip to back Letwin. The amendment was passed by a majority of 27.
MV3	**29 March 2019:** MPs rejected Theresa May's Brexit deal by 58 votes.

meaningful defeat of a prime minister was in 1924, when Ramsay MacDonald's short-lived minority Labour government lost by 166 votes. The defeat thus represented the biggest defeat a government had suffered in modern history.

As a consequence of the parliamentary impasse and May's EU withdrawal proposal having been thrice rejected, the House of Commons Exiting the EU Select Committee suggested a series of indicative votes to test the sentiment of MPs and narrow down the range of options. The series of indicative votes saw a range of proposals being presented by backbenchers in April 2019. The indicative votes were not legally binding, but if one proposal had come out on top, it might have become a rallying point as the Brexit deadline approached. A proposal to see the UK join a customs union came the closest to being passed – losing narrowly by three votes, in part because some Remain MPs decided to hold out for a second referendum where Brexit could be rejected. A motion in favour of 'soft Brexit' – staying in the European single market and customs union – lost by twenty-one votes, while another to support a second referendum lost by seventeen.

Further defeats and an inability to gather the requisite support to push her withdrawal agreement through parliament prompted May to try to cobble together a majority with opposition support, which led to intensive negotiations between the Conservatives and Labour frontbench team, including discussions on a customs union and a second referendum. The risk of compromises being made further alienated the Clean Break Brexiteers who sought to revise the rules of the 1922 Committee to enable another leadership challenge. The likely risk of being defeated in a vote compelled May to announce she would resign and leave office in July 2019.

May had sought to fuse mainstream Conservatism with the populist ethos of Brexit, but the reality and hard choices of the EU negotiations did not sit easily with the populist assumptions of Brexit and ultimately led to May being unwilling to leave the EU without a deal, which in turn ended her premiership as her support ebbed away. The leadership election to replace May would determine whether a leader more in the populist mould might more effectively complete the political transition that May had attempted. Yet the process appears to confirm Polanyi's assumption that in times of economic crisis and upheaval elites can be drawn into forms of authoritarianism. Brexit and changes in the Conservative Party reflected global economic trends where some economies such as the United States were reorienting their economic strategies in the wake of the global financial crisis to achieve greater competitivity.

Conclusion

As noted as the start of this chapter, a fundamental change took place within the Conservative Party which was in a state of flux following the Brexit referendum. The Conservative Party appeared to be recasting itself in a populist form, returning to the political trajectory established by Conservative leaders such as Hague, Duncan Smith and Howard. That model had been jettisoned by Cameron, who felt a more centrist position would deliver electoral success. The key problem with the populist stratagem from 1997 to 2005 was that during a period of prosperity and affluence it afforded limitations in terms of mobilizing a reasonably content electorate. In the wake of the financial crisis and a decade of austerity, in terms of electoral success the Conservatives may have felt justified in not just returning to the populist model but accentuating it in terms of language and polemics directed at the establishment and status quo. Reflecting the degree of shift, Conservative MEP Julie Girling, who lost the party whip for supporting a motion in the European Parliament critical of the British Government's Brexit strategy, noted in a statement: 'I have been active in the party for 40 years – 20 as an elected representative – and for 39 of those years our policy has been pro-Europe. I have never considered myself a rebel and have not altered my beliefs. It is the party which has changed' (Boffey, 2017a). Boris Johnson's success in the leadership contest and appointment as prime minister in July 2019, with senior cabinet positions going to Priti Patel and Dominic Raab, and with Dominic Cummings being made a key advisor in Downing Street, confirmed the degree of this shift.

The popular contention is that social movements are collective efforts by those at the margins to redress their disadvantage. With its emphasis on challenges to hegemony, the Tea Party in the United States can be viewed as something of a deviation from social movement theory. The Tea Party invokes the language and rhetoric of anger directed at vested interests, offers empowerment and seeks to mobilize the disenfranchised – yet aside from appealing to the dispossessed, it also aligns with the interests and agendas of elites, especially as the Tea Party favours a strongly hyperglobalist deregulatory frame based around an insular and restrictive form of identity (Dietrich, 2014). The same processes were at work in the Conservative Party. Hence, the Brexit phenomenon can be interpreted as the 'Tea Partyization' of British conservatism. As becomes evident in Chapter 4, conservatism was not alone in facing a process of deep and fundamental change; Labour was also undergoing a radical transformation.

4

Politics in Focus: Labour

The chapter gives an overview of the strategy of Labour in response to Brexit and covers the period up to the summer of 2019, detailing the words and actions of key Labour figures in the wake of the referendum. Labour's response to Brexit and course of developments between 2016 and 2019, as with the Conservative Party, is a story of paradigm change, tension and struggle between the different strands and traditions of a party in a state of flux.

Setting the context

Brexit confronted Labour with supreme challenges but also highlighted the different attitudes and stances to the European Union (EU) evident within the party in the postwar period. Labour had been influenced by the Churchill doctrine of welcoming greater unity in Europe but at the same time placing relations with the empire and commonwealth and the English-speaking world, primarily the United States, as a greater priority. Labour's caution and lack of imagination on Europe after the war is reflected in comments made to officials by Labour Foreign Secretary Ernest Bevin on the possibility of closer ties with Europe. Bevin exclaimed, 'If you open up that Pandora's box, you never know what Trojan horses will jump out' (quoted in Klos, 2018). Speaking at the annual Labour Conference, Labour leader Hugh Gaitskell (1962) had cautioned against British entry into the European Economic Community (EEC) by stating it would inevitably pull Britain into a federal structure, leading to 'the end of a thousand years of history'. Harold Wilson, though, abandoned his earlier ambivalence to the EEC and made Britain's second application in 1967, believing it might remedy the nation's economic woes. The application was vetoed by France for a second time.

In the 1970s, following Heath's successful application to the EEC, Labour's position on Europe became fractured, with concerns about the potential interference the EEC might pose to a socialist agenda. Such concerns were orchestrated by left luminaries such as Tony Benn, prompting Wilson to circumnavigate their opposition through Britain's first referendum on Europe in 1975. However, signalling a move to the left, in its 1983 manifesto under Michael Foot's leadership, Labour pledged to leave the EEC – a factor seen as being partly responsible for Labour's electoral humiliation in 1983 (Pugh, 2010).

Under the modernization programme of Labour opposition leader Neil Kinnock, the party embraced EEC membership in 1988, a stance accentuated during New Labour and the premierships of Tony Blair (1997–2007) and Gordon Brown (2007–10). Once in government, New Labour joined the social chapter, which the Major government had opted out of, but was far from being an ardent supporter of federalism. Just prior to his election victory, in 1997 Blair wrote in *The Sun*: 'I will have no truck with a European superstate. If there are moves to create that dragon I will slay it' (cited in MacShane, 2016, 91). Measures would be taken, Blair assured, to protect British identity. Anti-federalism prompted New Labour, primarily under the influence of Brown, to avoid Britain's entry into the euro currency, but it was enthusiastic in supporting the extension of the single market.

Dovetailed to Labour's more positive embrace of the European project was the fact the party had transformed itself from a statist party based on a redistributive egalitarian discourse to one that fused a social democratic and neoliberal outlook and thus accepted the rationale of the single market (Levitas, 1998). These aspects of New Labour policy prompted a small group of parliamentary Eurosceptics, including figures such as John McDonnell and Jeremy Corbyn, to defy the party whip and vote against a number of measures to accentuate European integration, perceived by these rebels as being designed to bolster neoliberalism. On assuming the party leadership in 2015, Corbyn's Euroscepticism became less pronounced and in the referendum of 2016 he became what can be termed a reluctant Remainer, seeking to retain EU membership but to reform it from within.

These differing stances, as reflected in this brief historic overview of Labour's views towards Europe, continue to have resonance in Labour's post-referendum strategy. As with the Conservatives, Labour's line was not a homogeneous one. To capture the essence of these positions, I have created a typology: The *Lexiteers* – radical socialists who saw Brexit as part of the socialist transformation of Britain but including centrists who felt Britain must exit a federalist project and respect the referendum result.

In contrast, *Labour Europhiles* wished to retain close links with Europe or even retain full membership and were broadly drawn from the centrist strands of the party. A third strand were the *Radical Left Europhiles* who generally supported Corbyn but included soft left factions; they favoured remaining in the EU and working for radical reform in Europe.

To understand further these strands of opinion, it is necessary to consider a series of demographic and socio-economic forces at play since the late 1980s, which were brought to the fore by the referendum. The deindustrialization of large parts of the UK has diluted working-class identity and traditions based on labourism (see Chapter 1), prompting forms of English nationalism tinged with nativism to take root among the working class. Such hostility to migrants from the working class has in fact been a feature of British politics since the seventeenth century, where sections of the British working class have been antagonistic towards migrant groups such as the Irish, Jews and Afro Caribbeans (Gough, 2017). In the 2010s, parts of the traditional Labour vote were prised away from Labour by the UK Independence Party (UKIP) and the Brexit Party, prompting some to assert that Labour has an English identity problem unable to appeal and entwine notions of English and Labour identity (Robinson, 2016). These changes in part accounted for how the Labour vote splintered in the referendum, with urban, more educated Labour supporters being passionate Remainers, while those mainly older less educated voters in post-industrial towns voted Leave with enthusiasm (Bailey, 2017).

Labour's dilemma was that while a large majority of the membership and parliamentary party were pro-EU, two thirds of the parliamentary constituencies held by Labour voted Leave. The perception that if Labour rejected Brexit it would lose northern seats was an important point of argumentation for those calling upon Labour to accept the referendum result.

Corbyn's and Labour's position on Brexit

A perceived lacklustre referendum campaign and the belief that Corbyn was still a Eurosceptic who secretly welcomed Brexit led to a large section of the parliamentary Labour Party, primarily on the centre and right, to denounce Corbyn's leadership, thus triggering a leadership contest. Despite convincingly winning a second leadership election with 60 per cent of the vote, the section of the party that had opposed him in that contest despaired of his and the party's Brexit strategy; others, though, hailed it as astute and realistic.

In the wake of the referendum, Corbyn's initial response – one that was frequently reiterated – was that the referendum result and the 'will of the people' had to be respected. McDonnell announced Labour would not frustrate the triggering of Article 50, the start of the legal process to leave. McDonnell stated that 'to do so would put us against the majority will of the British people and on the side of certain corporate elites, who have always had the British people at the back of the queue ... Labour accepts the referendum result as the voice of the majority and we must embrace the enormous opportunities to reshape our country that Brexit has opened for us' (Bienkov, 2016). McDonnell was inferring that the EU bolsters the interests of corporate elites to the detriment of the working class, a classic piece of Bennite argumentation. Labour set a three-line whip to support the passing of the government's Article 50 motion, but it also sought to map out a positive vision of Brexit. In the 2017 election manifesto, Labour pledged to respect the referendum result and leave the EU. However, Labour opposed a no-deal hard Brexit.

Labour pledged to support Brexit, but only where it fell within six tests defined and set by Keir Starmer, Labour's Brexit spokesperson. The tests included: (i) ensuring a strong and collaborative future relationship with the EU; (ii) delivering the exact same benefits as Britain currently has as a member of the single market and customs union; (iii) ensuring the fair management of migration in the interests of the economy and communities; (iv) defending rights and protections and preventing a race to the bottom; (v) protecting national security and Britain's capacity to tackle cross-border crime; (vi) delivering for all regions and nations of the UK (Bean, 2017). This position was instrumental in Labour refusing to endorse Theresa May's Brexit strategy.

Although a small group of Labour parliamentarians supported key votes in the House of Commons which set out the government's vision of a hard form of Brexit, there was a strong degree of unanimity from Labour on the dangers of such a position. Labour perceived May's Brexit strategy as heralding an attempt to adopt a new neoliberal model. In a series of leadership speeches, Corbyn sought to set out Labour's Brexit position, typical of the genre of leadership speeches. Through highly formal speech acts with short and clear sentences, Corbyn sought to develop his thoughts and main points step by step in a way that was comprehensible to a wide audience and designed to maximize the chance of accurate media coverage. As is typical of the genre, through a formal, serious and concise presentation the leader seeks to portray themselves as statesmanlike and with gravitas. As Corbyn (2017) noted in his address to the Trades Union Congress (TUC): 'The Tory approach to Brexit is to use the process of leaving to deliver a deregulated free market tax haven on the shores of

Europe, underpinned with a race-to-the-bottom trade deal with Donald Trump – a Shangri-La for bosses and bankers but nothing of the kind for everybody else.'

Here, Corbyn was clearly using a radical socialist frame to highlight what he considered to be the ultra-neoliberal agenda of the Conservative vision of Brexit, which was seeking to strengthen economic competitiveness a 'Shangri-La for bosses and bankers'. This reorientation of the economy was a shadowing of the United States under the Trump presidency, seeking to compete more effectively with China and new and emerging economies by moving away from social protections and workers' rights, coded as a 'race to the bottom'. Using Wallerstein's world-systems theory (see Chapter 1), such a perception can be interpreted as viewing attempts by Britain and the United States to reorient their economic models as seeking to preserve their positions within the core of leading capitalist countries. In a rare moment of agreement and radicalism, Tony Blair echoed this point by stating Brexit was driven by people who wanted to complete a 'Thatcherite revolution' (Stone, 2018a).

Corbyn accepted the referendum result and believed that a form of Brexit could be achieved that would protect social rights. Labour offered what Corbyn (2017) described in his address to the TUC as a 'jobs first Brexit', where Britain would be outside of the EU but in a relationship guaranteeing 'full access to the European single market as part of a new trade agreement and relationship with the EU'. Outlining this vision further, Corbyn stated that he sought '[a] jobs-first Brexit that maintains and develops workers' rights, and consumer and environmental protections and uses powers returned from Brussels to support a new industrial strategy. A jobs-first Brexit where work pays, employees have security and decent conditions and prosperity is shared by the true wealth creators – that means all of us' (topos of social justice).

Basically, Labour hoped a new economic agenda outside the EU would allow unhindered new forms of public ownership and lower rates of VAT to help those on the lowest income and allow state aid to support sunrise industries; in contrast to the Conservative position, this would benefit 'all of us' rather than just a privileged few. The repetition of the slogan 'jobs-first Brexit' by Corbyn, which was used frequently by Labour in campaigning, including for the 2017 General Election, was to emphasize that unlike the perceived dangers of a Conservative 'race to the bottom' Brexit, jobs would not be lost or undermined under a Labour Brexit. In fact the reverse was promised, with active job creation strategies and this explains Labour's decision to showcase its elaborated Brexit position at a TUC event.

In a further elaboration of this economic message, Corbyn (2018a) gave a speech where reference was made to plans for a 'UK first' approach in government funding, in the form of contracts and slogans such as 'build it in Britain', which in fact was also the title of a campaign Corbyn unveiled: 'We will build things here again that for too long have been built abroad because we have failed to invest.' In his speech, Corbyn said a Labour government would ensure the state used 'more of its own money to buy here in Britain'. He proceeded to list a series of contracts that government departments had awarded to foreign contractors. In order to raise the hackles of more nationalistic sentiments, Corbyn included in his list the case of the government using a French supplier to provide British passports. At the end of the catalogue, he announced: 'Labour is determined to see public contracts provide public benefit using our money to nurture and grow our industries and to expand our tax base.' Such rhetoric could be described as economic nationalism and veering towards protectionism, at least in the sense that it wished to avoid the free-marketism of global capitalism which successive governments, including New Labour, had subscribed to. It was a stratagem that might counter the nationalism of a Conservative Brexit, with a variant that promised rewards for the working class – not just an economic elite.

Corbyn was in effect seeking to revive the Bennite socialist economic strategy of the 1970s and 1980s, albeit a much diluted one, countenancing state intervention, much higher levels of taxation, and capital and trade controls. One Conservative MP, Andrew Bridgen, attacked the policies, remarking that they would make Britain into a statist and command control economy – 'Move over Venezuela, we're coming in. This is all part of the Marxist plan' (quoted in Davidson, 2018). Although such a comparison is a gross over-exaggeration the new Labour position was a sharp contrast to a British economic model dependent on personal and corporate debt, high immigration, flexible labour markets and low taxation (Gamble, 2017) that had formed an economic consensus since Thatcher.

Another point of departure appeared to occur in Labour's stance towards migration. Acknowledging the concerns that working-class communities held on migration, Labour recalibrated its position on this issue. The change of mood was apparent shortly after the referendum. Addressing a fringe meeting at the Labour Party Conference, the centrist Labour MP Rachel Reeves noted that her constituency was like a 'tinder box' and voters' concerns about immigration and lack of control over their lives could 'explode' onto the streets if they remained unaddressed (Mason and Stewart, 2016). On the left, figures such as Angela Rayner MP, shadow education spokesperson, also voiced concerns about the impact of migration on employment opportunities for British workers.

In an interview on the BBC with presenter Andrew Marr (2017), Corbyn now acknowledged that after leaving the EU there would still be European workers in Britain and vice versa but under Labour's Brexit vision there would be limitations under a 'managed' migration approach – a term that implied the existing system of free movement was the reverse of being administered and coherent. In fact, 'managed migration' had been a clarion call for Conservatives for a number of years, with a group active within that party called Conservatives for Managed Migration. Such a line of argument evokes the topos of burden. Corbyn justified this measure as ensuring there would no longer be 'the wholesale importation of underpaid workers from central Europe in order to destroy conditions, particularly in the construction industry'. A key point in the interview was as follows (Marr, 2017):

Andrew Marr: But to be absolutely clear you don't stop people coming from Latvia or Poland who want to come and work here, you don't stop them at the airport of the border and say let's see your papers?

Jeremy Corbyn: Listen, they would come here on the basis of the jobs available and their skill sets to go with it. What we wouldn't allow is this practice by agencies, who are quite disgraceful the way they do it, recruit workforce, low paid and bring them here in order to dismiss an existing workforce in the construction industry, then pay them low wages. It's appalling. And the only people who benefit are the companies.

Without directly saying it, the reply by Corbyn strongly indicated that free movement would end and be replaced by a quota system where migrants would only be admitted on the basis of requisite skills and labour shortages. Labour was seeking to address the concerns of those who voted Leave because of anxieties about migration, but this had to be done in a way which was not overtly nativist in order not to offend the Labour Europhiles and cosmopolitans committed to free movement. The general anecdote Corbyn provides, referring to how agencies exploit migrant and domestic workers in the construction industry, is a stratagem to give the policy shift a more radical spin that would make it attractive to Corbyn's radical support base. But some on the left were disheartened by this new position. The former Greek finance minister Yanis Varoufakis commented: 'It's a sad day when the Labour Party is defending the end of free movement and, indeed, promising its end' (quoted in Dallison, 2017). The customs union was a serious bone of contention in the Brexit negotiations as the European Commission complained that Theresa May's refusal to remain in the existing union or something similar and her making this a red line created a major stumbling block in talks, as there was a danger of creating a hard border in Northern Ireland. In February 2018, Corbyn pledged support for a bespoke customs union, with exemptions for Britain on a number of issues.

In a leader's speech at Coventry University's National Transport Design Centre, Corbyn no doubt hoped that in a setting of science and innovation located in a city noted for manufacturing he would be able to highlight the key theme of his speech: the need for a customs union (contextualization). Corbyn (2018a) told the assembled students and local politicians that 'Labour would seek to negotiate a new comprehensive UK–EU customs union to ensure that there are no tariffs with Europe and to help avoid any need for a hard border in Northern Ireland.' He was aware of the accusations that with such a soft form of Brexit, Britain would be a 'rule taker' – in other words, having to adhere to EU rules without the ability to shape and change them as it would no longer be part of EU decision-making processes. Corbyn sought to nuance these comments with reference to autonomy by demanding Britain had a continued say in trade deals: 'Labour would not countenance a deal that left Britain as a passive recipient of rules decided elsewhere by others. That would mean ending up as mere rule takers.' Labour would seek protections, clarifications or exemptions where necessary for privatization, public service competition directives, state aid and procurement rules.

Given that a significant number of Conservative MPs also supported a customs union, Labour had established a clear point of collision with the government that could lead to its parliamentary defeat. Although Labour countenanced the possibility of remaining in the single market during an interim transitional phase, Corbyn ruled out retaining membership, the argument being from the leadership that this would mean the UK was still effectively in the EU and not honouring the referendum result. Furthermore, it was maintained that membership could impede Labour's new economic strategy and interfere with a managed migration policy.

The vagueness of Labour's Brexit approach was referred to as 'constructive ambiguity'. It prompted Corbyn to tread carefully and cautiously in terms of rhetoric and pledges as Brexit progressed, allowing the Conservatives to take the lead and ultimately the responsibility for Brexit, in the process possibly destroying their party. Constructive ambiguity was described by Jonathan Lis (2017), deputy director of thinktank British Influence, as Corbyn following Napoleon's advice not to interrupt his enemy while they are making mistakes. Lis noted, 'he is not showing great courage, or even perhaps acting in the immediate national interest – but he is playing a clever long game that in the end could benefit us all'.

An added advantage of constructive ambiguity was that, like May, Corbyn needed to straddle a diverse range of groups with different agendas in order to preserve party unity and the Labour vote. In the 2017 General Election, Remainers had voted Labour despite its manifesto pledge to leave, because they saw the party as the best viable option for a soft Brexit or to actually retain EU membership, while the pledge and rhetoric of Corbyn also convinced some Leavers to vote Labour. The different strands of opinion on Brexit are described in the next section; they formed deep cleavages and cut across the left and right of the party.

The Lexiteers

Lexiteers (Labour supporters in favour of Britain leaving the EU) encompassed a diverse range of groups and included elements of the radical left supporters of Corbyn influenced by Bennite Euroscepticism. Lexiteers Guinan and Hanna (2017) note:

> Under successive leaders Labour became so incorporated into the ideology of Europeanism as to preclude any clear-eyed critical analysis of the actually existing EU as a regulatory and trade regime pursuing deep economic integration. The same political journey that carried Labour into its technocratic embrace of the EU also resulted in the abandonment of any form of distinctive economics separate from the orthodoxies of market liberalism ... Given that the UK will soon be escaping the EU, what opportunities might this afford? Three policy directions immediately stand out: public ownership, industrial strategy, and procurement. In each case, EU regulation previously stood in the way of promising left strategies. In each case, the political and economic returns from bold departures from neoliberal orthodoxy after Brexit could be substantial [topos of left Euroscepticism].

This quote displays some of the classic tropes of left Euroscepticism, namely that the EU is a hierarchical and bureaucratic body serving the interests of a neoliberal market and that New Labour, seduced by market economics, had lost its objectivity and propensity to critical analysis. Once Britain 'escapes' this restraint, the authors assume government will be free to introduce 'bold' forms of socialist economic policy. Such arguments had been part of the Bennite left position and had reached their zenith when Labour's 1983 election manifesto pledged to leave the EU. With the advent of New Labour, such arguments were marginalized. Now, the proponents of Lexit reasoned that the left in Britain and the rest of Europe had become disconnected from the working class and poor – a process accentuated by German hegemony that had divided Europe into an unstable core and dependent peripheries (Lapavitsas, 2018). A Lexiteer argument was that a socialist government would need freedom from EU law on competition, state aid and procurement to tackle the growing trade deficit that had bedevilled the British economy and to boost productivity, reducing dependence on the service sector (Whyman, 2018).

Hostility to the EU from this section of the left was bolstered by actions the EU took to advance austerity measures in the wake of the financial crisis and its interference in the governance of Greece while under the left populist administration of Syriza. It was the contention of these left Eurosceptics that the economic model that nurtured the crisis was largely still in place. For Lexiteers, the referendum result was also an act of resistance by working-class communities to the power and hegemony of the market. Yet the Lexiteers were accused of peddling deluded and serious mistruths about the ability of the EU to frustrate a socialist programme. Ben Chu (2017), economics editor of *The Independent*, asserted that while the EU has a bias against monopoly, it is not opposed to public ownership. The operation of more radical socialist governments in Portugal and Spain also undermined claims that the EU could not be compatible with radicalism.

Some Lexiteers advocated forms of internationalism, which stressed the importance and value of a European and globalist social movement committed to the overthrow of capitalism, while others subscribed to left nationalism, with socialist veterans such as Arthur Scargill and Dennis Skinner advocating an emphasis on the national struggle for socialism. For some, Lexit was at the heart of the new left populist turn within the Labour Party. The Harvard University Professor of Government Richard Taylor (2017) wrote: 'Without Brexit the Labour Party will revert to its role of providing an alternative managerial class for late-stage capitalism, and the enthusiasm of its new-found supporters will wither away or find new and more troubling outlets.' In a similar vein, a Labour activist and supporter of Corbyn declared: 'If the People's Vote campaign is successful, there will be a powerful narrative told by a populist right alliance that the elites of this country colluded to usurp the democratic will of the people. Asking Labour to campaign for remain in a second referendum in leave-voting, post-industrial cities such as Stoke would make Corbyn part of the same political elite they feel have betrayed them' (Rigby, 2018). In some respects, Labour's pro-Leave position became an article of faith in Corbyn and the party's commitment to socialist values, with those seeking to see the party support a referendum and/or a Remain position perceived by some Corbyn supporters as using this policy position as a proxy to undermine Corbyn and a radical left agenda.

Within the parliamentary party, though, there was also a small band of right-wing and maverick MPs like Frank Field and Kate Hoey whose Euroscepticism had far more in common with the right wing of the Conservative Party. The group also included MPs such as Caroline Flint who represented Leave constituencies; although they had campaigned in the referendum to Remain, they now felt the result had to be respected and such an outcome would enable a form of managed migration. These MPs were sympathetic to May's deal. There were also centrist MPs such as Stephen Kinnock who promoted a soft Brexit conception, the 'Common Market 2'.

Critics of the Lexit position, primarily from the more Europhile wing of the Labour Party, levelled a number of accusations, with the charge that Labour was failing to hold the government to account by not setting out sharply contrasting positions and was in the process undermining Labour values. This was all part of a narrative that Labour under Corbyn was out of sync with the mainstream of public opinion. As one critic noted: 'One of the more bewildering things about Britain's current politics is the spectre of a socially liberal, internationalist Labour Party apparently siding with the English, nationalist right-wing of the Conservative Party over Brexit' (Tilford, 2017b). Thus, for critics Labour was enabling and facilitating Brexit.

Labour Europhiles

The principal group within the Labour Europhiles were the remnants of New Labour. The Labour Europhiles were active in their support for a second referendum. Key arguments deployed for a second referendum were that the first referendum had been dominated by lies and distortions and that key pledges could not be honoured.

Former Labour leader Tony Blair, now claiming the mantle of an 'insurgent', urged people to 'rise up' (Castle, 2017). In the use of such language, Blair insinuated that Corbynism – rather than his own brand of centrist, pro-business politics – was reactionary and that an anti-Brexit position should be the default stance of genuine radicals. Blair argued that there were serious faults in Labour's line of strategy:

> We're actually in the same position as the Tories, which is to say we'll get out of the single market but we want a close trading

relationship with Europe. Your risk is that, at a certain point, you get exposed as having the same technical problem that the Tories have, which is: here's the Canada option, here's the Norway option, and every time you move towards Norway you'll be accepting the rules of the EU, but you've lost your say in it, and every time you move towards the Canada option you're going to be doing economic damage.

Blair also contended that Corbyn should show greater assertiveness but despaired of the argument that the public were, as reflected in the referendum, tired of political elites and would resent any interference in frustrating the outcome of the referendum: 'Guys, come on! I mean, what the hell are you in politics for? Of course, you've got to listen to people, but you've also got to lead them.' With his Leave strategy, Corbyn was in the eyes of Blair acting as the handmaiden of Brexit, facilitating and helping to nurture and prepare the ground for a hard Brexit. As is typical of the genre of the conversational media interview, Blair spoke in everyday, blunt language to engender trust and convey sincerity.

Despite the profession of radicalism, Blair seemed to have little to say on the structural causes of Brexit and alienation of left-behind communities who supported it. Working-class communities had supported Brexit as a survival strategy because socialist militancy had not materialized in the form of governmental policy and neoliberal individualism had failed to share the rewards of growth with them, hence they voted Leave in the hope of primarily seeing curbs on migration materialize (Winlow et al, 2016). The referendum result, in the language of Polanyi, constituted a revolt against market fundamentalism (Pettifor, 2016). The Labour Europhiles seemed to not acknowledge this aspect of the Brexit phenomenon and in the absence of any reference to strategies to address the core resentments of left-behind communities, it appeared that for them it was merely a case of 'business as usual' – returning to Third Way New Labour policy.

Radical left Europhiles

Radical left Europhiles were part of the left surge that had come to the fore of the Labour Party. While committed to transformative politics and conversely critical of New Labour, this group had deep reservations about a Lexit position on Brexit. The academic Mary Kaldor (2018) reasoned that retaining full EU membership or even single market membership could facilitate a socialist and transformative Labour programme – a topos of social justice: 'let's begin to talk about the extraordinary possibilities open to a Corbyn government inside the EU. In his speeches, Corbyn rightly emphasizes the need to tax multinationals, to control the volatility of financial markets, address climate change and end global conflicts. But this is not something the UK can do on its own. It is only through the EU that it is possible to envisage seriously dealing with such global challenges.' Kaldor envisaged, through transnational governance, a reformed EU managing interconnected economies and societies by closing tax havens for multinational companies, regulating global financial flows or controlling carbon emissions – and overcoming inequality, bringing peace to conflict zones, managing migration and refugee flows. Yet Kaldor was sensitive enough to temper such comments with profession of support for Corbyn's desire to reign in multinationals, so as to avoid her comments being construed as an attack on the Labour leader. Kaldor also acknowledged how Corbyn had changed the narrative of debate on issues like austerity but that he now needed to do so on Europe. Kaldor issued the following clarion call for action: 'With Labour's sister parties in crisis and people crying out for new ideas, a Corbyn government could act as a catalyst for transformative change in Europe.' Thus, Kaldor implied that it was part of the destiny of the Corbyn project to rekindle radical socialism in Europe, a line of reasoning that would appeal greatly to the internationalist sentiments of the party (rational legitimation).

The possibility of Labour softening its Brexit stance through single market membership or a strategy that could reverse Brexit raised deep concerns from pro-Leave sections of the party. For example, Labour MP Kate Hoey said Labour risked 'reviving' UKIP if voters felt let down by Labour (Maidment, 2017). Gareth Snell, Labour MP for Stoke-on-Trent Central, which voted Leave, also expressed concerns about Britain potentially still complying with EU regulations and remaining within its frameworks: 'What message are we, as a Labour party, sending to voters in these seats if we simply turn away from the spirit of the referendum result? What hope can we have to win back those traditional seats we need to win in order to form the next government if we tell the voters in those communities that we know better than they do?' (Stewart and Elgot, 2018).

In 2019, the pressure grew for Labour to more robustly endorse a referendum. Labour Party chair Ian Lavery stated: 'It does feel that a certain portion of "left-wing intellectuals" are sneering at ordinary people and piling on those trying to convey the feelings of hundreds of thousands of Labour voters' (quoted in R. Mason, 2019). These statements by Snell and Lavery insinuate that elitists within the Labour movement, outside of and lacking understanding of or respect for working-class communities, were being arrogant and condescending. Both statements also imply that the Labour movement should follow the whims and mood of the most exalted sections of its voting base, namely the working class, and by implication acquiesce to those demands even when reactive. Both imply a certain authenticity, being elected from northern working-class constituencies (legitimation of authority based on status/experience).

In the latter stages of the Brexit negotiations, a question vexing parliament was to what degree MPs should be swayed by the views of their party, locally or nationally, and the way their constituency had voted in the referendum. The need to exercise representative judgement was outlined by the Labour MP David Lammy (2019): 'We have a duty to tell our constituents the truth, even when they passionately disagree. We owe them not only our industry but our judgment. We are trusted representatives, not unthinking delegates, so why do many in the House continue to support Brexit when they know that it will wreck jobs, the NHS and our standing in the world?' According to Lammy, many who voted Brexit had been lied to and manipulated by powerful forces in the media and political class – 'Blame us; blame Westminster: do not blame Brussels for our own country's mistakes. And do not be angry at us for telling you the truth; be angry at the chancers who sold you a lie.' For Lammy and other MPs, the topos of representative judgement and democracy meant that politicians should not always be harnessed to the will of the people, a view more aligned to a traditional view of representative democracy. Tellingly and reflecting the mood of the times, such sentiments seemed to now be located at the radical fringes of political debate. In Lammy's view, Brexit was a 'con, a trick, a swindle, a fraud' and there was a need for politicians to make a stand: 'This country's greatest moments came when we showed courage, not when we appeased: the courage of Wilberforce to emancipate the slaves in the face of the anger of the British ruling class, the courage of Winston Churchill to declare war on Hitler in the face of the appeasers in his Cabinet and the country, and the courage of Attlee and Bevan to nationalise the health service in the face of the doctors who protested that that was not right.' Such an analogy centred on historic figures was likely to appeal to national pride centred on liberal, conservative and socialist sentiments. The repetition of and emphasis on 'courage' indicates legitimation centred on morality, tradition and custom.

Thus, Labour, as the Conservatives, was deeply troubled and fractured on one of the most pressing and important issues of the postwar period. Prior to the election of 2017, Labour, as reflected by a deeply polarizing leadership contest held in the wake of the Brexit result, a flurry of poor opinion polls and local and by-election results, seemed to be trapped in a deep downward spiral which might well result in the demise of the party.

Some had predicted that the election of 2017 would be as bad if not worse than Labour's dire performance in 1931 when a deeply divided party had been left with around fifty MPs.

None of these things came to pass, as Labour's election performance in 2017 surpassed all expectations and deprived May of her majority, indicating that Corbynism might, with further development, be an election-winning formula. Labour's policy of 'constructive ambiguity' had successfully straddled the wide body of opinion within the party and beyond among its voters, giving all something they could live with. However, constructive ambiguity was severely tested as Brexit reached a stage in the parliamentary process where hard decisions needed to be made. A second referendum/confirmatory vote emerged as one of the strongest alternatives to Labour's official position.

The people's vote

Labour policy on Brexit was a process of evolution. In 2016 a composite motion had been passed that contained a short clause calling for an election or second referendum, but Labour's national executive committee discounted that motion from having any provenance in shaping party policy (Eaton, 2016). The 2017 manifesto stated Labour would honour the referendum with a 'jobs-first' Brexit and that free movement would end after leaving the EU. In 2017 efforts were made to ensure motions on the single market and freedom of movement were debated, but delegates refused to prioritize them for debate in part because the influential campaign group Momentum recommended to delegates an alternative set of issues for debate. Instead, the national executive submitted a motion to conference elaborating upon the party's manifesto position.

In 2018 a prominent campaign was organized by various pro-Labour referendum groups to see the conference debate a second referendum; 150 Constituency Labour Parties endorsed such motions. The left-wing campaign Another Europe is Possible was instrumental in achieving a policy shift in Labour's position on a second referendum – a goal achieved in part through creating some distance between themselves and more centrist Remain advocates through arguing that the transformative potential of Corbynism could be fused with EU membership. In the face of such huge support for a referendum, the Labour leadership sought to maintain some room for manoeuvre by drafting a composite conference motion which stated that Labour would 'support all options remaining on the table, including campaigning for a public vote' should it not be able to secure a general election (Labour List, 2018).

This was a position that could accommodate business where, as Corbyn wryly noted, the Confederation of British Industry which opposed a hard Brexit now seemed to have more in common with Labour as opposed to the Conservatives. It was also a position that could reach beyond the party itself and placed it in closer alignment with the views of the Liberal Democrats, Greens and Scottish and Welsh nationalists – and even one nation Conservatives. Through its vision of job creation and redistribution to the working-class, it also might appeal to communities left behind who had supported Brexit in large numbers. At the same time, through entreaties for close ties and cooperation with Europe, reflecting Labour's cosmopolitan traditions, it might appeal in particular to the aspirations of the intelligentsia. In forging such an alliance, Labour had ultimately reflected the tenets of consensual compromise, rather than the sharp divisions of left populism.

McDonnell and UNITE trade union leader Len McCluskey had sought to dilute the power of the conference commitment to a possible public vote by stating that Remain should not be on the ballot. However, to rapturous applause, Keir Starmer (2018) stated: 'Campaigning for a public vote must be an option … and nobody is ruling out remain as an option.' The issue of a referendum remained a contentious one, especially in the wake of Labour's no confidence motion tabled against May in 2019, as some reasoned that this failure in accordance with the conference policy meant Labour should more directly back a second referendum.

Labour's Brexit position unravels

By the start of 2019, Labour's hybrid approach on Brexit had started to unravel. In late 2018, May finally presented her EU Withdrawal Bill to parliament. Corbyn vociferously attacked the proposal. In his mind, the negotiations had been 'botched' and there was no consensus for the proposals. In an article for the *Guardian*, through metaphor and antithesis Corbyn (2018b) stated of May's approach: 'Instead of taking back control, it gives up control. Instead of protecting jobs and living standards, it puts them at risk by failing to put in place the basis for frictionless trade. For two and a half years the Conservatives have been negotiating with themselves, rather than the European Union.' For Corbyn (2018c), this was a 'blindfold' Brexit, a dangerous 'leap' in the dark as there was no clarity over future trade relationships.

Some on the left perceived May's withdrawal agreement to present a loss of status. As is typical of the genre of political blogs, through provocation, antithesis and irony, the trade unionist Cortes (2018) sought to mobilize support for a Labour remain position: 'So, it comes to pass that Brexit is not a British liberation strategy. It is vassalisation; the annihilation of our equal-rights status as a European country. The dawn of a new age of British colonialism. But this time round it is Britain that is the colony. This is where the Tories' 40-year war with Europe has landed us. Brexiters who thought their leave vote was going to set Britain back on course to rule the waves should be feeling humiliated.'

Both Corbyn's and Cortes's speech acts are examples of antithesis – a rhetorical device used to strengthen an argument by using either exact opposites or simply contrasting ideas. Corbyn contended that the Conservatives had achieved the opposite of what they had promised in a chaotic and dangerous exit strategy, while Cortes, in a reference to the Brexit mantra of reversing EU hierarchicalism, argued that the Conservative plans for Brexit had achieved the opposite. Contrasting Conservative promises with the now evident reality of Brexit was an astute tactical move, as opinion polls indicated the public was increasingly dissatisfied and disillusioned with May's handling of Brexit. In March 2019, social research organization NatCen released the results of a survey that revealed a consensus view that the government had been handling Brexit badly. Only 7 per cent of those surveyed believed that the government had handled Brexit well, while 81 per cent reckoned it had done so badly (Quinn, 2019). Despite broad agreement within the Labour Party on the inherent defects of May's exit position and the fact that only a small number of Labour MPs supported May in her failed attempts to pass the Withdrawal Bill (see Chapter 3), divisions became more accentuated as to what the Labour alternative should be. Corbyn, like May, seemed to feel that the referendum and the 'will of the people' had to be honoured. Corbyn was attacked at the end of 2018 for stating in an interview with *Der Spiegel* that Brexit could not be stopped and that if he won an election Brexit would still go ahead (Schindler, 2018). He continued to express the view that a Labour government's programme could be hemmed in by EU state aid rules.

In January 2019, Corbyn sought to trigger an election by tabling a no confidence motion against May, but this was defeated. In the wake of this defeat, proponents of a second referendum now argued Labour's principal position should be to support a second referendum in accordance with the 2018 conference motion line that if a General Election could not be secured then Labour must support all options remaining on the table, including campaigning for a public vote. Further criticism was generated by Labour's initial decision to abstain on the government's migration bill that would end freedom of movement and introduce rigid restrictions on migration. Protests from within the party led to Labour deciding to whip

MPs to vote against the measure, but members were now realizing the reality of Labour's Brexit position that meant in effect the party supporting an end to freedom of movement. By late 2018 the unity of the left seemed to be fracturing, with some starting to ponder whether Corbyn represented their best chance. Was the left of British politics failing to show decisive leadership and seize an opportunity to stop Brexit? Centrists within the Labour Party were also deeply dissatisfied. Change UK – The Independent Group was established in parliament in February 2019, with seven Labour MPs including Chuka Umunna defecting to the group, along with four Conservatives including Anna Soubry. To add to Labour's woes, the party performed very poorly in local elections in the spring of 2019. The Conservatives lost 1,334 councillors but Labour also lost 82 seats while the Lib Dems gained 703 seats. Critics argued that Labour was losing votes to the Lib Dems because of its indecisive Brexit position.

These concerns were greatly accentuated in the European Elections of 2019, which Britain was compelled to participate in on account of the extension of EU membership May had secured to provide extra time to finalize parliament's support for a withdrawal agreement. Some pro-Remain Labour members had hoped that the party would use the election to shift its policy and thus within its EU election manifesto contain a pledge to stage a referendum, with Remain being on the ballot paper. However, Labour decided against jettisoning its hybrid position, where another nationwide poll should only be 'an option' if it could not force a General Election. Prior to the election, Labour had even been involved in negotiations with the government to determine whether there was a means to frame a cross-party agreement to facilitate Brexit, but a lack of concessions in areas like a customs union led to the collapse of the talks.

In the European elections, the newly formed Brexit Party led by Farage (see Chapter 6) won twenty-eight of the seventy-three British EU seats. The Lib Dems took about 20 per cent of the vote and fifteen seats – up from one. Labour came third with ten seats, followed by the Greens with seven. The ruling Conservatives were in fifth place with just three seats and under 10 per cent of the vote. Labour's 14 per cent of the vote share was its worst performance in a national poll for a century. Critics argued that Labour's intransigence on the referendum had led to a revival of the Lib Dems, a strategic blunder that could cost the party dearly in the next election. The Lib Dems were further bolstered when a number of Change UK MPs, including Umunna, joined them.

Following the European elections, the shadow chancellor John McDonnell changed his position and declared support for a referendum. Increasing anger was directed at Corbyn for not changing his position too, but the UNITE leader Len McCluskey and party chair Ian Lavery, as well as key advisors such as Seumas Milne, were said to be resistant to a policy change in the party, fearing the threat posed to northern working-class seats from the Brexit Party. In contrast, figures such as Margaret Beckett, a vocal supporter of another referendum and former foreign secretary, acknowledged Labour's efforts to bring a divided nation together with its hybrid strategy and desire for a softer Brexit but felt that voters were confused or dismayed and that this would lead to a haemorrhaging of votes. Beckett (2019) concluded that any policy change had to be done swiftly: 'If we do this in the next few weeks we can still change the course of history. If we don't, we risk becoming history ourselves.' Beckett's presentation of two sharp contrasts highlighted the dilemma facing Labour.

Voices on the left were also deeply critical of Labour's position. The Corbyn-supporting journalist Paul Mason (2019a) used the topos of threat and danger:

> But the leadership's Brexit position and the woeful performance of senior officials have now become an impediment to defending the left project. I will enthusiastically circle the wagons around Corbyn. He has grown since 2015 into a politician who thrives on adversity and class struggle and will do so now. But the officials who designed this fiasco, and ignored all evidence that it would lead to disaster, must be removed from positions of influence … We have to begin from the facts: the struggle against rightwing authoritarianism and fascism is now the main priority. No amount of pledges to nationalise stuff, or appeals to class solidarity, wins that war. We are engaged in a culture war over values and narratives. Labour's narrative has to be built around resistance to Brexit as a project of the racist and xenophobic right, and a story of communities revived by hope and solidarity.

Mason was careful to stress his strong support for Corbyn, to allay accusations of being disloyal, arguing that the Corbyn project could only be saved by adopting a referendum and a Remain and reform position, which would be the polar opposite to the forces of authoritarian populism that it was now ranged against. For Mason, Lexiteer pledges and old-style working-class labourism were redundant in the struggle ahead. Mason also tried to insulate Corbyn from growing anger by placing most of the blame on his key aides Karie Murphy and Seumas Milne, calling upon them to be dismissed. Corbyn's left support base was fragmenting. Critics of such a position, such as Jon Cruddas MP, argued that left thinkers like

Mason were prioritizing the aspirations of more urban and networked members over traditional working-class communities. For Cruddas (2019), the cosmopolitanism of the radical left presented real difficulties 'as it embraces a global network rather than being anchored around more parochial concerns of place, community and nation'. The positions of both Mason and Cruddas highlighted the dilemma facing Labour: How could a policy position be devised that could straddle both the educated cosmopolitan section of the Labour vote base with left-behind working-class voters attracted to nativism? Was such a compromise possible and compatible with Labour values?

Corbyn declared that a wide-ranging consultation would take place in order to reach a position on Brexit. As anticipated, the initial results of Labour's internal consultation were unveiled in July 2019. In an email to party members, Corbyn set out Labour's new thinking. After setting out the rationale for attempts to find a compromise to bring the country back together, Corbyn stated:

> Now both Tory leadership candidates are threatening a No Deal Brexit – or at best a race to the bottom and a sweetheart deal with Donald Trump: that runs down industry, opens up our NHS and other public services to yet more privatization, and shreds environmental protections, rights at work and consumer standards. I have spent the past few weeks consulting with the shadow cabinet, MPs, affiliated unions and the National Executive Committee. I have also had feedback from members via the National Policy Forum consultation on Brexit. Whoever becomes the new Prime Minister should have the confidence to put their deal, or No Deal, back to the people in a public vote. In those circumstances, I want to make it clear that Labour would campaign for Remain against either No Deal or a Tory deal that does not protect the economy and jobs. (Corbyn, 2019a)

The temporal deixis 'now' indicated the Brexit debate had entered a new phase: the certainty of a Conservative leader committed to a no deal being elected as part of the Conservative leadership race. This new phase was used to justify Labour's repositioning on the grounds of timeliness (kairos) for as Corbyn indicated, 'no deal' is part of an ultra-neoliberal frame that is the antithesis of Labour values and would undermine key social protections (topos of justice). A new and pivotal commitment was that Labour would campaign to remain in the EU. However, Corbyn did attract some criticism, with the party indicating that if it were elected to power before the completion of Brexit it would seek to negotiate a compromise deal with the EU and subject that to a referendum. Some critics argued this was a continuation of Labour's policy of constructive ambiguity.

Conclusion

The radical insurgency of Corbynism as a characteristic of left populism often stressed conflict and polarization as requisite features of transformative change. There was a need for an 'us' and 'them' in an 'agonistic struggle' counterposed to liberal pluralistic conceptions of politics and the trivialization of political debate, which had bolstered the hegemony of neoliberalism and deprived citizens of real and meaningful choices in post-democratic societies (Mouffe, 2016). This was a deep contrast to the third-way technocracy of New Labour, which through luminaries like Giddens (1995), decried the tribalism of socialism and sought to craft a more consensual approach to politics. However, the third way had encompassed huge concessions to the neoliberal order and alienated large swathes of Labour's traditional body of support, namely the poor and working class. Labour under Corbyn had developed a more radical set of policy positions in a number of areas, perhaps most importantly on austerity and economic policy, areas where former leader Ed Miliband had been accused of timidity. Ironically, such radicalism was absent from the question of Europe, with Labour behaving like New Labour in its desire to find compromise and consensus and being averse to a more challenging stance. Labour under Corbyn had also antagonized a large section of membership, including his own grassroots support base, by being slow to make the transition to a fuller backing of a referendum, undermining claims that Labour had become a member-led party. Moreover, it appeared that by the summer of 2019 and the onset of the Johnson premiership Corbyn had failed to shift the ground of the debate and mobilize public opinion behind a compromise Brexit. An important question was whether Labour recalibration on its Brexit policy was sufficient, timely and would bend further to meet the demands of remain campaigners – questions that are returned to in Chapter 7.

5

The Nationalists: Exclusionary and Civic

Defining and understanding nationalism

This chapter explores how forms of nationalism interacted with the Brexit process, focusing primarily on the Scottish National Party (SNP), UK Independence Party (UKIP) and the Brexit Party, giving some consideration also to smaller groups such as the Northern Irish Democratic Unionist Party (DUP) and Plaid Cymru. The chapter covers the period up to the summer of 2019. These political groupings can be placed on progressive and reactive points of the political spectrum; the progressive SNP opposed a hard Brexit and UKIP and the Brexit Party militantly agitated for such an outcome. Scottish nationalists believed a hard Brexit would inevitably revive support for independence but sought to avoid a hard Brexit by advocating that Scotland should retain close links or even membership of the European Union (EU); they campaigned for a more cosmopolitan and egalitarian vision of the future. In contrast, UKIP and the Brexit Party advocated for a Britain free from the restraints of EU regulation and free to limit migration.

Before reviewing the speech acts of the various nationalist groups, this chapter summarizes prominent and competing insights into the nature of nationalism. Identity in a nationalist sense can be related to space but may also consist of a series of shared symbols and codes utilizing myth, history, tradition and language which can create a sense of solidarity and answer the questions: Who am I? Who and what are we? (Smith, 1991). For some (primordialists), national identity derives directly from a priori ethnic groupings and is based on kinship ties and ancient heritage (Bellamy, 2003). Others (constructionists) perceive national identity as something that is imagined, being constructed through the interpretation of history and culture; indeed, for some (instrumentalists) it is perceived as a phenomenon that can be manipulated and orchestrated by political elites (Anderson, 1991). The likes of Gellner (1983) have argued that nations are essentially a modern phenomenon, facilitated since the eighteenth century by modernization and industrialization, bound and nurtured through state institutions and apparatus, education and mass communication.

The world order was compelled to review the danger and allure of radical forms of nationalism in the form of fascism in the wake of the Second World War. The genocide and economic havoc of that conflict gave rise to a human rights regime and forms of supranationalism, of which the EU is one example, that were designed to safeguard the world from nationalist excesses. Fukuyama (1992), following the collapse of communism in the then USSR, proclaimed an 'end to history' in the sense that civilization would remain on a trajectory pioneered by the West, where liberal democracy, human rights and the free market would guide and shape the world. However, weaknesses in these variables have presaged forms of nationalism that Fukuyama might have anticipated being consigned, along with communism, to the dustbin of history. In an age of globalization and what might appear to be more fluid and flexible cultural borders and markets, one might assume that the power of cosmopolitanism could be a great force in eroding adherence to national identities, at least in more radical identarian forms. Huntington (2012) has contended that globalization itself and the cultural change it has heralded has created a cultural backlash, where people have sought solace in more basic and traditional forms of identity in which a weakened and diluted nation state fails to articulate a meaningful sense of identity for them. He controversially argues that this would lead ultimately to civilizational clashes between the West and civilizations such as that encompassed by Islam. Observers such as Delanty (1996) have reasoned that a crisis in the modernization project has created new forms of nationalism centred on exclusion, as opposed to previous incarnations emphasizing inclusion. Thus, rather than being centred on ideology, nationalism has identity at its core and can be viewed as a form of cultural nationalism. Economic, cultural, political and territorial crises have been key drivers in radical forms of nationalism in recent decades.

Ramet and Adamovic (1995) describe such crisis-fuelled nationalism as 'traumatic nationalism' which centres on a sense of injustice and suffering and is bolstered by a notion of being besieged and under threat. Ramet and Adamovic applied this model to an interpretation of the tragedy of the war in the former Yugoslavia. The war in Yugoslavia characterized by ethnic strife and cleansing, was a rude reminder to the postwar order of the profound dangers that could still be aroused through forms of identarianism, despite four decades of effort to curb and restrain such manifestations. Some would argue that the crisis within the modernization project was accentuated from 2008 with the financial crisis of global capitalism, which has fanned the flames of radical identarianism and populist nationalism (see Chapter 1).

The rise of radical forms of identarianism have been articulated in a desire to assert forms of self-determination and notions of monocultural identity which nationalists feel have been compromised by the ideals and policies of cosmopolitanism and supranationalist projects such as the EU. These were a principal factor in leading to the British referendum result to leave the EU in 2016 and explain the *exclusionary nationalism* of UKIP and the Brexit Party that seeks to exclude people and practices perceived to be at odds with the integrity of an idealized vision of British identity and society. In contrast, the SNP has rejected these more narrow and rigid conceptions of nationhood and has sought to promote a *civic nationalism* based on territory, which is inclusive and welcoming of diversity and based on the guarantee of rights (Seidler, 2018). Alongside some of the principal theoretical interpretations of nationalism centred on primordialism, constructionism and instrumentalism, these contrasting visions of nationhood provide an important framework for the analysis of speech acts related to Brexit by various nationalist groupings. Set alongside this, it is worthwhile to consider that identity is a performative act; as Goffman (1956) notes, this is a form of dramaturgy in which people use certain codes, symbols and cultural narratives in formulaic and routine scripts to assert who and what they are. Brexit thus provides a screen onto which competing versions of nationalism, both civic and exclusionary, articulate and project their core values in political discourse.

The Scottish National Party

The SNP was founded in 1934 but it was not until the 1970s that it became an important force in Scottish politics, when its growth prompted the Labour government of Jim Callaghan to stage a referendum on devolution. Earlier incarnations of the party had had a more nationalist hue, its traditionalism and conservatism leading some opponents to deride the Scottish nationalists as 'Tartan Tories'. Disappointment with the New Labour project and the creation of a Scottish Parliament in 1998 helped create a revival of Scottish nationalism. The SNP was the largest party in the Scottish Parliament in 2007 and gained a majority of seats in 2011 and despite falling just short of a majority in 2016 was still able to form an administration. Under First Ministers Alex Salmond (2007–14) and Nicola Sturgeon (2014 to date) the party developed a more progressive and centre-left persona. Although the SNP lost the independence referendum in 2014 by a decisive margin (55.3 per cent voting against independence with 44.7 per cent voting in favour), the strength of Scottish nationalism was reflected in the 2015 General Election where the SNP won 50 per cent of the vote in Scotland and a staggering fifty-six out of fifty-nine Scottish seats in the Westminster parliament.

The advance of the SNP can be credited to the success of its civic nationalism. Scotland lacks clear and homogeneous ethnic markers such as religion and or language and thus emphasizing a civic and residential conception of nationalism has been astute (Agnew, 2018). It is a vision of nationalism based on 'inclusive citizenship', where citizens from a diverse range of backgrounds can feel part of a nation centred on rights and residence, blending an aspiration for self-determination (political nationalism) with forms of social (equality and rights) and soft cultural nationalism (Moskal, 2016).

The divergence between civic nationalism in Scotland and the influence of exclusionary nationalism in England was evident in the 2016 EU referendum result, with 62 per cent of voters in Scotland opting to remain in contrast to a majority of English voters opting to leave. In the wake of the referendum result, the First Minister Nicola Sturgeon (2016) made a formal address in which she framed Scotland's vote in terms of civic nationalism:

> Scotland voted to stay inside the single market and to protect the jobs, investment and trade that depend on it. We chose to be an open, inclusive and outward-looking society in which other EU citizens are welcome to live, work and contribute. We voted to protect the freedom and prosperity that comes with our rights to travel, live, work and study in other European countries, and we endorsed the principle of independent countries working together to tackle global issues such as climate change, energy security and the fight against terrorism.

In this extract, Sturgeon justifies the SNP support for a softer form of Brexit by outlining a series of positives which were attuned to civic and progressive conceptions of civic nationalism (orientation to difference – acknowledgement of difference and openness towards it). Nationalism often projects a self-image by contrasting itself with an opposite. According to social identity theory (Tajtel and Turner, 1979) identities are constituted in relation to others, so by comparing the characteristics of one country to another a sense of 'who we are' is construed. The Scottish vote had been heavily in favour of Remain; as far as Sturgeon was concerned, this demonstrated Scottish alignment with a range of values and principles that England had turned its back on. Thus, opposition to the Brexiteers' aims and the government's negotiation strategy, primarily centred on the aspirations of English politicians and voters, enabled Sturgeon to demonstrate a civic concept of Scottish nationalism.

The call for a second Scottish referendum

One immediate response to the EU referendum result was to claim that since the independence referendum of 2014 there had been a material change, in effect a major change to the terms under which Scottish citizens had agreed to stay in the UK (Sturgeon, 2016). Sturgeon indicated that even if Britain left the single market she would explore means by which Scotland could retain membership in what has been termed the 'reverse Greenland' option where, as in the case of EU member Denmark, part of its territory – namely, Greenland – is classified as being outside of the EU (Morphet, 2017). Sturgeon also indicated that if May achieved a hard Brexit after negotiations in Europe then Scotland would call for a second referendum. In Scotland, Labour revived the argument that had worked successfully in the referendum that the SNP's aspiration to retain the pound without its own central bank would make independence a fallacy and would be a distraction from Scotland's real needs. The Scottish Labour leader Richard Leonard stated: 'Scotland does not need, and the people of Scotland do not want, this tired argument again. The SNP should recognize that, and focus instead on jobs, schools and hospitals' (Cowburn, 2018).

The UK Prime Minister Theresa May interpreted the material consideration argument as a stratagem by the SNP to revive its nationalist aspirations, which had been defeated in 2014, and denounced the SNP by deriding such thoughts as 'tunnel vision'. May said that '[i]nstead of playing politics with the future of our country, the Scottish government should focus on delivering good government and public services for the people of Scotland. Politics is not a game' (quoted in Stone, 2017a). An extremely intense way of doing politics is to accuse others of politicking (political performance) while denying doing it oneself, affirming that one's own view is objective, scientific and so on (Wiesner et al, 2017). Sturgeon had ensured independence would be centre stage in the General Election in Scotland by declaring during the campaign: 'The issue at the heart of this election is, whether you support independence or oppose independence' (quoted in Shipman, 2017, 387). Accusations of blinkered nationalism and fears of seeing a return of the division and polarization of the bitter independence referendum in 2014 were central factors leading to something of a revival in Scottish conservativism. In the 2017 General Election, with 36 per cent of the vote the SNP's Westminster seats fell from fifty-six to thirty-five, while the Conservatives in Scotland, with their 28.6 per cent, moved from one seat to thirteen – a result that played a key and unexpected role in helping May to form a government. This reverse led to Sturgeon moderating her appeals for a rerun of the independence referendum.

In the wake of this election setback, Sturgeon (2017a) remarked that

> having spoken to many people who voted Yes in 2014 and to many others who did not but who would be open minded in future, what has struck me is the commonality of their views. They worry about the uncertainty of Brexit and the lack of any clarity about what it means. Some just want a break from the pressure of big political decisions. They agree that our future should not be imposed on us but feel that it is too soon right now to make a firm decision about the precise timing of a referendum. They want greater clarity about Brexit to emerge first – and they want to be able to measure that up against clarity about the options Scotland would have for securing a different relationship with Europe.

In consensual and placatory language, Sturgeon emphasizes that she is aware of and even sensitive to voters' fears about a possible independence referendum, which was adding to the already great anxiety being caused by Brexit. But in pledging to tackle worries about Brexit by gaining greater clarification of its impact, Sturgeon indicates that this could lead to Scotland seeking to retain a relationship with Europe that differs to that secured by England (orientation to difference – attempt to go beyond difference and reach consensus).

Sturgeon pledged to be constructive in giving advice and opinions on May's Brexit strategy and, although Scotland had voted Remain, she was prepared to countenance a form of Brexit that would enable Britain to remain within the single market and a customs union. Thus, Sturgeon sought to appear conciliatory and pragmatic, a position she often contrasted with the perceived inflexibility of the May government. As a visible demonstration of the SNP's consensual approach, Sturgeon indicated that the question of another independence referendum would be deferred so that her administration could focus on Brexit.

Scottish Nationalist positions on Brexit

To emphasize their more consensual approach to politics, the SNP highlighted what they considered the dogmatism of Brexiteers. In a *Guardian* article that set out the SNP position on Brexit, Sturgeon (2017a) stated: 'If Brexit is to happen, then it must happen in a way that limits the damage as much as possible. The unedifying experience of the past few months – with irrational and unreasonable threats of no-deal, insults flying across the Commons chamber and across the Channel, and the utterly despicable attitude and ignorance of the extreme Brexiteers towards Ireland and Northern Ireland – is only adding to the harm being done by the Brexit decision to the UK's reputation at home and abroad.'

By highlighting the widely reported antics of Brexiteers, which some critics held had been bellicose and chauvinistic creating reputational damage for Britain and threatening the Irish peace agreement, Sturgeon sought to depict the SNP as responsible and mature. Thus, according to Sturgeon, the SNP administration in Scotland had a willingness – unlike the Brexiteers and their extreme positions – to be flexible.

For the SNP, Brexit presented grave economic risks. Sturgeon raised concerns that 134,000 jobs in Scotland depended on trade with the EU and claimed that business was anxious for answers on the transition. For the SNP, a strong economic case could be made for retaining in the transition the single market and customs union. Sturgeon (2017b) declared with reference to her support for a softer form of Brexit: 'Yes, that will mean accepting the jurisdiction of the European court of justice; but to continue to put ideological totems before the jobs of hundreds of thousands of people would be to compound and accelerate the damage Brexit will do.' Again, Sturgeon is indicating that forms of political extremism as manifested in Brexit were jeopardizing stability and security. In the economic case against Brexit, heavy reference was made to analysis by the Scottish Government which revealed that Scots could face a loss of £2,300 per person each year, with GDP around £12.7 billion lower by 2030.

Brexit was also presented by the SNP as being indicative of the England/London-orientated focus of the Westminster government in which Scottish interests were ignored. In this sense, Brexit was framed within a longstanding nationalist trope of English domination and arrogance towards Scotland. In the Westminster debate on the EU Withdrawal Bill, a mere nineteen minutes were devoted to devolved matters, which were taken up by a ministerial statement. The lack of time afforded to devolved matters infuriated the SNP in Westminster. The SNP leader in Westminster Ian Blackford described the allotted short timeframe as a 'democratic outrage' and argued that the government lacked a democratic mandate for the Brexit it envisioned in Scotland. Evoking topoi of abuse and justice Blackford (2018) stated that '[t]he prime minister gave a commitment that she would treat Scotland as part of a "union of equals". Yet, last night, she pressed ahead with a power grab in direct opposition to Scotland's elected parliament. The Tories haven't won a democratic mandate from the people of Scotland for over 60 years, yet they press on to claw back powers from Holyrood without consent. History will remember this defining moment when the UK Parliament chose to reject devolution. This will haunt the Scottish Tories for a generation.' On his refusing to sit down, the speaker ordered Blackford to leave the chamber, which prompted the SNP MPs to stage a mass walk-out in solidarity with their leader. The statement and the refusal to sit down, which Blackford knew would lead to expulsion from the chamber by the speaker, and the mass exit can be construed as a performative act that symbolized the exclusion and alienation Scotland felt in the political context of Westminster – symbolized by unwarranted interference in Scottish affairs by the perceived English 'power grab'.

As the risk of a 'no-deal' seemed to draw nearer, Sturgeon raised her rhetoric on another possible independence referendum. In Sturgeon's 2018 SNP annual conference speech in Glasgow, she derided the Brexit negotiations as 'shambolic, chaotic, and utterly incompetent' and castigated the notion that the UK was a 'partnership of equals' on account of May's rejection of Sturgeon's compromise plan to remain in the single market. As far as Sturgeon was concerned, the previous two years had emphasized the need for Scottish independence but she would only release details of potential next steps once it had become clear what the UK's future relationship with the EU would be, that is, once negotiations had been concluded. At the conference in Glasgow, Sturgeon also signalled that the SNP would support a second referendum on Brexit.

In April 2019, Sturgeon introduced to the Scottish Parliament legislation to enable another independence vote by 2021. In these efforts, she called for cross-party talks and stated the Scottish government would set up a so-called citizens' assembly, drawing people from across the country and the political spectrum, and chaired by an independent figure, to start a debate on its constitutional future. Sturgeon declared: 'We have seen in Westminster what happens when parties fail to work together; when leaders take a "my way or the highway" approach and when so many red lines and inflexible preconditions are set that progress becomes impossible' (Carrell, 2019). Sturgeon was again drawing a contrast between her approach and aspirations and those of the Brexiteers, hoping that her emphasis on negotiation and conciliation might create genuine support for independence, changing what was once considered to be a radical and reckless political action into the antithesis of Brexit and an antidote which might spare Scotland from its worst extremes. Emphasizing this strategy at the launch of the SNP manifesto for the European elections, Sturgeon (2019) stated: 'The fact is, Westminster politics is in a pretty dark place right now. That places an obligation on the SNP. Our obligation is to provide a beacon of light and hope.'

Whether another independence referendum and possibly independence was the remedy to the dilemma facing Scotland was debatable. In the 2014 independence referendum, the European Commission President José Manuel Barroso noted that it would be 'extremely difficult, if not impossible' for an independent Scotland to join the EU, as Scotland would have to apply for membership and get the approval of all current member states (Holehouse, 2014). Given Spain's belligerent attitude to separatist groups within its own borders, it was one state among others that might veto such an application. Likewise, the reversal experienced by the SNP in the 2017 election indicated a sense of exhaustion with the independence question. However, a hard Brexit was perceived by many to be a material consideration and a decisive factor in prompting the Scottish electorate to escape the consequences some feared would emerge from a hard Brexit.

Smaller nationalist parties

At this point in the discussion, it might be useful to briefly survey the position of the smaller nationalist parties in the Brexit debate – the Welsh nationalist party Plaid Cymru, the Democratic Unionist Party (DUP) and Sinn Fein. Plaid Cymru lacked the power and presence of the SNP. Prior to the 2019 election it only held four Westminster parliamentary seats out of forty and ten out of sixty seats in the Welsh Assembly. As well as lacking the political platform the SNP enjoyed, Plaid Cymru was unable to match the strength of feeling of the SNP on Brexit and relations with the EU because the Welsh electorate had supported Brexit in the referendum, with 52.5 per cent of voters choosing to leave the EU. However, Plaid Cymru had, over decades, sought to cast itself as a progressive party with more of a civic nationalist orientation, which also closely aligned itself to the EU. The Plaid Cymru leader Leanne Wood reflected the pessimism of the SNP by declaring with reference to Brexit that she had no confidence in the UK government's ability to reflect the specific Welsh national interest. Wood also argued that if Scotland was to vote 'yes' in a second independence referendum then Wales would need to start a serious conversation as to whether to follow its example. Her successor as leader, Adam Price, supported a 'people's vote with remain being an option on the ballot paper and predicted a "no-deal" Brexit would be an economic disaster for Wales which would 'accelerate the path towards independence' (Morris, 2018).

The central objective of the DUP is to ensure Northern Ireland remains part of Britain. With its core support coming from the protestant community, it is considered to be very right wing on gay and women's rights (MacShane, 2017). Its political nemesis is Sinn Fein, the republican party, which is committed to seeing Northern Ireland integrated into the Republic of Ireland. In a critique of Sinn Fein, Arlene Foster, the DUP leader, gave some insights into the central values of her party: 'It is time that Sinn Fein started to respect our British culture. For too long they have shown nothing but disdain and disrespect for the national flag, the Royal Family, the Armed Forces, British symbols, the constitutional reality and the very name of this country' (quoted in Peck, 2017a). For Foster, Sinn Fein clearly constituted the antithesis of British identity and the Union. Conversely, Irish nationalists had deep concerns over the unionist Brexit position. The Sinn Fein President Mary Lou McDonald, speaking of those agitating for a hard Brexit, stated: 'They are people who have acted with absolute contempt for this country, utter disregard for the experiences of Irish people north and south, with utter disregard for the peace process that has been collectively built over decades' (quoted in Schaart, 2019). Again, as with the unionists, charges of disrespect are highlighted and both extracts contain Manichaean dichotomies and the topos of culture. In terms of perceptions and divisions in Northern Ireland, Brexit seemed to have been transposed onto the decades-old political fractures and dividing lines between Catholics and Protestants and North and South. Brexit was thus a proxy for deep political and cultural tensions within Northern Ireland.

Indifference to Ireland was not confined to the political class. In a survey, respondents were asked whether the unravelling of the peace process in Northern Ireland was a price worth paying for Brexit: 83 per cent of Leave voters and 73 per cent of Conservative voters in England agreed that it was (Centre on Constitutional Change, 2018). The DUP had supported Brexit during the referendum and, despite the province of Northern Ireland narrowly voting in favour of remaining in the EU, gave important support to Theresa May following the 2017 General Election, when May failed to achieve a majority. In return for DUP support in parliament, most importantly on Brexit legislation, the DUP were promised £1 billion of increased revenue. This agreement led to charges that May was buying votes and turning the rationale of austerity on its head. Despite this support, the DUP insisted on a frictionless trade border with the Republic of Ireland or any form of agreement that left Northern Ireland under different arrangements to the rest of Britain.

Northern Ireland constituted a huge area of concern in the EU negotiations, as the EU asserted that if Britain left the customs union then a hard border would return to Northern Ireland, which would have huge implications for the peace process. The fear was that border controls could return, as these had been a focus of tension and attacks during the Troubles, before the Good Friday Agreement of 1998, which brought peace to the region. The issue of Brexit and related speech acts became entwined with the simmering tensions and complexity of Northern Ireland politics, with one side being perceived as slavish to English Conservative aspirations and the other as wishing to rekindle Irish reunification. The issue of the border between Northern Ireland and the Republic of Ireland was to prove a serious stumbling block in the closing stages of the Brexit process.

The UK Independence Party

When founded in 1993, UKIP was at first a left-of-centre Eurosceptic party initiated by London School of Economics historian Alan Sked, but drifted to the right and eventually eclipsed the UK Referendum Party as the principal Eurosceptic force in British politics. In terms of policy, UKIP became what can be considered as ultra-Thatcherite, with a tough immigration policy and a desire if in government to secure the closest possible ties with the United States (Winlow et al, 2016).

In the years prior to the Brexit referendum, the rise of UKIP was phenomenal. In 2010 UKIP had secured just 3.1 per cent of the vote but by 2013 seemed to have usurped the Liberal Democrats as the third force in British politics. In 2014 UKIP in effect won the European election, achieving 27 per cent of the vote with Labour on approximately 24 per cent and the Conservatives on 23 per cent. Generally, UKIP attracted the older white working class, who tended to be less educated and were frustrated with the established parties (Thrasher et al, 2018). In the wake of the 2008 financial crisis and with the growing impact of austerity, UKIP's anti-EU and anti-migrant rhetoric resonated with a growing number of voters (Ford and Goodwin, 2014).

Exclusionary nationalism

Insurgent right-wing parties like UKIP, most notably the Republicans under Trump in the United States, Le Pen in France and the Five Star

Movement in Italy had during the preceding decade been able to align with a sense of economic grievance and corresponding perception of socio-cultural threat and a political distrust of the establishment, which articulated a combination of nationalism and nativism as part of an exclusionary political discourse (Mudde and Kaltwasser, 2013). In the populist tradition, UKIP was able to deliver a series of easily understood policy antidotes which seemed pragmatic and decisive and were often marketed in the language of ordinary people in contrast to the perceived out of touch, self-interested and timid political establishment. At the heart of the solution was severing Britain's links with Brussels and freeing it from excessive bureaucracy and regulation (Clarke et al, 2016).

Although UKIP proclaimed it was not a racist party, as did much of the nationalist populist movement in Europe, for the new right migration was a proxy for race. UKIP's (2015) manifesto observed that 'even our prime ministers have labelled good, decent people "closet racists" and "bigots"' and asserted that '[i]mmigration is not about race; it is about space.' The 2016 EU referendum witnessed the transition of UKIP into a fully fledged form of insurgent populism. As Dennison (2018) notes, whereas Vote Leave focused on the economic arguments and was relatively restrained in the opening stages of the referendum campaign, the UKIP campaign Leave.EU did not shy away from highly emotive language. Such emotive language centred on the economic, cultural and even sexual dangers associated with migration (see Chapter 2). In accordance with nationalist populist narratives, UKIP liked to portray itself as trying to defend 'pure people', in contrast to outsiders who were deemed economically and culturally subversive. Such groupings could be taken as coded language for ethnic insiders from the dominant ethnic population, while foreigners/migrants were the impure/outsiders (Donovan and Redlawsk, 2018). UKIP was thus able to tap into the latent racism of British society.

British identity was closely aligned with the imperial project, which nurtured a sense of entitlement and supremacy and in turn British imperialism and English identity became closely entwined, leading to a residue of nativism and exceptionalism that can be felt in the present day (Kumar, 2003). This phenomenon may explain why the great bulk of UKIP votes were located in England and how English nationalism had taken a more exclusionary tone than nationalism in Wales and Scotland. This latent and insular nationalism could be activated through coded language about immigration which, although avoiding forms of direct racism, was about keeping the nation Christian and white (Virdee and McGeever, 2018).

An example of exploiting this reservoir of exceptionalist nationalism is evident in the following statement by former UKIP politician Nigel Farage, when in a podcast interview with the former Liberal Democrat leader Nick Clegg he declared it was Britain that had lost the Second World War: 'We were the losers. We were bankrupted. Our imperial possessions started to disappear. We had a massive crisis of confidence as a nation that went all through the fifties, sixties, seventies' (quoted in Smith, 2018).

Such rhetoric was typical of Farage, who had a keen eye for a controversial and provocative line which might generate headlines. In this case, by using a nationalist trope that contended Britain had been in a deep spiral of decline since the end of the war, he was reflecting a feeling of sadness that the older generation, in particular, held for a loss of empire and prestige but also resentment – in the sense that despite being on the winning side, postwar Britain had not found the place it deserved in the world. These sentiments also reflected another trait of populist nationalism, which interpreted modernization and liberal values, features of the postwar period, as elements of decline.

Answering a question from Clegg about whether the past was 'better', Farage said: 'No actually, I'm very bullish about Britain as it is right now. Yeah, we've got our problems, we've got our divisions. We've always had them. But I actually think that there is a great feeling. A great national spirit out there. We've changed' (quoted in Smith, 2018). This comment also reflected another important aspect of the UKIP narrative, namely that once Britain had left the EU there would be a renaissance of the country's greatness.

Despite his privileged background, the style of language that Farage frequently exhibited in writing and speaking is very much everyday. This is a key factor in his image construction (face work). Such tactics are redolent of populism, where politicians speak and act like popular television hosts in terms of their simplicity of language but also through the use of rhetorical gimmicks and entertaining style (Inglehart and Norris, 2016). Elwes (2014) notes the flair Farage demonstrated in playing the common man, which included props such as drinking beer and smoking while giving supposedly impromptu interviews to journalists. An important component of the populist style of speech acts is heightened emotion, dramatization and use of colloquial language to increase newsworthiness (Ekström and Morton, 2017). All of these traits are very much evident in the extracts featuring Farage in this chapter.

Leadership and political fortunes

As with most nationalist populist movements, a central aspect of UKIP's success was having a strong and charismatic leader. Nigel Farage (UKIP leader 2006–09 and 2010–16) saw himself as a man of the people. Farage had attracted huge levels of opprobrium during the EU referendum when he suggested the reported sex attacks that had taken place in Cologne by migrants could happen in Britain. Baroness Shami Chakrabarti described these comments as resorting to 'an age-old racist tool'. Equally controversial was UKIP's 'breaking point' poster, which implied Britain was being besieged by a flood of migrants (see Chapter 2). A popular claim by Farage was that he was standing up for the 'honest and decent' people of Britain, the 'pure'. On the night of the referendum result, Farage triumphantly stated: 'This will be a victory for real people, a victory for ordinary people, a victory for decent people ... Let June the 23rd go down in our history as our independence day.' In similar vein, Farage derided the predictions of economic woe following Brexit by asserting: 'Do you know something? There is more to this country, there is more about this community than just being competitive ... What I'm saying is that it's wrong, wrong, wrong for average decent people in this country, their living standards are falling by about 10%. It's about time we were not thinking about GDP, the rich getting richer, and think about ordinary decent people who are having a rotten time' (Phipps, 2016).

Following the EU referendum result, Farage decided to step down from the UKIP leadership role, announcing in the fashion of an anti-politician that he wanted his life back and that the central goal of his political career had been achieved. From the date of the referendum to the premiership of Johnson, UKIP had eight leaders who through various mishaps all fell from grace. In the 2017 election UKIP secured a mere 3.2 per cent of the vote.

The betrayal of Brexit

As the 2018 departure date for Britain drew near, it was evident there would be serious delays and possibly that Brexit might even be cancelled. UKIP vehemently opposed delays and perceived there to be efforts by the political class to undermine Brexit.

Farage castigated those calling for parliament to be given a vote on triggering Article 50, the formal process of leaving the EU, characterizing this as a betrayal: 'I worry that a betrayal may be near at hand ... I now fear that every attempt will be made to block or delay the triggering of Article 50. If this is so, they have no idea of the level of public anger they will provoke.' Such rhetoric implied that the referendum created a 'super-mandate' which precluded second thoughts or a change of mind; any such action for Farage was a 'betrayal' (Griffin, 2016). Typical of populist frames, Farage believed that attempts to thwart Brexit would come from the establishment, a group he described through reification and a topos of hierarchicalism as a 'unholy trinity of big banks, big business and big politics' (quoted in Khan, 2017). Farage later warned, invoking bold and militarist language, that establishment threats to subvert Brexit would lead to serious disorder and violence; he himself would be compelled to take direct action '[i]f they don't deliver this Brexit that I spent 25 years of my life working for, then I will be forced to don khaki, pick up a rifle and head for the front lines' (Peck, 2017b). Through the use of such militarist language, Farage presented himself as a man of action and bold resolve deeply committed to the cause – classic populist traits. Here Farage demonstrates his ethos; his expertise to make such a pronouncement based on the longevity of his involvement in the cause, but we can also see in these comments moral legitimation and exigencies being evoked to justify his indignation.

Farage's cultivation of an outsider image is evident in an address he made in 2017 to the European Parliament, which he referred to as 'you' (use of pronouns to polarize). Farage (2017) described what the EU was doing to Britain as 'vindictive, nasty, like the mafia'. This elicited protests from fellow MEPs and a reprimand from the chair, leading to Farage mischievously rephrasing 'mafia' as 'gangster'. Such pieces of theatre bolstered Farage's outsider, anti-establishment persona. These antics resonated well with his support base, too. A tweet (anon) indicative of the many in support of Farage's statement declared: 'Just caught @Nigel_Farage sticking it to the #EuropeanParliament a few home truths, spectacular.'

Unsurprisingly, Farage was highly critical of what became known as the Chequers proposal, a plan for the final phase of negotiations (see Chapter 3), which was deemed closer to a 'soft Brexit' rather than the clean/hard exit that Brexiteers like Farage felt was the decision the public had expressed a desire for in the referendum. Farage argued: 'May's response shows that she is controlled by the civil service. For Brexit to succeed we must get rid of this awful, duplicitous PM.' Farage proceeded to contend that the blueprint May presented was a betrayal of the government's earlier pronouncements on Brexit: 'Mrs May and her cabinet have wilfully broken the direct promises they made to the electorate and their behaviour could even sink the Conservative Party' (quoted in Embury-Dennis and Buncombe, 2018).

The possibility of a new movement emerging increased as UKIP fragmented in the final stages of the Brexit referendum process under the controversial leadership of Gerard Batten (leader 2018–19), who caused division by seeking to align UKIP more closely with radical Islamophobic sentiments. Tensions were also created by Batten appointing

Tommy Robinson, the controversial former leader of the English Defence League, as an advisor. In protest Farage and Banks abandoned UKIP and established the Brexit Party just prior to the 2019 European elections, which Britain was compelled to participate in under the terms of the extension given by the EU to finalize the details of Britain's departure.

The Brexit Party

The new Brexit Party greatly strengthened the dominant position that Farage enjoyed on the radical right of British politics. The party was constituted as a company rather than political party, with registered supporters rather than a membership with voting rights. The only body that could dismiss Farage was the Brexit Party board, but Farage had the power to appoint the board and thus held huge clout. The Brexit Party did not issue a manifesto: Farage said policy would emerge after the election. At the official launch of the Brexit Party, Farage displayed central elements of his populist nationalist rhetoric with hints of insurgency and an anti-establishment agenda. He promised 'a revolution in British politics' and pledged that there would be 'no more Mr. Nice Guy'. Farage accused Britain's politicians of 'managed decline', adding: 'I genuinely believe this nation, right now, we are lions led by donkeys.' He went on to proclaim: 'I do believe that we can win these European elections and that we can again start to put the fear of God into our members of parliament in Westminster – they deserve nothing less than that after the way they have treated us' (quoted in Dallison, 2019). The public in large numbers accepted Farage's invitation to shake up and unsettle the establishment. The European elections saw the Brexit Party attain first place with 30.52 per cent of the vote, securing twenty-nine out seventy-three of the MEP positions. The Brexit Party completely eclipsed UKIP, which lost all its seats and secured a mere 3.2 per cent of the vote. Farage's electoral triumph allowed him to continue to place pressure on the political establishment, encouraging the Conservatives in their 2019 leadership contest to see Boris Johnson as the only leader who could possibly counter the appeal of Farage.

At the opening of the new session of the European Parliament, the Brexit Party members made a provocative statement by turning their backs as the EU national anthem 'Ode to Joy' was played. The former Conservative minister and television personality and now Brexit Party MEP Anne Widdecombe gave a speech using the topos of history/lessons learnt and Manichaean dichotomies which caused much controversy when she likened Brexit to a colony rising up against an occupying empire. Widdecombe (2019) stated: 'There is a pattern consistent throughout history of oppressed people turning on the oppressors: slaves against their owners, the peasantry against their feudal barons – colonies, Mr Verhofstadt, against their empires. That is why Britain is leaving.'

This anger was in part prompted by the delaying of Brexit and the disappointment of the Brexit Party MEPs that they were even present in the parliament, as Britain should already have left. Guy Verhofstadt, the European Parliament's representative on matters relating to Brexit, was a principal target for attack in Widdecombe's speech. Verhofstadt was perceived by Brexiteers to be part of an establishment elite seeking to thwart Brexit (topos of hierarchicalism). The language of oppression, as noted, is a standard trope of nationalist populism, but what alarmed some was the degree of ferocity and emotion in Widdecombe's words (pathos) accompanied by finger-jabbing (expression structure/kinetic signal). An important aspect of populist nationalist rhetoric is building up a sense of crisis through emotive discourse in order to maintain social tension and legitimize radical action against the 'people's enemies' (Moffitt, 2016). Through populist performance, prominent public figures embody the values, emotions and aspirations of the populist cause – hence Widdecombe's dramatic display of anger and defiance.

Populist ascendancy?

A key question, in what some deemed to be a time of crisis, was whether Britain, alongside other countries, would succumb to nationalist populism. Would Brexit lead to a shift in political culture? Would the uprising Farage predicted materialize in the event of a soft Brexit? Who would be blamed in the event of a no-deal outcome? Some considered that in all these potential scenarios, forms of nationalist populism might be the beneficiary. The assiduous courting of President Trump by Farage and his increasing cooperation with the president's former advisor and populist guru Steve Bannon – by supporting his efforts to establish a foundation called 'The Movement' to bolster the anti-EU faction in Europe – also indicated increasing alignment with the radical right. Critics such as the Liberal MEP Layla Moran saw within such posturing ominous indicators as to the implications of such ideological alliances: 'Now they want dark elements of the far right in America to help plot their nasty agenda. The dangers stirred up by this kind of right-wing populism are obvious, but terrifying for the many people who fear history might be repeating itself' (quoted in Stone, 2018b). The fear was that with a strong Brexit Party poised to take large numbers of seats in a future election, a Tory prime minister in the populist mould and Conservative talk of an electoral pact with the Brexit Party could mean that the centre ground of British politics and representative democracy was irreparably damaged.

Some would argue that populist nationalism is ill placed to take the reins of power, being a 'thin' ideology that lacks the potential for governance because it is restrained in its actions by its primordial intuitions, which preclude negotiation, compromise and efficiency (Freeden, 2017). It can also be stated that the irrationalism of nationalist populism presents another barrier to its progress, if we accept that it is an anti-globalist phenomenon. The strength and power of market globalism and the ability to undermine and punish states that defy its agenda (generally socialist but in some cases governments of the radical right such as Berlusconi's in Italy) has led to nation states being compelled to fall into line and accept the will of the market and supranational institutions. In the case of Italy it had to accept imposed austerity measures to stabilize the euro. In effect, in a globalized world national government autonomy in policy making is limited (Clarke et al, 2016). In the aim to maintain human rights and forms of collectivity based on global economic, social and environmental challenges, justice-orientated globalism centred on supranational and non-governmental organizations committed to global wealth and power redistribution as well as social and environmental protection holds a certain logic and potency. Although nationalist populists may be at odds with these entities and sentiments, they present a substantive moral restraint for populist discourse (Scotto et al, 2017). Despite the logic and allure of such a position, an emboldened version of justice-orientated globalism seemed a distant dream in the present political landscape.

Some would argue that the strength of nationalist populism in the UK, or Brexit nationalism as it can be termed, reflects the fact that despite British society's pretensions to multiculturalism and celebration of diversity it is characterized by white communities and ethnic groups still living largely separate lives (Rosman and Rubel, 2006). In addition, white working-class communities have in some cases been part of a white 'backlash' against liberal multiculturalism, resenting the perceived privileging of ethnic cultures to the exclusion and detriment of their own (Back, 1996). Yet such views seem to be more predominant among the older age groups and with time, it has been argued, the more cosmopolitan views of the younger generations will prevail (Gilroy, 2004), possibly creating new, non-racialized conceptions of Englishness. Moreover, it has been argued that improved access to education and information, particularly among the young, who have developed post-materialist traits and achieved levels of political sophistication, make them less inclined to accept Euroscepticism (Fox and Pearce, 2018).

Given the ongoing cultural changes we have touched on, it could be argued that in future English nationalism might be more adept at rejecting the legacy of British imperialism and exceptionalism and imitating more tolerant and inclusive forms of nationalism – as are evident in Scotland. Perhaps the exclusionary and nationalist rhetoric of Brexit was the final spasm of a form of national identity that is facing demographic decline, reducing perhaps to virtual oblivion the primordial ethnic core that has thwarted attempts to square national identity with cultural pluralism. Such a process might be assisted by forms of critical multiculturalism which seek to explore the interplay between race, gender and class and oppressive behaviours and practices (Farrar, 2012). These can be described as a more dialogic and negotiable form of multiculturalism which challenge oppressive outlooks in both majority and minority society. Such a notion can be articulated as 'two-way integration', where the identities of all ethnic groups, including white majoritarian society in the UK and Europe, undergo processes of change as the overarching national community and sense of identity emerges (Modood, 2012). Such conceptions may be the antidote to the new assimilationism that emerged post-9/11 along with the rise of nationalist populism. This is a theme that will be returned to in Chapter 8.

In the summer of 2019, with the onset of a Johnson premiership various forms of nationalism seemed to be in good health. A poll by Lord Ashcroft published in August 2019 indicated that a majority of Scots now favoured independence, with 46 per cent for and 43 per cent against (Christie, 2019). Various opinion polls also indicated that support for Brexit was still large, with Remain only enjoying a narrow lead. In the Brecon by-election in August 2019, despite the seat changing from Conservative to Liberal Democrat, the combined vote of the Conservatives and other pro-Brexit parties was greater than the votes for other parties, indicating a Leave-favouring majority. The strength and resilience of both support bases for the SNP and Brexit Party is testament to the astuteness of these parties' strategies and speech acts.

6

Brexit: Views from Europe

Crisis in Europe

This chapter describes the views of the European Union (EU) on Brexit up to the summer of 2019. The realist theory of international relations contends that a country's foreign policy is not governed by internal affairs but rather by rational self-interest, which seeks to maximize national advantage in a world perceived as conflictual and competitive. In contrast, liberal theorists stress the importance of internal factors in shaping a state's international behaviour and offer a more idealized vision of international affairs shaped by cooperation (Williams, 2018). As will become evident in this chapter, both of these theories have relevance in understanding the international context of Brexit and indeed the speech acts and resulting actions of policy actors, where Brexiteers' notions of reclaiming national power and self-interest were often pitted against and contrasted with the ethical and idealistic sentiments of those who wanted to preserve the European Project.

These debates and discussions took place within and were shaped by a profound paradigm shift provoked by an economic and cultural crisis in which competing philosophies were set against each other. Cosmopolitanism versus nationalism presented one clash of paradigms – a discourse in which international cooperation, integration and cultural diversity are juxtaposed against narrow national self-interests and monocultural and reactive forms of identity, creating frames (interpretations and perspectives) that can mobilize and galvanize populations and political elites (Adler-Nissen et al, 2017). Alongside identity discourse, there was a socio-economic cleavage which revolved around the tensions between neoliberalism and conceptions of the state centred on statism and welfare, where social justice rather than profit was the central governing force. Both discourses (identity and socio-economic) were accentuated and inflamed by the financial crisis of 2008 and a populist backlash against globalization, with some propounding a theory of 'European disintegration' leading to the unravelling of the democratic capitalist compact with which European integration has been so firmly entwined through the European project.

Brexit took place in a profound moment of crisis for Europe. The eurozone crisis that started in 2009 threatened economic chaos and created huge political resentment as a consequence of German-led measures to protect the currency, which were perceived to infringe national sovereignty. The Syrian migration crisis (2015) and a spate of terrorist attacks by Daesh, which were particularly intense in France, caused deep trauma across Europe. In the wake of the Brexit referendum, there were also very real fears that Marine Le Pen might triumph in the presidential election in France (leading to a Frexit) and that Geert Wilders, another arch Eurosceptic, might win power in the Netherlands. In addition, the radical right seemed in 2016 to be dominant in some Central East European states such as Hungary and on the rise in Germany and Austria (Taggart and Szczerbiak, 2018). Michel Barnier (2017a), chief EU negotiator on Brexit, described the contextual crisis that Brexit had taken place in and asserted the need for solidarity:

> To many of us [The Brexit result] came as a great shock. It was a decision taken against the backdrop of a strategic repositioning by our American ally, which has gathered pace since the election of Donald Trump. It was a decision that came after a series of attacks on European soil, committed by young people who grew up in Europe, in our countries. It was a decision that came six months after the French minister of defence issued a call for solidarity to all his European counterparts to join forces to fight the terrorism of Daesh. Never had the need to be together, to protect ourselves together, to act together been so strong, so manifest. Yet rather than stay shoulder to shoulder with the union, the British chose to be on their own again.

Barnier implied the Brexit decision should be seen in the wider context of the United States repositioning itself, which had sent out a ripple effect touching one of its key allies, namely Britain, and could thus be construed as part of the Trump phenomenon. Barnier also asserted here that Britain was turning its back on Europe in a time of crisis and danger as presented by terrorist threats, implying that the British had a serial habit of not working collectively or in unison with European partners. There is also the insinuation that by not standing 'shoulder to shoulder' with the EU,

Britain was not acting in accordance with honour and duty and would be vulnerable outside of the European alliance (topos of European unity).

It is within this broad context of crisis and contestation that the frames and speech acts utilized by political elites have to be considered. The speeches of European elites outlined in this chapter are performative, providing an opportunity for EU political elites to reaffirm and defend a democratic capitalist and integrative conception of Europe from the challenges now facing it in the space of what can be described as a pan-European communicative sphere – a space or arena for (broad, public) deliberation, discussion and engagement in societal issues (Barth and Bijsmans, 2018). Habermas (2001a) has decried the weakness in the European public sphere as a 'deficit in democracy' which is undermining the functioning, transparency and evolution of the EU. The media in Europe, in particular that located in Britain, has limited interest in the detail of EU decision-making, with the tabloids being especially active in mendacious and partisan reporting with frequent references to waste, bureaucracy and elitism.

Despite the impediments to a functional European public sphere, the crisis within the EU provoked greater European news coverage and in fact prompted EU political elites to be more attentive in tuning their political messages to wider audiences. This was very much at the centre of the speech acts and strategizing of Barnier, who stated he would use the negotiations and his statements as an educative process: 'There are extremely serious consequences of leaving the single market and it hasn't been explained to the British people.' In a later point of clarification, Barnier elaborated on this by describing the Brexit process as an 'occasion to explain single market benefits in all countries, including my own' (Khan, 2017).

As well as trying to reach out to the British public and cut through the perceived misinformation, EU political elites in all probability had an eye to a European and domestic audience, with Britain being seen as a potential outlier triggering a domino effect across Europe for referendums in other countries. The less educated, low paid and older members of the electorate had voted for Brexit in the referendum – demographic groups prominent across Europe and with the potential to rise up (Hobolt, 2016). Brexit could therefore be perceived as an illustrative example of the danger of Euroscepticism from which the European public could learn, thus acting as a deterrent (Walker et al, 2018).

Central frames and positions on Brexit

The decision by Britain to leave the EU was one received with deep regret by elite European political actors. Donald Tusk (2018) President of the European Council, said Brexit was 'one of the saddest moments in 21st century European history – in fact, sometimes I am even furious about it.' Dealing with Brexit was said to be distracting Tusk and others from the challenges of integration.

Outgoing German Ambassador to Britain, Peter Ammon, also expressed concern: 'I spoke to many of the Brexiteers, and many of them said they wanted to preserve a British identity and this was being lost in a thick soup of other identities. Obviously, every state is defined by its history, and some define themselves by what their father did in the war, and it gives them great personal pride' (quoted in Wintour, 2018). Thus, Brexit was seen in some quarters as a desire for a monocultural and nativist vision of society tinged with exceptionalism and nostalgia, as evidenced by Britain's perceived obsession with the Second World War.

Some deemed Brexit to be aligned with emerging populist forces where truth and reality were discounted. As another German commentator observed, Britain had 'fired the starting pistol on an era of post-truth' (Zimmerman, 2017). For some, Brexit was an act of supreme irresponsibility. German President Frank-Walter Steinmeier stated: 'Take back control is a strong slogan we hear everywhere. Nationalists will be unable to deliver it … We are not losing sovereignty in Europe we are gaining strength through it … It is irresponsible to lead people to believe that in a world that is becoming more complex that the answers are becoming simpler. It is irresponsible to say that in this world, a European country alone and without the EU can make its voice heard or its economic interests' (quoted in Mansfield, 2017). The use of repetition to stress 'irresponsibility' reflected a central concern of many European elite actors who contended, as evident in the cited quote, that nationalist populists were being deceptive through their use of simplistic frames. The logic of such thinking was that the world we live in is a complex one, where governance requires technocratic and mature expertise. These are valid points but elite political actors like Steinmeier failed to appreciate the disconnection between political elites and European voters – a point I return to later in the concluding chapter.

Generally, though, unlike the supporters of Brexit who berated EU negotiators as bullies seeking to punish Britain (see Chapter 3), the EU sought to avoid what Barnier described as 'emotional' language and positions, and rather emphasized the power of core principles as set out in treaties, along with need to retain the integrity of the European Project. In the guise of his envisioned educative role, Barnier often seemed to be like a rather serious school headteacher explaining the school rules to a truculent child. Yet the EU is experienced in dealing with such challenges, in particular from Britain which has often been viewed through the frame of being an awkward and a contrarian member.

The European Project has been marked by countries trying to evade the principles of shared sovereignty and integration and seeking to carve out some autonomy. The EU's history has also been characterized by member states organizing referendums which have opposed or defied treaties and deep-held principles of the EU. In response to such challenges, through concessions which do not violate core treaties or the fundamental principles of policies, the EU has sought to placate recalcitrance, and where this fails has invoked the rule of law (Rose, 2018). In Switzerland a referendum was held which succeeded in gaining support for an initiative in favour of limits and quotas on migration, which the EU deemed would contravene treaty agreements on free movement between the EU and a single market member. The threat of penalties led to the Swiss diluting their proposals so as to merely oblige employers in regions or sectors of high unemployment only to notify local job centres of vacancies before recruiting outside Switzerland, and to interview local applicants.

In such conflicts the EU has tended to rely on what can be described as Weberian legal rationalism, a formal conception of rationality dependent on the power of universally applied rules, laws and regulations and bureaucracy. For Max Weber (1958), capitalism was a rational system in the sense of being calculating, efficient, reducing uncertainty and increasing predictability and thus seeking to maximize labour and market freedoms and commercialization of economic life (promotion of market mechanisms). Adherence to such notions of authority explains the EU's deep commitment to uphold the 'four freedoms' (free movement of goods, services, capital and persons) as set out in the Treaty of Rome, the Single European Act and the Lisbon Treaty.

In a major speech which set out the EU position on Brexit, Barnier (2017b) stated:

> The free movement of persons, goods, services and capital are indivisible. We cannot let the single market unravel ... I have heard some people in the UK argue that one can leave the single market and keep all of its benefits – that is not possible ... I have heard some people in the UK argue that one can leave the single market and build a customs union to achieve 'frictionless trade' – that is not possible [legitimation through law].

Here, Barnier is seeking to refute the claims and promises of Brexiteers by expressing the impossibility of such pledges. A key word in the extract is 'unravel'. The fear of the EU was that agreeing to the concessions and exemptions the British expected would undermine the integrity of the

EU. Barnier, although strong and forthright in his language, seeks to neutralize some of the invective by not listing the names of the British politicians propounding fallacies by instead referring to 'some people' or use of the neutral 'one'. Such diplomacy and restraint was a central feature of the EU's response to Brexit. There is also a matter-of-fact style or 'low profile' rhetoric that implies facts are being referred to and that there are no alternatives.

In its negotiations with the EU under Theresa May, Britain was not seeking a clean break – although the threat of such was often raised. It was seeking to gain concessions on EU treaties to forge a future trading relationship that would enable its vision of 'taking back control' coupled with promises of being able to retain the same benefits as when a member of the EU. Barnier was forcefully emphasizing the illusion of such an assertion: that the EU's very legitimacy, and the integrity of its single market, rest on the rule of EU law, the autonomy of EU decision-making and the acceptance of EU regulations and standards. Fears about the logic and coherence of Britain's position formed a central frame for European leaders' arguments against the type of Brexit the British Government aspired to.

Views on Britain's negotiating strategy

In an address to the German Bundestag, Angela Merkel was blunt that in the EU negotiations Europe would put its interests first and not hand out large concessions. Merkel observed that some in Britain seemed to have a contrary 'illusion' (Wagstyl, 2017). As noted, a series of promises and pledges had been made during the referendum which Prime Minister Theresa May was grappling to translate into negotiating positions, even though critics complained they had no basis in reality and were illusionary and deceptive. In addition, as is the nature of negotiations, unrealistic positions are sometimes proposed in the hope of securing generous concessions in a game of 'bluff'. Britain's preparedness for the negotiations in fact had poor foundations. The challenges facing the British government were compounded by the fact that the former prime minister David Cameron had failed to instruct the Civil Service to carry out preparatory work in the event of a Leave vote. Barnier captured the indecision at the heart of the British position by remarking that '[t]he impression is of a huge underestimation of the implications, the consequences, of their decision. We also have the feeling that there is a certain reticence to accept the consequences of this choice: "We want to leave, but we're not really ready to fully assume the inevitable consequences"' (Henley, 2017b). However, the major factor in Britain's inconsistency was that the British cabinet was deeply divided, with a vocal faction agitating for a hard Brexit while others were inclined to support less traumatic variants.

An EU analysis paper noted that May's rhetoric on Brexit had a tendency to address 'her domestic audience, trying to bridge the gaps between the two poles of the debate on Brexit in the UK', rather than face the hard realities of the negotiations (Asthana et al, 2018). A leaked confidential report from the Irish Government quoted senior EU figures as being alarmed by 'chaos in the Conservative government' with deep concerns that the British cabinet was incapable of forming clear and coherent views (Boffey, 2017b). At one point, Barnier compared the British government's negotiating position to 'hide and seek' (Barker, 2018). Jean-Claude Juncker, President of the European Commission observed: 'I don't want to lecture Theresa May, but I would like our British friends to make clear their position. We cannot go on living with a split cabinet. They have to say what they want and we will respond to that' (Boffey and Stewart, 2018).

A lack of detail and ongoing ambiguity were a central factor in delaying the progress of Brexit negotiations and were a frequent bone of contention for the EU negotiating team. Barnier revealed his frustration at Britain's repeated demands for more flexibility by saying it was impossible for him to bend until he knew 'two points – our point, and their point' (Henley, 2017b). Within Europe there was also a growing sense of exasperation at the more radical Brexit-supporting members of the British government, such as Boris Johnson, who agitated for and pressurized May to take up hard Brexit positions.

Phil Hogan, the Irish Commissioner for Agriculture at the EU, reflected the aforementioned exasperation by warning of the damaging influence of hardline Conservative Brexiteers (pathos and topos of abuse):

> What becomes more obvious day-by-day is that the Brexiteers are hooked on brinkmanship – and have been since the beginning. Unfortunately, their only approach is the tough-guy approach. The hardliners cannot get out of their head the idea that if they bully their way towards the wire, the 'Union's nerve will crack'. I fear that in the UK debate, common sense left the building a long time ago. Unfortunately, facts and details are derided by the Brexiteers. (Quoted in Smyth, 2017)

EU negotiating positions and frames

The Brexit negotiations came in a sequence, with the EU commission insisting that separation issues were to be dealt with first before exploring

Britain's future relationship. Thus, the initial talks focused on issues like the financial settlement (divorce bill), citizen rights and the issue of the Northern Ireland border. With respect to all the stages of negotiations and central issues raised, a common complaint from the EU was that the UK was being unrealistic in its demands and expectations. A key criticism made of Britain in the negotiations by EU leaders was of there being a delusion that Britain could secure one-sided and significant concessions from the EU on its own terms.

Some hard Brexiteers assumed that once Britain left there would be no more financial contributions to the EU. The EU contended though that long-term projects Britain had sanctioned while a member, it would continue to need to supply financial support. In expressing his concerns on these points, Juncker used the analogy of a bar: 'If you are sitting in the bar and you are ordering 28 beers and then suddenly some of your colleagues are leaving without paying, that is not feasible. They have to pay' (quoted in Henley and Walker, 2017a). Eventually, once Britain had accepted a need for some form of payment, there was much quibbling as to how much that sum should be. Barnier expressed concerns, in a moral tone, at perceived British efforts to backtrack on earlier agreed financial commitments: 'So there's a moral dilemma here: you can't have 27 paying for what was decided by 28, so what was decided by 28 member states, that has to be borne out by 28 member states right up to the end, it's as simple as that' (quoted in Stone, 2017b). The use of British idioms and popular metaphors is discussed later in this chapter, but it suggests a carefully considered public relations strategy by the EU eager to connect with British voters.

The citizens' rights of the 3.6 million EU citizens residing in the UK was another important issue in the opening stages of negotiations with the EU, which was eager to ensure there was no diminution of rights. The President of the European Parliament Antonio Tajani struck a defiant note by declaring: 'The EU will not step back one millimetre from its position in defence of the rights of European citizens' (Stone, 2017c). Guy Verhofstadt, the European Parliament's Brexit representative, an instrumental figure in the negotiations given the fact the parliament had the power to veto a final deal, called Britain's initial offering on the rights of EU citizens 'a damp squib'. Verhofstadt threatened to veto any Brexit deal if pledges on citizens' rights were not improved: 'We will never endorse the retroactive removal of acquired rights. The European Parliament will reserve its right to reject any agreement that treats EU citizens, regardless of their nationality, less favorably than they are at present' (quoted in Payne, 2017). A similar threat of veto was made when Britain sought to limit the rights of EU citizens coming to Britain during the transition period and was denounced by Verhofstadt as 'penalising citizens' and would not be accepted (Boffey and Walker, 2018).

Northern Ireland was another difficult point in negotiations, with fears being expressed that unless Northern Ireland was in some form of customs union then a hard border would return between it and the Republic of Ireland. The fear centred on the potential damage to the two highly interconnected economies but also tensions that could potentially fragment the peace agreement, as the previous border with its checkpoints had been a focus for terrorist attack. One proposal from the EU was that Northern Ireland should remain in the customs union, but this was resisted and some feared it would compromise the unity and uniformity of the UK. Juncker gave strong support to Ireland's concerns by declaring: 'We have Ireland backed by 26 member states and the Commission – this will not change. I am strongly against any temptation to isolate Ireland and not to conclude the deal on Ireland. Ireland has to be part of the deal' (Young and McHugh, 2018). With this he was basically indicating that no overall deal could be concluded unless Ireland was satisfied.

Ireland was particularly successful in lobbying and persuading the EU to hold firm. Others noted the EU's function as a peacekeeping instrument and thus that it was integral for the EU to seek to preserve the Good Friday Agreement. For some in Ireland, the desire of Clean Break Brexiteer Conservatives to discard the backstop was redolent of a form of British arrogance that had impacted negatively on Ireland for centuries, by not understanding or valuing Ireland. In lobbying for the backstop to be retained and bolstering the determination of the EU on this question, the Irish were demonstrating to the British that now they had real influence and, in contrast to the past, could not be pushed aside by their powerful neighbour by virtue of the power of being in a union of twenty-seven countries – a power the British, or so it appeared, failed to appreciate and value.

A central focus of negotiations was the future trading relationship with the EU – with Theresa May hoping to see Britain achieve frictionless access to the single market but simultaneously be free to place limits on migration and forge new trade deals outside of the EU. The British aspirations were strongly rejected by the EU on the grounds that they undermined core treaties of the EU and the four freedoms. Barnier (2016) asserted: 'Being in the EU comes with rights and benefits – third countries can never have the same rights and benefits. The single market and its four freedoms are indivisible. Cherry picking is not an option.' Cherry picking was an idiom frequently used by EU negotiators. Another idiom employed to convey EU negotiators' frustrations at Britain's perceived lack of coherence and reasonableness was 'having one's cake and eating it'. Tusk denounced May's position in the following terms: 'It looks like the [have your] "cake" [and eat it] philosophy is still alive. From the very start it has been a key principle of the EU27 that there can be no cherry picking and no single market à la carte. This will continue to be a key principle, I have no doubt' (quoted in Randerson, 2018).

The use of these idioms suggested that Britain was being unreasonable and selfish in its Brexit strategy, which sought to accrue unfair trading advantages over Europe. The attraction of such metaphors embedded in popular British idioms is that it allowed EU politicians to cut through complex arguments related to Britain's future trading relationship with simple everyday language that could be grasped by the British electorate. Indeed, the public often respond well to messages that explain proposed actions with reference to familiar experiences. In other words, messages become persuasive when they evoke what is known or is familiar (Charteris-Black, 2005). Idioms are perfect for such needs, containing archetypes with great expressive and emotive power. Idioms also have important cultural resonance and EU actors were no doubt aware that idiomatic charges of being selfish or not paying its dues would alarm the British sense of fair play and honour.

The EU seemed keen to convey its message to the British people, perhaps hoping this might lead to the reining in of British demands. A key concern was that Britain seemed steadfast in its desire to jettison freedom of movement, while the EU asserted that acceptance of this convention was a prerequisite for enjoying the benefits of the single market. Martin Schulz, President of the European Parliament (2014–17), cautioned against Britain's aspiration for a bespoke deal with exemptions from the four freedoms: 'I refuse to imagine a Europe where lorries and hedge funds are free to cross borders but citizens are not' (Lowe, 2016). The EU was keen to impress on Britain that the only means by which it could 'take back control', that is, to be free of EU law while rejecting free movement of people and contributions to the EU budget, was to have a clean break. As Tusk (2016) remarked: 'This approach has definitive consequences. Regardless of magic spells, this means a de facto will to radically loosen relations with the EU – something that goes by the name of hard Brexit. The only real alternative to a hard Brexit is no Brexit, even if today hardly anyone believes in such a possibility.' Thus, the British public needed to be alert to the consequences of their choices and live with them.

The need to ensure that post-Brexit Britain was in an inferior position did not stem from a sense of vindictiveness, as some Brexiteers asserted, but the need to protect and preserve the integrity of the union. As Juncker observed: 'If we don't insist that full access to the single market is tied to complete acceptance of the four basic freedoms, then a process will spread across Europe whereby everyone does and is allowed what they want' (Henley and Elgot, 2017). This rigidity meant that the EU was reluctant to endorse what was considered May's softer and more pragmatic policy position on trade in what became known as the 'Chequers proposal' (see Chapter 3). Barnier (2018) was clear in his rejection of that proposal: 'The UK wants to keep free movement of goods between us, but not of people and services. And it proposes to apply EU customs rules without being part of the EU's legal order. Thus, the UK wants to take back sovereignty and control of its own laws, which we respect, but it cannot ask the EU to lose control of its borders and laws.'

It seemed that in view of the 'red lines' May had set on free trade and migration, at best the EU was willing to offer a deal similar to that given to Canada but probably with 'level playing field' stipulations in taxation, environmental protection, labour standards, state aid and competition – or if Britain was prepared to relinquish its positions, an agreement like Norway's membership of the single market could materialize. Barnier was adamant that he was seeking an agreement, expressing his fears about the consequences of a no deal scenario: 'In practice, "no-deal" would worsen the "lose–lose" situation which is bound to result from Brexit. And I think, objectively, that the UK would have more to lose than its partners. I therefore want to be very clear: to my mind there is no reasonable justification for the "no-deal" scenario. There is no sense in making the consequences of Brexit even worse' (Crisp, 2017).

A deep concern on the part of the EU was that there were sections of the British government and Conservative Party actively agitating for a hard Brexit, with the intention of establishing an alternative socio-economic model to that of the EU with a greater neoliberal focus on deregulation and closer relations with the United States. Barnier cautioned about this danger: 'The UK has chosen to leave the EU. Will it also want to move away from the European model? There is behind the European regulatory framework the fundamental societal choices we hold: the social market economy, health protection, food security, fair and efficient financial regulation … It is up to the British to tell us whether they still adhere to the European model. Their answer is important because it directs the discussion on our future partnership' (quoted in Cooper and Ariès, 2017). Barnier was trying to convey, through the protections incorporated in the European model, the dangers facing the British public through their potential departure (politics building).

A profound fear on the part of the EU was that social protections could be undermined if Britain was working outside of this regulatory framework, reducing wages and workers' rights and managing to pour cheap products into the European market, a 'race to the bottom' scenario.

Britain had long been torn between the attractions of its close relationship with the United States and trading benefits of the EU and had tried to straddle the two. The Trump administration and its desire to reorient its economic and trade strategy was one factor that had unsettled some of the British political class in their affiliation to the EU. Verhofstadt observed Britain's economic overtures to the United States and interpreted the whole scheme as efforts by agitators like the arch-populist Steve Bannon to realize the 'disintegration of the EU' (Henley and Walker, 2017b).

The fall-out from Brexit

Little support was expressed by EU member states for Britain's negotiating positions. In fact, the level of cohesion for the EU negotiating position was unprecedented. Barnier detected a new sense of united purpose. 'Following the UK referendum, many people assured us that divisions would spread', he said. 'And yet, in an act of collective responsibility, Europeans suddenly woke up and responded by choosing unity' (quoted in Stewart, 2017). Attempts by Britain to use separate talks with lead EU members, such as France and Germany, to circumvent Barnier were given short shrift. Manfred Weber, Leader of the European People's Party in the European Parliament, was blunt: 'There is only the European commission negotiator, Michel Barnier: he will be sitting next to David Davis. If you split up Europe into different interests it will not be easy to get unanimity at the European council' (quoted in Henley, 2017a). Such unity as noted stemmed from a fear that large concessions could lead to the unravelling of the EU but also inspire populist nationalist movements in other member state countries to attempt to secure referenda.

The so-called Visegrad countries of the Czech Republic, Hungary, Poland and Slovakia had some sympathies with Britain's desire for autonomy, mindful of their own historic break from Soviet domination. Moreover, in states where the radical right was in the ascendancy, such as Hungary, there was a perception that the bureaucracy and regulation of the EU was in some cases overbearing. A sense of apprehension in the region was also accentuated by growing fears about the impact of migration to these countries and what was considered a liberal hegemony on the part of the EU (Taggart and Szczerbiak, 2018). Nationalist leaders in Hungary and Poland expressed some sympathy for Britain and appealed for flexibility, but generally expressions of support for Brexit from this region were muted – in part because these countries had large numbers of migrants living and working in Britain and were concerned about the citizens' rights of these people post-Brexit.

As well as political elites shying away from support for Brexit, popular support across Europe was also lacking. Many populations seemed to recoil from the idea of breaking away from the EU; the dramatic example of chaos and uncertainty as reflected by the British case may have deflated Eurosceptic ardour – a number of opinion polls showed a lessening of support for leaving the EU in the remaining twenty-seven member states (De Vries, 2017). Illustrative of this process was Ireland, which although it had had a number of clashes and tensions with the EU, most notably on the referendum it held on the Lisbon Treaty and subsequent revote and the eurozone crisis. In the wake of the Brexit vote, Ireland expressed a more Europhile outlook. In a poll for the *Irish Times*, when asked if the UK was right or wrong to leave the EU, more than four out of five voters (81 per cent) said that the decision was wrong. Just 12 per cent said the UK was right, while 7 per cent said they didn't know. Of those polled, 86 percent said Ireland should remain in the EU (Leahy, 2016). Some of the Irish population identified anti-EU sentiments with the worst excesses of English nationalism. As in Ireland, in France euroscepticism seemed to be in decline. The radical right in France dropped the possibility of a Frexit during the presidential election of 2017.

The failure of the radical right to make significant advances in France and Holland, combined with the victory of Emmanuel Macron and a period of renewed growth and stability in the European economy in comparison to the economic stagnation of Britain, created a new sense of confidence in the EU in contrast to the sense of panic and alarm following the Brexit referendum. These factors also partly explain the determination and unity that the EU was able to maintain in the negotiations. This mood of renewed confidence may also have created a sense of complacency, where political elites within the EU failed to consider some of the lessons they needed to draw from Brexit. Neo-functionalists, those who favour the steady integration of EU member states, propound that EU integration as driven by elites and technocrats would eventually lead to wider populations identifying with the European Project based on the positive results of EU integration (Fromage and van den Brink, 2018). Yet elite-driven integration only served to alienate European populations from the EU – a process that had been accentuated by the bureaucratic machinations by political elites to save and bolster the euro in the eurozone crisis (Habermas, 2012). Juncker to some degree recognized the mounting resistance to deeper integration when he famously said: 'I think that in the end too much Europe will kill Europe' (Wiener, 2017, 151). However, the dynamics and practices of integration appeared to remain unchanged.

Former Italian prime minister Enrico Letta (2016) declared Brexit to be a wake-up call for the EU and called for a fundamental rethink: 'A relaunch of the EU must rekindle popular enthusiasm at a time when crisis and uncertainty have destroyed the perception of gradual but inevitable and universal progress. This offers us the opportunity to return to the origins of the European ideal that has, in recent years, lost its way and ended up in bureaucratization.' Others made similar appeals, but new and bold plans failed to materialize. One of the leading voices for radical reform was Macron, who set out plans for a bold transformation and claimed an isolationist attitude had returned to Europe 'because of blindness ... because we forgot to defend Europe. The Europe that we know is too slow, too weak, too ineffective' (quoted in Chrisafis and Rankin, 2017). Macron sought to revive the notion of concentric circles, with a core Europe engaged in the main European integration projects like the euro, and with countries at the periphery only engaged in some, such as the single market. Macron envisaged fiscal union for core Europe, with a finance minister and parliament for the eurozone (Mallet, 2019). To counter the appeal for the radical right, Macron sought to promote tax harmonization and a minimum wage.

The impetus for such reforms seemed to be deflated by the continual caution and ordoliberalism of Germany, which seemed reluctant to embrace bold new plans, while political and economic crisis in Italy alongside Brexit seemed to sap the vigour of the European Commission. Support for new bold initiatives, such as the Keynesian-fuelled economic stimulus and interventionism of the 'New Deal' advocated by radical Greek socialist Varoufakis (2017), remained on the fringes of political debate. As Weber outlined in his discussions on legal rationalism, upon which much of the defence of the EU in the wake of Brexit has been centred, formal rationality is hegemonic, with substantive rationality declining in importance. In other words, organizational bureaucracy crowds out other forms of rationality and limits the possibilities of creative social action (Kalberg, 1980).

Despite lacking the imagination to develop far-reaching structural solutions that might eradicate the groundswell of anger which was fuelling disquiet and unrest across Europe, as outlined earlier, Brexit was an illustrative example of the dangers of leaving the union. Some in Europe could sense such a process at work in Britain. EU Commissioner Phil Hogan (2018) felt the British public were finally seeing through the 'deception and lies' of politicians like Michael Gove and Nigel Farage – 'The tide is finally starting to go out on the high priests of Brexit, and not before time.' Tusk, with the endorsement of Juncker, also made an impassioned plea, saying that EU 'hearts are still open' to 'our British friends'. Tusk felt it was possible for Britain to reverse its decision to leave (Wilkins, 2018). Such appeals might have struck greater resonance if simultaneously the EU had embarked on a major transformation of not just its bureaucracy but also the policy restraints of austerity. Austerity caused the economic dislocation that had been the motor for populist nationalism in Europe, a point discussed in more depth in Chapter 8.

Conclusion

It can be conjectured that the strategy of the commission on Brexit and the spectacle of Brexit itself had helped to some degree to bolster centrism in Europe. Despite Macron and Tusk both proclaiming in 2019 that the EU would be embarking on a 'European renaissance', there was a sense of business as usual. With the resignation of Theresa May, Brexit would continue to vex the mind of the EU and it would face what many considered to be its nemesis and the epitome of a Brexit populist in the form of the new British Prime Minister Boris Johnson – events described in the next chapter.

7

Boris Johnson: Getting Brexit Done?

This chapter provides an overview of the premiership of Boris Johnson between July and December 2019, detailing the progress of Brexit negotiations and the General Election – events that shaped the final trajectory of Brexit but also, in all probability, the course of Britain's future for the coming decades.

From its inception in 2016, Brexit had brought extreme convulsions, drama and chaos to society and politics – and those characteristics were especially evident in the Johnson premiership, prior to the election. These traits were compounded by the fact that under the Johnson premiership, Brexit resembled a game theory stratagem. More than ever, game theory (in which individual agents or institutions are assumed to interact strategically) became an apt instrument to try and decipher the machinations and tactics of the political class.

Perhaps the most relevant example of game theory that could be used to help decipher Brexit is the 'chicken game', a situation where two cars are heading for each other – if one driver does not swerve and give the road to the other there will be a collision (Muthoo, 2019). Who will blink first? Who will swerve? In the context of Brexit, would Johnson's gambit to either get a deal he was happy with or otherwise leave without a deal succeed or lead to the destruction of his premiership. Here Thomas Schelling's (1960) 'madman theory' also has some relevance, where a principal player in the strategic game conveys sufficient irrationality to convince other players that more than a game of bluff is being played out and is thus able to yield major concessions. Possibly, Johnson wanted to use the threat of no deal to actually secure a better-negotiated deal than May had achieved. In this sense, Johnson's actions could be construed as those of an astute political fixer and operator. As noted in Chapter 3, Johnson had contemplated how Trump and his political antics might have secured more success in pressing the EU for concessions in Brexit negotiations. Johnson's love of showmanship and bravado also made him well suited to play the role of the volatile 'madman'. On the other hand, Johnson may have merely been playing out a charade that gave the pretence of seeking a deal when in fact he aspired to no deal. This chapter assesses the degree to which Johnson's and other politicians' rhetoric and stratagems achieved optimal outcomes.

People versus parliament

Dominic Cummings, who had steered the Vote Leave campaign (see Chapter 2) was appointed as Johnson's key advisor. Unsurprisingly therefore, Johnson's administration resembled the Leave referendum campaign itself by demonstrating bombast, challenge and a form of emergency politics – all common traits of populism. As with May, Johnson placed the 'will of the people' argument at the centre of his strategy and sought to depict the dissenters in parliament as an obstructive elite. In one of his live broadcasts on Facebook, titled 'peoples' question time', Johnson (2019d) stated: 'There's a terrible collaboration, as it were, going on between people who think they can block Brexit in parliament and our European friends.' Johnson was accused of framing his opponents as collaborators and weaponizing his rhetoric with the intent of demonizing Remain politicians, a charge that gained increasing traction through his tenure as prime minister.

Johnson's central aim appeared to be to outflank the Brexit Party and, through a harder Brexit position than that advocated by Theresa May, stem the flow of support to the Brexit Party. Johnson also wanted to remove the Northern Ireland backstop (see Chapter 3), which in tandem with the hard Brexiteers in his party he denounced as undemocratic. More broadly, Johnson seemed to aspire to a much looser relationship with the EU than that outlined in May's proposal and was more avowedly hyperglobalist in the sense Britain would diverge more sharply from the 'European model' under his vision.

At the Conservative's national conference, invoking topoi of history, modernization and national test, Johnson (2019a) declared:

> This country has long been a pioneer. We inaugurated the steam age, the atomic age, the age of the genome. We led the way in parliamentary democracy, in female emancipation. And when the whole world had succumbed to a different fashion, this country and this party pioneered ideas of free markets

and privatisation that spread across the planet. Every one of them was controversial, every one of them was difficult, but we have always had the courage to be original, to do things differently, and now we are about to take another giant step to do something no one thought we could do. To reboot our politics, to relaunch ourselves into the world, and to dedicate ourselves again to that simple proposition that we are here to serve the democratic will of the British people.

Such rhetoric seemed to imply that Brexit could herald a return to the buccaneering ethos of the nineteenth century that had brought unprecedented economic dominance to Britain. Johnson was promising transformative change and a return to greatness, a promise that rested on the trope that Britain had stagnated. Such sentiments were also reflected in a parliamentary exchange between Johnson (2019c) with Jeremy Corbyn, where the former relied upon mythopoesis as a rhetorical strategy: 'Since I was a child, I remember respectable authorities asserting that our time as a nation has passed and that we should be content with mediocrity and managed decline, and time and again. They are the sceptics and doubters, my friends. Time and again, by their powers to innovate and adapt, the British people have shown the doubters wrong, and I believe that at this pivotal moment in our national story, we are going to prove the doubters wrong again.'

Johnson appeared to want to achieve this aim by departing more radically than any previous prime minister from notions of the social contract and policy of alignment that the EU had done much to nurture in order to avoid downward competitive spirals in social, consumer and economic protections. Hence, the political declaration for the Withdrawal Agreement that Johnson negotiated appeared to indicate a looser relationship with the EU than that envisaged by May in the agreement she negotiated. Instead of writing into the legally binding withdrawal agreement that the UK would abide by EU standards on workers' rights and the environment, level playing field commitments were moved to the forward-looking political declaration. Some believed this afforded room for interpretation and possible divergence (Busby, 2019). During the Conservative leadership contest, in an article for the website Brexit-Central Johnson (2019b) clearly signalled his desire for non-alignment: 'We will be free to substantially diverge on tax and regulation … I have had enough of being told that we cannot do it – that the sixth biggest economy in the world is not strong enough to run itself and go forward in the world.'

The thirst for non-alignment and deregulation seemed at odds with Johnson's frequent claim in the leadership contest and declarations of intent to be guided by 'one nation' Conservative thinking as reflected in his flagship policies to develop the National Health Service (NHS) and sanction a more interventionist economic policy, ostensibly based on expansion in public spending. In reality though, such economic activism would clash with the hyperglobalist agenda that Johnson's 'buccaneer' and 'non-alignment' vision of Brexit implied. The reality of a rightward direction being implicit in Johnson's Brexit policy was reflected in the composition of his cabinet, which contained a number of radical hyperglobalist Conservatives. Cabinet ministers such as Dominic Raab (Foreign Secretary), Priti Patel (Home Secretary) and Liz Truss (Secretary of State for International Trade) had contributed to the book *Britannia Unchained* (Kwarteng et al, 2012), which argued that Britain 'rewards laziness', that British workers were 'the worst idlers in the world' and that 'too many people in Britain prefer a lie-in to hard work'. The book also opines: 'If we are to take advantage of these opportunities, we must get on the side of the responsible, the hardworking and the brave ... We must stop bailing out the reckless, avoiding all risk and rewarding laziness.'

Further confirmation of the intent of Johnson was received when the Conservative MP John Baron, a Clean Break Brexiteer, informed the BBC that ministers such as Dominic Raab and Michael Gove had told him that if the trade talks with the EU did not produce a deal by the end of 2020, the country would leave the transition and trade with the EU on no-deal (i.e. World Trade Organization) terms (Merrick, 2019). Some felt that Conservatives such as the hardline Brexit European Research Group were being slavishly loyal to Johnson's Brexit strategy, as although this initially involved a negotiated deal it could afford an opportunity to crash out later in 2020 without a deal if the scheduled trade talks faltered. The former chancellor Philip Hammond felt the withdrawal proposal Johnson eventually presented was a 'camouflage to no deal' (Syal, 2019a), a deceptive stratagem designed to lead to eventual failure in the negotiations on a trade agreement at the end of the transition period that would present a trapdoor to no deal. Such fears were bolstered by Johnson seeming to emphasize the importance of the 2020 deadline to frame a trade deal with the EU and expressing a refusal to sanction any extension beyond that date. Given that it took many years to frame a trade deal between the EU and Canada, few believed Britain could finalize the nature of future trade in a period of just months.

As with May, Johnson's vision of Brexit resisted the continuation of free movement. Johnson favoured a new points system that would prioritize skills in sanctioning entry into the British workforce. In her keynote speech to the national conservative conference, Patel (2019) as Home

Secretary extolled the righteousness of a more nativist stance to migration by resorting to legitimation through experience/status: 'This daughter of immigrants needs no lectures from the North London metropolitan liberal elite.' The reference to North London here could be interpreted as having antisemitic connotations, as this part of London has a high proportion of Jewish residents and certainly conforms to populist notions of a privileged metropolitan liberal elite. Patel proceeded to state: 'As home secretary at this defining moment in our country's history, I have a particular responsibility when it comes to taking back control. It is to end the free movement of people once and for all.' Thus, the end of freedom of movement is equated to the 'take back control' and 'will of the people' topoi.

Although Johnson expressed a preference for a negotiated withdrawal agreement over a no deal in the first months of his administration, there was scant evidence of efforts being made to find a new agreement with the EU. Johnson was accused of 'running down' the clock in pursuit of a no deal Brexit, a fear accentuated by Johnson's bravado in declaring that if the EU did not give concessions on the backstop then Britain could crash out without a deal on 31 October 2019. Such fears moved dissenting MPs to seek to constrain Johnson's room for manoeuvre. In what became known as the 'Benn Act', named after its principal sponsor Hilary Benn, MPs seized control of the House of Commons agenda and mandated Johnson to seek an extension on Britain's departure from the EU in the event of a deal not being negotiated by the latter part of October. Benn's proposal was passed in parliament with a number of Conservative MPs in support, which led to the party whip being withdrawn from twenty-one Conservative MPs including prominent figures like Philip Hammond and Ken Clarke. In sympathy with the rebel MPs, cabinet minister Amber Rudd resigned.

Johnson was vehement (2019f) in his opposition to the Benn Act, using the topoi of elitist manipulation he declared:

> This is not a bill in any normal sense of the word. It is without precedent in our history – it is a bill that, if passed, would force me to go to Brussels and beg an extension. It would force me to accept any terms offered. It would destroy any chance of negotiations or a new deal. And indeed it would enable our friends in Brussels to dictate the terms of the negotiation, that is what it does. There is only one way to describe this bill – it is Jeremy Corbyn's surrender bill. It means running up the white flag. I want to make clear to everybody in this house – there are no circumstances in which I will ever accept anything

like it. I will never surrender the control of the negotiations in the way the leader of the opposition is demanding. We promised the people we would get Brexit done. We promised to respect the result of the referendum and we must do so now. Enough is enough. This country wants this done. They want the referendum respected.

Johnson's emotive reference to 'surrender' and language that inferred Britain would be emasculated in the negotiations caused deep anger. Some critics charged Johnson with using populist language and tactics to create a cleavage between parliament and the wider public, with a fabricated image of an out-of-touch elite that was trying to frustrate Brexit being manipulated for electoral purposes. Tensions were ratcheted up further when Cummings was reported to have been responsible for an anonymous briefing to a Sunday newspaper that claimed the MPs behind the Benn Act had been liaising with the EU and would be investigated (Syal, 2019b).

Johnson had assumed the premiership just before the summer recess in July and did not properly face MPs in parliament until September. However, Johnson reduced further any chance of scrutiny of his Brexit proposals by proroguing (suspending parliament) for five weeks before a new Queen's Speech, even though the party national conferences would be held during this period. The length of this prorogation was exceptionally long. Critics charged Johnson with using the prorogation as a means to silence parliament and reduce their scope to challenge and question his Brexit strategy. Cameron, the former prime minister who was launching his memoir at this time, felt the prorogation was a 'sharp practice' on the part of Johnson (Proctor, 2019). This assertion was upheld by the Supreme Court ruling that declared the prorogation to be illegal and that given the critical situation regarding Brexit there was a need for parliament to scrutinize the government's intentions (Supreme Court Judgement, 2019). However, even this setback suited Johnson's narrative, as he could depict it as further evidence by a political elite to frustrate the will of the people. In a parliamentary exchange with Corbyn, Johnson (2019e) declared, again invoking the topoi of elitism: 'Worst of all, they see ever more elaborate legal and political manoeuvres from the Labour party, which is determined, absolutely determined, to say "We know best", and to thumb their noses at the 17.4 million people who voted to leave the European Union. The Leader of the Opposition and his party do not trust the people.'

The drama and tension of this political moment and the deliberate ratcheting of tensions between parliament and the people was evident in the rather masculinist approach Johnson took in his rhetoric calling on Corbyn to 'man up' and agree to an election, accusing him of being 'frit'(a colloquial shortening of 'frightened') and a 'girl's blouse' (slang for emasculated) for not agreeing to one. In one advert, the Conservatives depicted Corbyn as a chicken (Baker, 2019). On the day this advert was launched, Conservative party chair James Cleverly tweeted: 'Thinking about what to have for lunch. Large bucket of boneless (certainly spineless) JFC (Jeremy's Frightened & Chicken) perhaps.'

Johnson was rebuffed in his first attempt to secure an election. The opposition parties and rebel Conservatives effectively liaised to present a united front and stated they would only acquiesce to an election if and when crashing out of the EU was clearly not an option. Towards the end of October 2019, Johnson produced a new outline agreement that received a positive reception from the EU. As noted earlier, this proposal accorded opportunities for divergence from the EU regulations entailing that Northern Ireland remain aligned to EU regulations by remaining in the EU customs territory for the whole transition period of at least four years, removing fears around border checks between the Republic of Ireland Northern Ireland and in effect creating a new border between Britain and the EU down the middle of the Irish Sea. At no less a place than the Democratic Unionist Party (DUP) conference in Belfast, Johnson (2018) had himself denounced such a proposal as one that no British prime minister could agree to, because Northern Ireland would thus diverge from the rest of the UK and therefore undermine the level of uniformity between its various constituent parts. As a consequence of the policy change, the DUP withdrew its support for the government's Brexit stance, which along with the loss of support of Conservative rebels meant the Johnson administration did not enjoy a majority and would have trouble navigating its vision of Brexit through parliament. As will be noted in the next section, the opposition to this particular vision of Brexit was intense and centred on profound concerns regarding the economic and social implications of this hard form of Brexit but also the moral and constitutional probity of the Johnson administration.

Opposition to Johnson

Opposition to Johnson's Brexit strategy was mounted from across the political spectrum and included a small number of one nation Conservatives, the Corbynite left as well as centrist Labour MPs and the Liberal Democrats and nationalists. These groups sought to desecuritize the rhetoric and strategy of Johnson by emphasizing the inherent constitutional and economic dangers of Johnson's threat to allow Britain to crash out of the EU without a deal if his requests for concessions were not met and/or the dangers that non-alignment with the EU would augur in social and environmental protection.

A key area these disparate forces converged upon in their attacks was Johnson's rhetoric (topoi of threat and danger). Dominic Grieve, a former one nation Conservative MP now sitting as an independent, accused Johnson of behaving like a demagogue with his 'tub thumping populism' that Grieve claimed had led to him receiving death threats (Press Association, 2019). The charge against Johnson that he was imperilling the safety of MPs with his rhetoric was forcefully made by the Labour MP Paula Sherriff. Invoking the memory of Jo Cox, the MP who had been assassinated by a right-wing fanatic (see Chapter 2), Sherriff rose in a parliamentary debate and was visibly gripped by outrage and emotion. While pointing at the memorial to Cox in the chamber, she asseverated: 'We stand here, Mr Speaker, under the shield of our departed friend. Many of us in this place are subject to death threats and abuse every single day. Let me tell the prime minister that they often quote his words – surrender act, betrayal, traitor – and I, for one, am sick of it … he should be absolutely ashamed of himself' (Belam, 2019). Johnson, unmoved, was accused of crassness when he retorted, 'I have to say I have never heard such humbug in all my life' – which was greeted with howls of protest. Later in the debate, in response to appeals for Johnson to avoid inflammatory language which might endanger the lives of MPs like that of Cox, Johnson replied: 'The best way to honour the memory of Jo Cox and, indeed, the best way to bring this country together would be, I think, to get Brexit done.' This was a remarkably insensitive comment given the assassinated Cox was an ardent Remainer.

A prominent counterargument to Johnson's strategy was that he was undermining the fabric of British democracy. As the Labour MP Jess Phillips (2019) wrote in *The Independent*:

> False divides are opening up everywhere. People who have been left with nothing by years of cuts feel they have nothing to lose and need someone to blame. These are the seeds from which fascism grows … He [Johnson] has moved to close down parliament, close down scrutiny, and close down the voices of democratically elected representatives. It doesn't have to be a military coup to be dangerous. It doesn't have to be unprecedented to be unacceptable. It doesn't have to be illegal to be unethical. The warning signs for our country are flashing a burning, urgent red.

Others also summoned up sinister images of authoritarianism. Shadow attorney general and Labour peer Shami Chakrabarti, speaking to Sky News's Sophie Ridge stated with reference to Johnson's possible flouting of the Benn Act and refusal to seek an extension: 'Every tinpot dictator on the planet throughout history has used the excuse of having the people on their side to break the law to shut down parliament and all the rest of it. It's absolutely extraordinary and I think it's very un-British, as was the purge of the 21 MPs, who are Conservatives, they're not secret Corbynistas' (Ridge, 2019).

Some critics, such as former premier Gordon Brown (2019) and the former foreign secretary Malcolm Rifkind (2019), emphasized the political dangers of Johnson's strategy by drawing parallels with the constitutional crisis that triggered the civil war under Charles I (topoi of history and lessons learnt). Labour MP Stephen Doughty, a leading supporter of the People's Vote campaign, said: 'It is more than 320 years since the question of whether parliament or the executive is sovereign was settled, and parliament won. Instead of impersonating Stuart monarchs and claiming a divine right to rule, the prime minister and his retinue should recognise they have to submit to democracy and have no right to impose no deal or any vicious Brexit on us' (quoted in Woodcock, 2019).

A central concern of Corbyn was that Johnson was seeking to fundamentally change the economic and social model of Britain by securing a Brexit that would allow the country to radically depart from the EU in terms of regulatory frameworks. Corbyn (2019b) declared in his conference speech as leader that under the cover of no deal the Conservatives would extend privatization, deregulate and cut taxes for the elite.

> That would mean a race to the bottom in standards and workers' rights to create an offshore tax haven for the super-rich. And they want all of this locked in with a one-sided free trade deal that would put our country at the mercy of Donald Trump. That's why a no-deal Brexit is really a Trump-deal Brexit. That would be the opposite of taking back control. It would be handing our country's future to the US president and his America First policy. Of course, Trump is delighted to have a compliant British prime minister in his back pocket. A Trump-deal Brexit would mean US corporations getting the green light for a comprehensive takeover of our public services. I am not prepared to stand by while our NHS is sacrificed on the altar of US big business or any other country's big business [exigency].

The 'race to the bottom' interpretation of Johnson's aims and his potential links with Trump became frequent features of Corbyn's opposition to Johnson's Brexit, which traded upon the deep unpopularity of Trump among the British public but also the perception that Johnson was acting in accordance with the same populist playbook.

Many of the attacks against Johnson centred on his lack of moral probity (ad hominem). A frequent charge was that he was a compulsive liar. The former Conservative minister Chris Patten (2019) accused Johnson of being 'a mendacious chancer'. Patten proceeded to state: 'It is no exaggeration to say that Johnson has lied his way to the top, first in journalism and then in politics. His ascent owes everything to the growing xenophobia and English nationalism that many Conservatives now espouse.' For Patten, a lack of moral rigour in Johnson and the increasing influence of extreme nationalism within the Conservative Party was leading to Britain being a 'failed state' in terms of representative democracy, with its very institutions being undermined. Corbyn used the judgement of the Supreme Court on the proroguing of parliament in his 2019 conference speech (see earlier discussion) as evidence of Johnson's moral failings being combined with an elitist sense of entitlement, which meant the Tory leader felt he could ignore and discard convention:

> Resigning would make him the shortest serving British prime minister in history and rightly so. His is a born-to-rule government of the entitled who believe that the rules they set for everyone else don't apply to them. That's what today's supreme court judgment spells out with brutal clarity. There was no reason – 'let alone a good reason', the judges concluded – for the prime minister to have shut down parliament. He thought he could do whatever he liked just as he always does. He thinks he's above us all. He is part of an elite that disdains democracy. He is not fit to be prime minister. Let me quote the supreme court's conclusion: 'Unlawful, null and of no effect and should be quashed' – they've got the prime minister down to a tee. (Corbyn, 2019b)

Lack of trust in him was a principal factor in explaining why opposition MPs failed to be persuaded when Johnson did present his withdrawal proposal, pledging that he would seek the highest standards in regulatory frameworks. Such MPS were also unwilling to agree to approve the terms before the legal framework had passed through parliament. An amendment to enable such a sequence was championed by Sir Oliver Letwin, a Conservative grandee who had been among the twenty-one

MPs to defy the party whip. The Letwin amendment thus closed a loophole that would have allowed Johnson to stage a vote on the deal as mandated in the Benn Act and thus not have to seek an extension. But there was the danger that if the Withdrawal Agreement Bill did not progress through parliament Britain could still crash out of the EU. This delay meant it was no longer possible to leave the EU as promised by Johnson on 31 October, and thus under the provisions of the Benn Act he was compelled to write to the EU Commission asking for an extension. Johnson did indeed send a letter seeking an extension, but it was unsigned and accompanied by a second letter stating he did not really think it was a good idea – an act that further damaged his reputation for moral rectitude. Furthermore, some argued Johnson had broken the law by seeking to undermine the Benn mandate. Although Johnson's Withdrawal Agreement Bill received a second reading, parliament refused to agree to the short timetable (programme motion) for a debate of three days as set by the government, with MPs arguing that much longer was needed to scrutinize such an important piece of legislation. On the part of the government, there were fears MPs would amend the deal to frame a soft Brexit – for example by inserting a clause on a customs union or revising the bill to ensure there was no chance of crashing out of the EU sans deal or without parliament's approval.

As noted earlier, Labour had resisted Johnson's call for a General Election to resolve the impasse until a no-deal Brexit was taken off the table, something it was able to do under the Fixed Term Parliament Act that stipulated two thirds of MPs were needed to sanction an election. Sensing that an election was likely, the EU decided to agree to an extension until the end of January 2020; as the imminent threat of no deal had been removed, so had the obstacle to an election. Thus, parliament by a simple majority on an amendment to the Fixed Term Parliament Act, agreed to hold an election on 12 December 2019.

There was a great deal of apprehension among MPs as to the merits of such an election. Some argued it played into Johnson's hands by giving him the chance to play out his 'people versus parliament' rhetoric and could act as a silver bullet to rid the Conservative party of dissenting one nation MPs. Victory would give Johnson an effective majority of compliant MPs who would in all probability loyally support Johnson's hard Brexit or possible attempt to crash out in 2020. Some had argued for a referendum first, so the public could focus clearly on the Brexit question and then stage a General Election. Some supported the notion of a unity government following a possible no confidence motion in Johnson. Corbyn offered to lead such a government but insisted on staging a General Election first and then holding a referendum where

Remain was an option alongside a renegotiated withdrawal agreement based on membership of a customs union and close alignment with the EU. However, Liberal Democrat leader Jo Swinson, who replaced Vince Cable as leader in July 2019, refused to countenance support for such an interim government, arguing that Corbyn was too politically extreme to warrant any support (see later discussion).

Difficulty in forming a partnership between these two parties was also accentuated by the fact there was a marked difference in their Brexit policies, with the Lib Dems now promising to revoke Brexit without a referendum if they won an election and Labour continuing to maintain its policy of ambiguity. In the 2019 European elections, the Lib Dems had secured many new seats and gained votes – in part at the expense of Labour – on account of their clear opposition to any form of Brexit. Hence, the sense of rivalry between Labour and a rejuvenated Liberal Democrat Party became more accentuated.

Hopes had been high prior to the Labour Conference that a motion might be passed committing Labour to campaign for Remain in any election. Instead, the views of the leadership prevailed, in part through the support of major trade unions, the influence of Momentum and appeals that if conference decided to diverge from the leader's preferred position it would be interpreted as a vote of no confidence in the leadership (Chessum, 2019). Thus, the Labour Conference endorsed a position that pledged to negotiate a new deal with the EU and only then stage a special discussion to decide if they would campaign for leave or remain. Corbyn promised to be an honest broker, who would impartially enact any decision that was made. The diverging opinions among the opposition made it difficult to promote any legislative attempts to get parliament to support a confirmatory vote on Johnson's deal.

Liberal Democrats appealed for a 'unity government' to be led by a figure like Ken Clarke or Margaret Beckett, as Corbyn was too divisive a figure; some sections of the Labour Party argued if Corbyn could not muster the numbers he should step aside for such a figure. Meanwhile, some contended that the proposed government should stage a referendum after a national conversation using regional deliberative forums, and that only after the Brexit question was resolved should an election be held (Ryder, 2019). The proposal of a unity caretaker prime minister was rejected by Corbyn; he argued he had the right to form a government as leader of the opposition. A refusal to support such an arrangement and stand aside may also have stemmed from a fear of Corbyn being bypassed and marginalized by Labour MPs critical of his leadership. The radical journalist Paul Mason (2019b) called for a popular front to be formed, replicating the progressive/left alliance of the 1930s against fascism, but here also the Labour leadership refused to consider entering into any form of electoral pact. In view of this unity in the opposition, though it was still fragmented, with the SNP and Lib Dems agreeing to support an election now that the immediate threat of a no-deal Brexit had been averted, Corbyn also decided to acquiesce and give his agreement. This was Johnson's fourth attempt to secure an early election; 438 MPs voted in support with twenty against. Almost half of Labour MPs did not vote, and the SNP and Lib Dems abstained as they were unable to secure their preferred date of 9 December for the poll.

The electoral chances for Labour did not seem propitious. The Conservatives enjoyed consistent poll leads over Labour. For example, after the party conferences and despite the censure of the Supreme Court, the Conservatives had a fifteen-point lead in an Opinium poll for the *Observer* (Helm, 2019). Furthermore, although opinion polls indicated a majority of the population now favoured Remain, the margin was slight. Prior to the election, YouGov estimated 53 to 47 per cent of the public (excluding don't knows) wanted to remain in the EU (Cecil, 2019). However, it was not clear whether Remain sentiment would be clearly translated into a parliamentary majority, given the fact that Remain was represented by a range of opposition parties but Leave was only represented by the Conservatives and the Brexit Party, and Farage made the arithmetic of voting simpler by pledging to withdraw candidates from Conservative-held seats.

Conversely, other surveys indicated a mood change on the part of the public that might facilitate Brexit. A poll conducted by Lord Ashcroft found that 63 per cent of Leave voters would prefer to leave the EU even if it meant Scotland, Wales or Northern Ireland leaving the Union (Gourtsoyannis, 2018). A survey by Cardiff University found that a majority of leave voters thought violence to MPs was a price worth paying for securing Brexit (Malik, 2019). The results of such surveys indicated that a degree of extremism had entered the mainstream of politics, which might make the election of 2019 even more volatile, one in which the mould of British politics of previous decades might be irrevocably changed.

The election of 2020

Some assumed that Brexit under the Johnson premiership would reach some form of closure or endgame, either crashing out without a deal or with some form of deal being negotiated. Johnson himself encouraged such a perception by declaring through an oft-used slogan – also the

Conservative national conference strapline and which was put on the side of the Tory campaign bus for the General Election – that he wanted to 'get Brexit done' and proceed to address other national concerns and bring the country together. The ingenuity of this simple slogan was that it appealed to and played upon the public frustration and exhaustion over Brexit, with promises of a return to political normality (Kirkup, 2019). The reality, of course, was that the wrangling would continue in the next phase of Brexit as negotiations would centre on the new trade deal with the EU, which presented a potential new cliff edge and chance still to crash out of the EU without a deal.

The Conservatives were adept at using simple visual devices to bolster the promise to 'get Brexit done', with Johnson wearing boxing gloves and a cooking apron with the slogan emblazoned on them and even driving a JCB with the banner 'Get Brexit done' and smashing through a polystyrene wall – the metaphorical wall of opposition to Brexit. Many of these photoshoots took place in blue-collar work environments and signalled the Conservative strategy to build a majority by taking working-class Labour seats that had voted heavily to Leave. Johnson also sought to appeal to these voters with his pledge to govern in the tradition of 'one nation' conservatism and, as noted earlier, he even promised a more active economic policy – arguing that once outside of the EU, the British government would be freer to intervene and subsidize economic activity.

Repetitive use of the slogan 'get Brexit done' was attributable to Isaac Levido, a key Conservative election strategist and protégé of Lynton Crosby (see Introduction and Chapter 2), who had helped coordinate a recent Australian election that was characterized by repetitive and relentless message discipline and fake claims about tax rises (Waterson, 2019). During the 2019 campaign, notable acts of deception by the Conservatives involved fabricating a video of Labour's Brexit spokesperson Keir Starmer to imply indecision and, during the leaders debate between Corbyn and Johnson, changing the name of their Twitter account to 'factcheckUK' so as to impersonate an independent fact-checking account, using this to disseminate anti-Labour propaganda. First Draft – a non-profit organization which works on debunking fake news – analysed every ad promoted by the UK's three main political parties on Facebook in the first four days of December 2019. It found that 88 per cent of the Conservatives' Facebook campaigning pushed figures challenged by Full Fact (Reid and Dotto, 2019).

Apropos Labour's strategy of calling for a second referendum with Corbyn playing the part of the neutral broker, some claimed it lacked the simplicity and clarity of the Conservative message. Corbyn's unwillingness to declare how he would campaign in such a referendum was depicted by Johnson as demonstrating a lack of leadership. Johnson repeated the Conservative mantra of the 2015 election, with the warning that a hung parliament would mean a coalition of chaos under an SNP-supported Labour government, with the prospect of two referendums, one on Brexit and the other Scottish independence, the price Labour would pay for SNP support.

Corbyn's personality and leadership was also a point of attack, with the print media depicting him as an extremist unfit to lead the country. Such a media strategy had been evident from the onset of Corbyn's leadership, with newspapers such as the *Daily Telegraph*, the *Daily Express* or *The Sun* having 15–20 per cent of their coverage depicting Corbyn as having historic links with the IRA, Iran, Hamas, Hezbollah and/or terrorism (Cammaerts, 2016). A study by Loughborough University Centre for Research in Communication and Culture (2019) found that press hostility to Labour in 2019 was more than double the levels identified in 2017. By the same measure, negative coverage of the Conservatives halved. Much of the negative media coverage focused on Corbyn and a large number of Labour candidates reported that while canvassing Corbyn was cited as a principal reason why some would not vote Labour. This was confirmed in an opinion poll by Opinium which found that among Labour voters of 2017 who had defected to the Conservatives in the General Election, 37 per cent cited Corbyn's leadership of the party as their main reason for doing so. In contrast, some Corbyn supporters sought to depict such defections and the election result as a consequence of anger at Labour's increasing policy tilt towards Remain. However, according to Opinium, 21 per cent of the sample said they defected due to the party's stance on EU membership while just 6 per cent said their main reason was Labour's economic policies (Cowburn, 2019).

The Liberal Democrats also faltered on Brexit. Their call for Article 50 to be revoked in the event of them forming a government distracted from a call for a second referendum, a point that even the previous leader Vince Cable acknowledged (Jankowicz, 2019). The Liberal Democrat pledge was seen to signal a certain contempt for those who had voted Leave and their aspirations, which was claimed by critics to mirror the arrogance of militant leavers. The call for a referendum was also hamstrung by the divisions within the People's Vote campaign for another referendum. Roland Rudd, campaign chairman, dismissed chief executive James McGrory, a former advisor to Nick Clegg, and Tom Baldwin, its director of communications who worked for Labour under Ed Miliband. In tandem with this, Rudd restructured the campaign around a new company. Staff staged a walkout and Rudd was accused of conducting a power grab with a view to preparing the ground for a new force in politics. As a consequence, the tactical voting campaign to oust the Conservatives initially planned by the People's Vote campaign was heavily scaled back (Savage, 2019).

Although opinion polls indicated that a majority now wished to remain in the EU, the opposition vote to Brexit was divided between Labour and the Liberal Democrats and a number of smaller parties. An alliance had been formed between the Liberal Democrats, Welsh Nationalists and Greens but neither Labour or the Lib Dems were prepared to form a pact, with Swinson stating she could not countenance supporting a Corbyn-led government: 'Look, Liberal Democrat votes are not going to put Jeremy Corbyn into Downing Street,' Swinson said in an interview with the *Financial Times*, 'He is not fit to do that job' (quoted in Hughes, 2019). In contrast, Farage assisted the Conservatives by withdrawing Brexit Party candidates in Conservative-held seats in part because he was encouraged by Johnson's declaration that he would not seek an extension beyond 2020 in negotiating a trade deal. Farage claimed that the Conservatives had encouraged the Brexit Party to withdraw candidates from Labour-held seats with promises of peerages being offered (Hughes and Parker, 2019).

To return to game theory, the opposition to Brexit, for its part, resembled something of a 'Mexican Standoff' – another game theory exercise, with three antagonists facing each other in a duel but with it being unclear as to who was the greatest threat or who might be worth forming a temporal alliance with to avert the most direct and immediate danger. As noted, one nation Conservatives, Labour, Liberal Democrat and nationalist MPs had, at times, before the election been able with some success to come together in efforts to thwart a hard Brexit. With reference to the election, another game theory has relevance: the 'Prisoner's Dilemma', where although it might appear to be in the interests of two actors to cooperate either might also be more willing to countenance turning against the other to maximize potential return. In this imagined scenario, if each prisoner cooperates and refuses to testify against each other they might be released or face reduced sentences, but if one testifies then a deal can be agreed and the police might release them, while the other prisoner faces a long sentence. However, in the election, cooperation by the opposition party machines and tactical voting by members and supporters was clearly not sufficient to thwart a Conservative victory. Some felt they had placed narrow party interests above the national interest.

In the election, the Conservatives secured a majority of seventy-eight; many of the seats gained were at the expense of Labour in northern working-class communities. Labour's tally of 203 seats was the worst result in terms of seats that it had suffered since 1935. The Conservatives secured

43.6 per cent of the vote, Labour 32.2 per cent and the Liberal Democrats 11.5 per cent, with the Brexit Party winning a mere 2 per cent. Despite Johnson's decisive victory, 52 per cent of voters had supported pro-Remain parties; in other words, 17 million people voted for parties that wanted a second referendum compared with fewer than 15 million opting for Leave. This result reflected a deep cultural divide between large cities that had sided with Remain parties and small towns, the countryside and deindustrialized communities that had voted Conservative. In a victory speech with populist slogan 'The People's Government' as a banner in the background, Johnson declared: 'We must understand now what an earthquake we have created. The way in which we have changed the political map in this country. We have to grapple with the consequences of that. We have to change our own party. We have to rise to the level of events. We have to rise to the challenge that the British people have given us' (quoted in Mikhailova, 2019). Some construed this as an effort to tilt his government towards one nationism, but the statement could be open to a different interpretation.

Conclusion

At the start of this chapter, I reflected on the relevance of game theory in understanding Johnson's political strategy, through strategizing that a winner can emerge through the use of bluff and bravado. However, such tactics can sow deep seeds of mistrust in other players and reduce the scope for compromise and more rational deal-making in the future, minimizing the chances of returning to normalcy. In other words, through such tactics you might win the battle but lose the war. It could be argued that even by feigning 'madness' as a temporal strategy to maximize a sense of bluff and potential concessions, there was a corresponding danger that such behaviour could become the political norm.

The American journalist Andrew Sullivan (2019) contemplated whether Johnson's actions were creating a new model for the centre-right across Europe that might present huge challenges for the European political establishment:

> What Cummings and Johnson believe is that the EU, far from being an engine for liberal progress, has, through its overreach and hubris, actually become a major cause of the rise of the far right across the Continent. By forcing many very different countries into one increasingly powerful Eurocratic rubric, the EU has spawned a nationalist reaction. From Germany and

France to Hungary and Poland, the hardest right is gaining. Getting out of the EU is, Johnson and Cummings argue, a way to counter and disarm this nationalism and to transform it into a more benign patriotism. Only the Johnson Tories have grasped this, and the Johnson strategy is one every other major democracy should examine.

It could be argued, though, that Johnson and the Conservative Party were merely reflecting trends seen elsewhere where the centre-right has moved further to the right in order to avoid being 'squeezed' by an emerging national populist right but which could also be seen as the accentuation and reinterpretation of values already evident in mainstream conservatism. A prominent view on the populist radical right is that it is alien to mainstream values in Western democracies – 'the normal pathology thesis' – and is caused by extreme conditions such as crisis and is thus an abnormal aberration. In contrast, paradigmatic shifts in political values could be construed as a 'pathological normalcy' – a radical interpretation of mainstream values where inherent and implied authoritarianism, nativism and populism are brought to the fore (Mudde, 2010). Of course, the two theories may be entwined and crisis may be the catalyst to the amplification of values that constitute forms of reactionaryism. During the course of this book, I have sought to explain how neoliberalism coupled with a sense of nostalgia and exceptionalism in British society, and how this was especially evident in the Conservative Party from the premiership of Thatcher onwards. As noted in Chapter 1, crisis has accentuated and rekindled a Thatcherite and nationalistic form of conservatism. Lucardie (2000) is right to note that nationalist right populism is a form of purification that objects to compromise and sees forms of consensus as betraying and diluting its core ideology. Thus, rather than being a new and novel aberration, Brexit nationalism was thus a reversion and accentuation of values deeply embedded in popular political consciousness.

Brexit nationalism was therefore a natural progression for conservatism. Johnson may have won an election, but he faced a series of challenges and dilemmas that could imperil his populist-driven political project. Corbyn had not been the only candidate to experience a stark examination of his probity and fitness to be prime minister. In the case of Johnson, the question of trust and integrity was repeatedly raised during the campaign. Johnson had made a series of promises – one being that he could 'get Brexit done' by the end of 2020. Many argued this was not possible given the complexity of negotiating trade deals. Michel Barnier, the EU's chief Brexit negotiator, who was now leading the EU taskforce on future relations with Britain, signalled doubt as to whether an agreement would be completed within the desired timeframe (Stone, 2019). Would Johnson be prepared to crash out of the EU without a deal? He had promised to align Britain to EU regulatory standards in a number of areas, but would this be compatible with a free trade deal with the United States and the hyperglobalist aspirations of a large section of his party? Johnson had promised a more active economic policy and one nationism, but would the hyperglobalists within his party countenance such policies? Would the economic health of Britain following its departure from the EU enable such policies, given the immediate and negative economic impact many expected? Another potential point of tension might be found in the allegiance radical right street politician and English Defence League founder Tommy Robinson proffered to Johnson. Robinson even claimed to have joined the Conservative Party after the election. Hannah Arendt (1973) famously declared: 'Only the mob and the elite can be attracted by the momentum of totalitarianism itself. The masses have to be won by propaganda.' Will street-organized and militant populists like Robinson remain satisfied with Johnson? Will Brexit nationalism nurture a more militant social movement? The convulsions, paradigmatic shifts and discord that have epitomized Brexit are likely to continue.

Addressing parliament after the General Election, Johnson (2019g) emphasized a desire to 'reunite' the country and 'to begin the healing for which the whole people of this country yearn'. However, evidence of concessions and compromise were sparse. In the wake of the election, Johnson appeared to be tilting his vision of Brexit into a 'hard' form as the Withdrawal Agreement Bill he presented to parliament specifically prevented MPs extending the Brexit transition period beyond the end of 2020. The bill was also shorn of previously pledged protections on workers' rights, though assurances were given they would feature in a separate bill. Ministers would also no longer be bound to provide updates on the future trading relationship or to make sure parliament approves the government's negotiating objectives. A mere three days were allocated for scrutiny. On 20 December, the bill passed its second reading by 358 votes to 234. In the debate on the Withdrawal Bill, both Boris Johnson and Keir Starmer indicated that the old labels of Remainer and Leaver were no longer apt. However, this did not mean that the strife and conflict of British politics would end or, indeed, the search for consensus and unity. These are themes discussed in the concluding chapter.

8

Antidotes to Brexit

This book has sought to highlight how serious flaws exist with the institutions and cultural and political norms of present-day Britain. The conclusion seeks to advance potential antidotes to the ills of Brexit Britain.

Through a study of the public discourse centred on Brexit, we can understand and witness certain stratagems deployed to prompt and manipulate public thought on identity and nationhood. Brexit can be perceived as a shaper of identity, a frame used to interpret the past and present. As noted throughout the course of this book, one prominent frame of Brexiteers was centred on British/English exceptionalism, monoculturalism and a rejection of European solidarity, which were perceived to impinge upon tradition, sovereignty and the freedom of markets. Brexit is a point of reference that helps us understand the nature and scale of political events and change since 2016, which can certainly be classified as 'tumultuous' but also reflect deep shifts in societal values. These shifts in values were reflected in the General Election of 2019; voters supported Boris Johnson for myriad reasons, but it was evident that sizeable sections of the electorate were prepared to support a radical government steered by hyperglobalist aspirations fused with monocultural and nativist conceptions of Englishness.

Brexit presents a paradigm shift (see Introduction), where a crisis of confidence in a vulnerable and dysfunctional paradigm has occurred. In this revolutionary phase, if the old model cannot adapt it is replaced with a new conceptual worldview, whose assumptions remain sovereign for some period of time, at least until the cycle repeats itself. However, although successfully fused, at least for the present, hyperglobalism and militant English nationalism may not always be in such complete harmony and alliance. Growing deregulation and divergence from the European economic model will have profound implications for the working-class/left-behind communities of the Leave-supporting electoral base, and social tensions can be anticipated to rise. What is more, the hyperglobalists may also wish to find means by which a cheap and much-needed supply of labour might be made available. Migration from Europe or other parts of the world may not abate to the degree that some nativist Brexiteers might hope for, especially as countries such as India may press for greater migration rights for their citizens in the event of any trade deal being made. It may also dawn on some that the heady mix of nostalgia and utopianism of Brexit is unrealizable. More tensions and division are, regrettably, to be anticipated.

Although there are a number of competing visions of Brexit, some may be left disappointed as the nature of Britain's departure becomes more defined. These tensions will also be evident within the elite. Some, such as the Confederation of British Industry, will continue to recoil from hard forms of Brexit. Others within the establishment will be chary of the cultural, political and constitutional changes that Brexit will herald which might signify unacceptable departures from traditional notions of identity and representative democracy, as well as the fabric of the Union. It is evident, therefore, that in the coming years there will be many points of expected tension and contestation, where Brexit will be a central point of reference in shaping ongoing popular political discourse. Through writing a book on Brexit it is all the more clear that there is no clear cut-off point in any attempt to describe the phenomenon; it is an ongoing process that will be a major thread in British politics and society for a generation.

This book has sought to understand the causes, nature and direction of Brexit, charting the flow of paradigm shift by detailing the speech acts of the various protagonists and placing them in a historical, cultural and socio-economic context. The final section of the book returns to some of the central concepts and schemes of argumentation (topoi) and rhetoric as set out in Table I.1 and referred to during the course of the book. Anticipating future flashpoints and tensions as well as noting the root causes of Brexit, I propose in the final section of the book a series of actions and interventions that have relevance to these concerns – and they are transformative in the sense they present profound socio-economic, cultural and political change.

A core message of this book is that authoritarian populism (Brexit nationalism) is a state of affairs where emotions are orchestrated by an increasingly demagogic subsection of the elite to polarize, mobilize and demonize – a reactive, illiberal and antagonist form of politics. It presents a threat in that although perhaps it has manifested itself in one of its most extreme forms in Britain through Brexit, it is in fact endemic to the whole of Europe. In January 2019 a group of thirty leading European thinkers, writers, historians and Nobel laureates declared that Europe as an idea was 'coming apart before our eyes' and the consequences would be 'calamitous' if the rising tide of populism was not challenged (Henley and Rice-Oxley, 2019). The final part of this book seeks to identify a panacea to the rise of authoritarian populism, both in Britain and Europe. Britain's future relationship with the European Union (EU) will be a key determiner in Britain's course as a nation; hence, the book advocates Britain's eventual re-entry into a reformed EU grounded within the concept of social Europe and a conception of identity that is inclusive and accommodated in a structural framework at once deliberative and egalitarian.

The power of speech

This book has illustrated that rhetoric has become a sophisticated but also securitized tool and in that sense a rather sinister one. As evidenced by Brexit, political rhetoric has been able to manipulate a range of dispositions, emotions and identities to the extreme. Such concerns are not new, in the time of ancient Greece, Plato, who was by no means a democrat, deplored the use of rhetoric and its propensity to obstruct rationality and reason (Plato, 2009). In the *Gorgias*, Plato decried that for the unprincipled demagogue rhetoric was a means to power rather than a path to truth. The use of surveys, development of social media and technology and the science of marketing have only accentuated the power and influence of rhetoric for the demagogue.

In what has been termed as 'plebiscitary rhetoric', according to Chambers (2009) a situation has arisen where campaigns are vapid and vacuous, voters have limited information at their command, the press stokes polarization as opposed to deliberation, and politicians literally say anything to get elected by a passive and largely compliant public. Rhetoric has become a honed weapon to give form and articulation to a broadly conceived popular 'will' that promotes an increasingly divisive political agenda. Lies and threats have accompanied the use of sharp rhetoric, thus coercion has become increasingly apparent. Jonathan Lis in *The Guardian* (2019) articulates effectively the dangers of current political invective: 'Politicians can no longer merely disagree. They must be acting in bad faith, or subverting democracy, or betraying the electorate. This finds its extreme form in the word "treason", which now peppers and pollutes the language of right-wing politicians and commentators.' Such invective narrows the scope for reconciliation and any pathway to escape strife and dissension. A much more bridging form of rhetoric needs to take root.

Bridging rhetoric is a more inclusive form of rhetoric that seeks to convey and uphold notions of unity and community that encompass a more cosmopolitan outlook and is therefore contrary to bonding rhetoric that is insular and deepens divisions and expands out-groups (Dryzek, 2010). We will perhaps never cease to resort to rhetoric, and a neutral form of political communication may be not only unobtainable but if it were achievable it might be undesirable – in the sense of the cultural hegemony it would constitute, whereby those whose dialect and idiom are representative of the margins might find their speech acts derided and marginalized. However, what is achievable and desirable is for an alternative set of political values to become the norm. Standards need to be set in society that preclude and impede the use of plebiscitary rhetoric in forms that are demagogic, base and divisive. That shift and the resulting change in the application of rhetoric will only come about when a series of cultural, political and socio-economic transformations take place within society – changes that the rest of this concluding chapter sets out.

Renewing democracy

Brexit and other tensions and deficiencies in representative democracy have prompted some commentators to call for a completely new political system. The British political system, with its unwritten constitution based on precedent, convention and tradition, has – with some degree of hubris – consoled itself with the notion that such a system has served the country well. However, in light of the events around Brexit few would agree with the statement by John Bright in 1865 that Westminster was the 'mother of parliaments' (Eaton, 2012), an accolade still used in recent times to infer Westminster is a model that others should copy and emulate. The functioning of British democracy was dependent on an assumption that the political elite could be trusted to act in good faith and honour, but Brexit has revealed fundamental weaknesses in the strength of the UK's democratic checks and balances and the integrity of some of the political class. Change has to come about. However, it may be a case of renewing the fabric of the existing system rather than wholesale replacement (Parvin, 2018). Reform and the British tradition of pouring 'new wine into old bottles' does not preclude comprehensive changes in decision-making.

Laclau and Mouffe (2001) are prominent critics of liberal democracy in its present form. They, among various other critics, have despaired of the stifling consensus, which is often grounded in neoliberal values, as was so evident in the third-way politics of New Labour, and which offers the public a limited choice. Instead, they advocate a form of radical democracy based on conflict. Radical democrats such as Mouffe (1999) wish to see antagonism develop into agonism, where polarization is encouraged between an 'us' and 'them', with the 'them' becoming not so much enemies but respected adversaries. Thus, agonism promises to return to politics passion and the prospects of fundamental egalitarian change.

However, there are inherent dangers with agonism. The divide and conflict of agonism can increase tensions and hostilities within society. The intense contestation by rival camps of their adversaries' values and identities can fragment cohesion, deepening and reifying the identities of besieged adversaries (Dryzek and Niemeyer, 2006). Agonism is, in fact, a product of populism, as has been illustrated throughout this book. It is a phenomenon susceptible to binary speech acts and irrationalism but also manipulation. And it is interesting to note that the German thinker Carl Schmitt (1888–1985) was one of the intellectual inspirations for the concept of agonism. For Schmitt, one identity could only be constituted by the suppression of an adversary, the other. Schmitt's concept of 'us and them' was nationalistic and nation-building and hence his case supportive of the Nazi movement. This is illustrative of the dangers that can be released when dialogue and compromise are pushed to the margins of politics, even through a left-wing interpretation. The Schmittian conception of antagonism creates a public enemy who ultimately cannot be engaged with in partnership – they can only be vanquished (Edwards, 2013).

Deliberative democracy, a discursive form of politics that encourages informed and collective conversation and decision-making, might be a more effective remedy to the current ills of the political system, as it offers the prospect of mediation and reconciliation. It is argued that wide-ranging dialogue and mediation hold the prospect of better-informed decisions being made which command respect and are perceived as having legitimacy (Schaap, 2006). Deliberative democracy can also bolster representative judgement (see Chapters 3 and 4). The former Conservative minister and champion of one nationism Chris Patten (2019) defines representative judgement thus:

> Voters elect individual members of parliament, who owe their constituents their best judgment about how to negotiate the predicaments of politics. MPs are not required to do what they are told by an alleged popular will, a system much favoured by despots and demagogues. Instead, they are part of a system that owes much to the conservative political philosopher Edmund Burke, not to the French writer Jean-Jacques Rousseau. We have always preferred caution, compromise and evolution to disruption and appeals to fleeting public passions.

Representative judgement may have its origins in Burke and conservative thinking and tradition but as was witnessed by the radical and transformative programme of the 1945 Labour government and other progressive landmarks, it has not always been a brake on radicalism. Michael Foot, considered a radical leader of the Labour Party, felt MPs should be independent minded rather than being delegates called to account by unrepresentative party organs and the cadre of membership. Foot thus revered parliamentary traditions and their instrumental use in furthering socialism and he was highly critical of the direct democracy reforms of the Campaign for Labour Party Democracy, which could be epitomized as the politics of leftist agonism (Pugh, 2010).

Deliberative democracy can be said to promote forms of reciprocity, where even those on the losing side of an argument might respect the outcome and decision made on account of the process and reasoning used to reach that decision (Smith, 2000). However, the form of deliberative democracy I advocate encompasses aspects of radical democracy by promoting notions of active citizenship and participation along with a rejection of the neoliberal consensus, and it thus holds the potential for transformative change. How can such notions of deliberative democracy be applied? Debates and proposals to reform British democracy and enhance debate and participation have grown apace since the turn of the millennium. Devolution has been probably one of the most significant reforms. Yet changes to the political system have tended to be tokenistic and superficial (Davidson and Elstub, 2014). A new and important dynamic in British politics would be to make greater use of deliberative innovations such as citizen's assemblies and juries, participatory budgeting and deliberative polls. Randomly selected but representative panels of citizens could provide decision-making processes with greater legitimacy and bridge the divide between elites and the wider public. Such fora need to be decoupled from institutions in order to retain legitimacy and should be counselled and guided by a neutral research team and independent secretariat so as to avoid partisanship. Such 'cold deliberative' settings are more effective in achieving shifts of opinion and consensus formation (Fung, 2003). Although such innovations have been experimented with in Britain, they have tended to be tokenistic and act more like focus groups than robust and independent-minded platforms.

It should be noted that deliberative forums can only work in a wider deliberative system – thus, the wider body politic and political parties need to become more inclusive and discursive. According to Habermas (1996), creating more effective channels of communication with political parties could make deliberative state bodies more 'porous' and grounded in the aspirations of the wider population. One potential reform is to introduce the American system of registered voters to candidate selection processes, an initiative that reaches out beyond party membership in the selection of candidates – ensuring selected candidates are potentially more reflective of communities they represent and grounded in the interests of their constituents. Interestingly, a similar experiment (open primary) that took place when David Cameron was leader of the Conservative Party led to the selection of a number of Conservative candidates, such as Heidi Allen and Sarah Wollaston, who were more independent of the party line than most and in fact vociferously opposed Brexit, leading to their eventual departure from the party. Alongside such a reform, the greater use of community organizers and case workers handling constituents' personal issues could do much to strengthen the bonds and understanding between MPs and their constituents.

The process of Brexit as chronicled in this book has undermined democracy and evidently the public's attachment to it. Britain has traditionally preferred what can be described as the Westminster model, that is, a relatively centralized form of political governance, as opposed to the continental model, where forms of proportional representation have a greater tendency to produce coalition governments, leading to an emphasis on consensus-building and deliberation. The Westminster system is more hierarchical and less inclined to compromise and negotiation. It is a restrictive form of representative democracy, compounding voters' sense of alienation from the political process and by appearing to act primarily in the interests of elites it appears to be distant and disconnected. The introduction of a form of proportional representation may facilitate more consensual and deliberative politics, similar to those on the Continent. As has been noted, the General Election of 2019 under a first-past-the-post voting system gave Johnson a sufficient enough parliamentary majority to leave the EU, but 52 per cent of the electorate had supported pro-second referendum parties. An election staged under proportional representation would have probably created a coalition government and in all probability a second referendum with a Remain or soft Brexit outcome.

A central question is whether political consensus will stifle transformative change. Despite her support for agonism and a trajectory of radical change, Mouffe (2005) acknowledges a certain degree of consensus can be achieved but it is a 'conflicting consensus' – a temporary concession that will eventually lead to the absorption of the out-group into the mindset of the wider public body. Here, there is an interesting parallel with notions of deliberative democracy, for radical proponents of deliberative politics contend that gradual and incremental changes can culminate in transformative change and a radical new consensus. Forester (1999) argues that deliberation should be centred on the needs of rival camps rather than values, as such a focus is more likely to achieve reconciliation. Forester notes the case of LGBTQ activists debating with fundamentalist Christians as to how to implement HIV/AIDS care in Colorado. Listening to each other's stories led to accepting specific interventions without direct challenges to value systems. Reciprocal recognition might be jeopardized by a robust, purist and ideologically passionate form of agonism.

Wilkinson and Pickett (2009), in their ground-breaking book *The Spirit Level*, argue that progressive social reform centred on redistribution and social justice can be to the benefit of the whole of society, creating higher levels of wellbeing and contentment and also having the propensity to stimulate economic growth. Such parameters of debate, invoking 'common sense' and efficiency, could do much to foster a new radical consensus, continuing the trajectory of that established during 'Les Trente Glorieuses', the 'Glorious Thirty' of postwar social democracy and interrupted by the Washington consensus (see Chapter 1)

Public sphere

As noted in Chapter 2, the public sphere, according to Habermas (1989), is the domain of social life, where public opinion is formed. Complex and multilayered, it is a cauldron of debate and information. It includes the media but also everyday interactions like political discussions, gossip and jokes at the bus stop, in a café, online or wherever some form of social interaction takes place. Heavily biased and marketized print media has followed the diktats of its owners, creating and bolstering a set of powerful tropes. Hostility towards the EU is one such trope that the media has framed over decades and which politicians have fed into and/or surfed upon. Social media, once heralded as having the potential to form a more emancipatory counter-public sphere that might challenge the bias of the mainstream media, has instead become a central arena for orchestrated and heavily financed campaigns of agitation, which in some cases rely on falsehoods and reactive tropes. Not in all cases, but in many, such media has been the prompt and cue to a vast number of social interactions or the formulation of views that have created a momentum behind Brexit and in general are counter to a deliberative public sphere and politics.

At times the dynamics between politics and the media has been intense, with the development of a plebiscitary rhetoric where politicians craft their dialogue to promote and mobilize frames reliant upon reactive and nationalistic sentiments (Chambers, 2009). Plebiscitary rhetoric in a 'tabloidized' form of politics provides the speech acts to manipulate and trigger audience emotions through carefully refined rhetoric designed to catch and fit into media headlines that invariably surf and steer longstanding and reactive public sentiments. Increasingly, such rhetoric has been binary, partisan and redolent of a post-truth political age.

How can the public sphere be made fit for purpose? Greater reform of the media is warranted, with the introduction of a more independent media watchdog for the print media. The Independent Press Standards Organisation (IPSO) was formed in the wake of the inquiry by Lord Leveson into the phone hacking scandal and the general conduct of the media. IPSO was established as an independent regulator of the newspaper and magazine industry. However, this new organization has reproduced many of the failings of its predecessor, the Press Complaints Commission, and doubts have grown as to the merits of self-regulation in its present form (Barnett, 2016). Obviously, any new reforms will need to be sensitive to freedom of speech considerations but the campaign for media fairness, Hacked Off (2018), has argued that Leveson's recommendations for the press to be regulated by a completely independent system – with punitive powers, arbitration and prominent corrections and apologies – has not been properly implemented. Likewise, many commentators agree that political advertising and communications on social media and the use of personal data need much greater regulation to prevent the misuses, as was reported in the Brexit referendum (see Chapter 2). Gans (2011) is right to appeal to the media to reorient and reinvent itself to give greater focus to the thoughts, views and experiences of those outside the governing class, especially those at the margins.

More broadly, within the public sphere the role of civil society needs to be rejuvenated and reconsidered. Civil society has suffered greatly from austerity cutbacks and/or been increasingly tamed through service delivery contracts and the application of market principles, which weaken the autonomy of civil society and relegate it to become an extension of the service sector. A stronger and more independent civil society, especially in left-behind and depressed communities, might have created a stronger deliberative counternarrative to the politics of nativism. Fraser's (1992) vision of a subaltern public sphere where, through forms of collectivity and social enterprise mini-public forums are created, would also be useful in the formulation of counternarratives – especially for marginalized groups who are poorly represented in the formal world of politics. In this sense, civil society has the potential to offer what Laclau and Mouffe (2001) describe as 'chains of equivalence', where marginalized groups can ally in opposition to forms of oppression but retain a different logic or political identities and strategies.

In order to help achieve a more informed and deliberative approach to politics, there is a need to enhance the role of civic education in schools.

A greater understanding by the electorate of how political and socio-economic processes work may equip the public to dismiss the worst excesses of manipulation by populist politicians and the media. As part of a process of educating people for citizenship, universities could have a central role to play in developing critical and independent thought, but the marketization of the academy has created an audit culture which limits the ability of academics to develop critical thought. Instead, the modern academic has to conform to performance-related managerialism where the focus is on sanitized and financially lucrative outputs (Brown, 2015). In addition, as was witnessed in the referendum campaigns, 'expertise' itself has been monstered. Independent and critical thinkers supported by creative and open academic environments, coupled with a fair media and deliberative political arena, might do much to restore the valuable role of intellectuals and experts in decision-making. More broadly, such change would create a purer and less tainted public sphere capable of nurturing a more deliberative, rational and open democracy.

Prior to the 2019 General Election, the Conservatives delayed the publication of a parliamentary intelligence and security committee report that raised serious concerns about the level of Russian money that had been injected into the political system to destabilize things and secure political advantage. Thus, more stringent limits need to be placed on financial political donations so as to nurture a fairer and more deliberative political environment.

Identity

In an age of turbulence and insecurity, identity has offered for some a form of shelter, a safe haven from the turbulence of profound economic and social change (Woodward, 2000). However, in this respect such forms of escapism and reliance on assumed cultural certainties have led to the formation of reactive forms of identity that foster and nurture conservatism and nativism and have proved to be fertile ground for the politics of nationalist populism. Britain once prided itself on its diversity and management of race relations. Today, though, those approaches are derided. Liberal multiculturalism is considered to have promoted tokenistic and static conceptions of minority cultures that essentialized the identities of minorities and created a backlash from white communities who felt their identity was ignored (Back, 1996). In more recent years, the focus has been on integration and allegiance to presumed core British values that could be interpreted as a return to assimilationism (Bourne, 2007). Such a governmental stance has often pandered to and bolstered conceptions of English nationalism that are nativistic and monocultural. English monoculturalism has been expressed politically in the guise of the UK Independence Party and the Brexit Party (see Chapter 5), which were a major driving force behind the referendum and Brexit.

How can English identity become more civic and inclusive? Scottish civic nationalism might provide some useful indicators as to how English identity can be refashioned (see Chapter 5). The former Labour minister John Denham (2019) has long lamented that the left has recoiled from embracing and articulating English nationalism because of a perception that such a form of identity is prone to nativism and exceptionalism. However, is the English identity of the South the same as that of the North or the South West? It may be useful to revive plans for English regional government that floundered under New Labour and allow regional English identities to have voice and take shape. The demographic fact that those with more insular conceptions of national identity are in the senior age brackets of British society – as opposed to the young who are more inclined to cosmopolitan viewpoints that embrace diversity, migration and membership of the EU – may mean that the passage of time will see dramatic shifts in how national identity is perceived.

Critical multiculturalism is another important dynamic that could challenge the cultural foundations of Brexit. It encompasses anti-racist education, critical race theory and critical pedagogy that challenges the social, economic and cultural drivers of exclusion and xenophobia (May and Sleeter, 2010). It is a more intercultural and deliberative form of identity management that recognizes identity is neither rigid nor static and that change and innovation are both possible and to be welcomed. Such an attitude might lead to the development of a form of British identity that not only embraces the Union but also a wide range of minority outlooks. Such a British identity should not be grounded solely in history and tradition but instead be steered by basic values, perhaps those encapsulated in what Gordon Brown (2007) described as a sense of fair play and tolerance. An ideal compass point in such moral arbitration, definition and application would be the Human Rights Act 1998, but this law has been widely disparaged by the right, while public support and understanding of this legislation is tenuous. An appreciation and support for human rights could therefore be seen as an important prelude to a more inclusive national identity.

Social Europe

Neoliberal forms of capitalism have created growing inequality and a twenty-first-century underclass open and susceptible to political agendas that promise fundamental change. A central driver in the Brexit phenomenon has been austerity and economic inequality, creating tensions that manifested in support of Brexit (see Chapter 1). Brexit can be viewed as part of the 'new neoliberal turn' – as former Conservative Chancellor of the Exchequer Nigel Lawson (2016) proclaimed, it presented an opportunity to complete the 'Thatcher revolution'. Hyperglobalism and the reorientation of the Conservative Party as a populist party has prompted some to reflect upon the predictions of Polanyi and Dahrendorf that capitalism might transform into forms of fascism and authoritarianism. Although these detours initially may appear to be in contradiction with globalization as reflected by sentiments favouring a retreat into the nation state and opposition to free movement of labour, the fusion of neoliberalism and nationalist populism (Brexit nationalism) seems to be a relatively simple form of political merger, facilitating further downsizing and dilution of social protections (Fekete, 2017).

In a globalized world, the notion that states can return to some form of postwar Keynesian mixed economy of the Attlee era are misplaced. It should be noted that much of the expansion of that period was based on rapid growth; today, growth and expansion are much more limited and economies will be unable to sustain redistribution as practised during the postwar Glorious Thirty, an age of unprecedented welfarism and consumerism. Such a model may also not be sustainable environmentally because of the level of resources that were and would be consumed in order to fuel rapid growth. Postwar growth was also based on cheap materials and the exploitation of low-wage labour from regions of the periphery, contributing to developing-world inequality (Benton, 2017). Furthermore, technological advancements and the increasing automation of production and services might mean that full employment is also an impossible goal in the manner it materialized in the postwar period. Clearly, we cannot replicate the precise pattern of the 'Glorious Thirty'.

Despite such restraints on future development, structural reorientation and change may be fundamental in frustrating economic, cultural and social patterns that fuel inequality, social tensions and environmental dangers. The economist Thomas Piketty (2014) has advocated improved and more egalitarian services and welfare, funded through forms of taxation targeting the wealthiest with a progressive global tax on capital. The strength of force opposed to such transformative change cannot be underestimated and it is for this reason that change will be hard to achieve at the national level. Given the globalized world we now inhabit, such change would need to be orientated in unison and collectively by large trading blocs such as the EU. Countries that ventured on such a path on their own would be subject to the wrath of markets that would retaliate through disinvestment. In other words, the only realistic option for such change in Europe is the realization of a social Europe within the EU that countenances intervention and redistribution. It will be evident to the reader that this book is advocating a 'return and reform' approach towards the EU which patently rejects the nationalism of Leavers and the misplaced notions of 'socialism in one country' of the Lexit variant of Leave.

However, change and reform within the EU do not appear to be immanent. Ordoliberalism, a technocratic approach to capitalism where the state upholds market freedom and which has been extended beyond Germany to the governance of the EU, has promoted forms of austerity through measures like the Stability and Growth Pact, designed to stabilize the eurozone. Ordoliberalism has been a contributory factor to political instability across Europe. The new President of the European Commission Ursula von der Leyen and the composition of the current commission does not suggest a radical change but instead a continuation of caution and conservatism. Fears had been great during the European elections of 2019 that there would be a surge in the populist vote, with the arch populist Steve Bannon becoming involved in the campaign and hoping to unite Europe's far right into an international alliance of populists, 'The Movement' (Mazza, 2019). The advance of nationalist populists in the 2019 European elections was not as great as had been anticipated but the danger remains of such predictions coming to pass if the EU is not able to create a more socially and economically cohesive vision for itself.

Final reflections

I would argue that the uniqueness and value of this book lies in the fact that it gives a comprehensive overview of Brexit, reaching beyond the referendum of 2016 and utilizing deeper historical, cultural and sociological insights to understand the phenomenon and its effects. Another point of difference between this book and others on a similar theme is the use of critical discourse analysis to understand the competing processes of securitization and desecuritization around Brexit and the charting of the impact of the populist turn on British politics and society.

At the start of the book, through a process of reflexivity I set out how my life experiences and activism had led to a point where I felt deep apprehension about the implications of Brexit. I outlined how writing this book was in part a personal exercise to help not only my readership to gain insights into these processes but to also enable me to make sense of what was happening in a world where old certainties are rapidly fragmenting. The last five years (2015–20) have been politically some of the most intense and emotive of my life. In the 2015 election, I was deeply disappointed by the failure of Labour under Ed Miliband to make greater progress and I was full of foreboding about the EU referendum that Cameron had pledged. Concerns about the impending referendum prompted me to support Yvette Cooper in the 2015 Labour leadership contest. Despite my commitment to more radical conceptions of socialism, I felt an experienced pair of hands such as Cooper would help Labour better navigate the challenges of that referendum. I had worked with Cooper closely on Gypsy and Traveller issues when she was a minister at the Office of the Deputy Prime Minister from 2003 to 2008 and knew she was highly competent and honest.

Corbyn was to prevail in the leadership contest. He offered the membership a clean break with the past, an appeal that was bolstered by the staid performances of the other candidates such as Cooper, Andy Burnham and Liz Kendall. Despite being attracted to Corbyn's calls to make Labour a members' led party, I was demoralized by the tribalism and factionalism this engendered – with the left and centrist factions of Momentum and Progress typifying the sterility of debate in a negative war of words between the two groups, centred on reified and binary frames. My disappointment was accentuated by Labour's lacklustre referendum performance and prevarication around Brexit, which saw the party accept the premise of Brexit for long periods, albeit with differing degrees of intensity. As reflected by this conclusion, I have been prompted by the research this book has entailed to seek a series of frames that might help to unify the left. Commitments to a social Europe and democratic reforms centred on fusing traits of direct and deliberative democracy could also do much to unify the left and centre.

Despite a desire for a new centre-left consensus, this journey of critical thought and discussion has reaffirmed my belief in the need for transformative change. And it has also clarified the importance of this process involving reform and the rejuvenation of established institutions, to revive more statist conceptions of economic management redolent of a 'golden age' in postwar British social policy. However, learning from the lessons of history, there is a need to avoid the disconnection and alienation engendered by past statist policy. I thus advocate a new and equitable trilateral balance between the state, business and civil society.

Populism has featured heavily in the discussion in this book. Conventional leaders of the capitalist order from established political parties and the media have been prepared to align with populism. Right and left forms of populism are a manifestation of the crisis in which capitalism and democracy find themselves in the twenty-first century. As has been set out in this conclusion, it is through economic, democratic and cultural change that the forces behind Brexit – including populism – can be quelled and or re-channelled.

To return to a key concept defined at the start of the book and revisited in this chapter, Brexit nationalism constitutes a paradigm shift. Society and political discourse are in a state of flux, out of which a new orthodoxy might emerge. It will be evident to the reader that the concluding section of the book has advocated a 'new orthodoxy' centred on the democratization of democracy through the reform of existing institutions within a policy framework that advocates a radical shift away from neoliberalism, entailing a new social contract and inclusive public sphere. However, around these reformed institutions I argue for a greater role for a renewed civil society and scope for greater participation. The book is thus seeking to fuse deliberative and radical conceptions of democracy and social change in order to achieve transformative change. Through attempts to renew and rejuvenate democratic practices and institutions and to link conceptions of democracy with social justice, the book seeks to foster an ethical discourse where genuine dialogue, cooperation and consensus can be nurtured through rational and informed speech acts which avoid the emotive invective and sharp practices of post-truth politics and populism. In other words, the ideal speech situation that Habermas (2001b) aspires to see must be nurtured, where reason and evidence steer deliberative debate and nonrational, coercive influences are minimized.

Although I am located in Hungary, many of the forces that gave rise to Brexit are evident in my country of residence: economic crisis, national trauma and insecurity, and a history of exceptionalism and empire have shaped the paths Britain and Hungary have followed. The nationalist populist Prime Minister Viktor Orbán has attacked liberal conceptions of society and proudly proclaimed Hungary to be an 'illiberal democracy'. In addition, he has orchestrated illiberal, xenophobic and Islamophobic campaigns against migrants and civil society and has instigated what have been construed as antisemitic attacks on the Jewish philanthropist George Soros. Some fear new government financial controls and limitations over the Hungarian Academy of Science will presage the withdrawal of support for challenging research in the social sciences. As part of a campaign against Soros and academia in general, the Hungarian government prompted the Central European University to relocate much of its teaching from Budapest to Vienna. Many of my former students seem to be leaving Hungary; they despair of the political climate and how it seems to be on the verge of becoming fascist. In the hushed tones of chance corridor conversations, colleagues whisper about the fate that may befall the country. Some yearn to escape and so speak of relocation; indeed, some have already left. Some are roused to activism and to speak out. Many have decided to keep their heads down and hope this dark moment may pass; others are complicit and ingratiate themselves and comply with power. I am a board member of a Soros-financed NGO and a faculty member of the Corvinus University, which is being transformed into a foundation that in theory is set to give the university greater autonomy but some fear that in practice this will prepare the ground to make the university more aligned and submissive to the government's agenda. I feel vulnerable and exposed.

What should I do? This is the question I increasingly ask myself. Is flight possible, given the global nature of the forces I and others seek to resist? I yearn most of all for what Paulo Freire (1994) described as a pedagogy of hope, a sense that change can happen. Over the years, I have found such sentiment on the frontline of grassroots struggles for social justice. To date, I have sought to combine critical pedagogy in the community with inclusive and collaborative research and knowledge production in the academy. Time will tell for how much longer such work in Hungary is feasible. I wonder whether it may be time to withdraw from the marketized and tamed academy and seek a greater role within the subaltern public sphere.

The role of the university should be, in the tradition of Socrates, to challenge and question hegemony. It is in that spirit that I have laboured upon and present this book. In an age of global crisis and anxiety, profound change and transformation seem inevitable. The nature and benevolence of that change will be determined by the contestation and argumentation between social movements and hegemony, both globally and nationally. Brexit has been one aspect of that wider arena of global struggle. History reveals that the progress of equality and even transformative change has often been triggered by moments of darkness, as reflected by forms of despotism and authoritarianism. A counter-revolution will come and I believe social justice and deliberative democracy should be vital components of that resistance and ultimate change.

In 2020 the rapid onset of the COVID-19 has had a huge social, economic and cultural impact on the world we live in, as great, if not greater, than the financial crisis of 2008. Communities entered into 'lockdown' mode and the world as we knew it was put on pause. Many of us have had to grapple with basic questions of how best to support our families, loved ones and wider community, those of us who have been lucky and faced little adversity in our lives have been tested. A whole range of developments, the trajectory and origins of which can be found in the wake of the financial crisis of 2008, exacerbated the crisis, in particular austerity as a response to that crisis, but also misconceptions as to what our priorities should be, left many societies with weak and crumbling care systems, poorly placed to meet the challenges of the COVID-19 pandemic. Boris Johnson though, in March 2020, insisted we must press on with delivering Brexit.

COVID-19 has put into perspective the importance of international cooperation in efforts to control the virus and find a vaccine and solution. In Europe as the new commission formulates its plans for the next term, many, as advocated in this book, would like to see a radical 'New Deal' across Europe that revives economies damaged by austerity and now COVID-19 and creates a new European social contract. If the EU gets its response right, many in Britain might deeply regret the decision to leave the EU. Old models and stances will no longer suffice, new radical models are needed that fundamentally change the world we live in through pre-distribution and social justice agendas. This would be a great leap but can be achieved through rational argument, deliberation and a radical consensus without having to resort to the populist frames of dissension, intolerance and falsehood. Winter is not coming, it is here! But change for the better could also be on the horizon. For the sake of humanity, let's hope so. I remain confident that one day Britain will rejoin the EU.

Bibliography

Adler-Nissen, R., Galpin, C. and Rosamond, B. (2017) 'Performing Brexit: how a post-Brexit world is imagined outside the United Kingdom', *The British Journal of Politics and International Relations*, 19(3): 573–91.

Agnew, J. (2018) 'Too many Scotlands? Place, the SNP, and the future of nationalist mobilization', *Scottish Geographical Journal*, 134(1–2): 5–23.

Alexander, J., Eyerman, R., Giesen, B., Smelser, N. and Sztompka, P. (2004) *Cultural Trauma and Collective Identity*, Oakland: University of California Press.

Anderson, B. (1991) *Imagined Communities: Reflections on the Origin and Spread of Nationalism* (revised and extended edn), New York: Verso.

Anthias, F. and Yuval-Davis, N. (1992) *Racialized Boundaries: Race, Nation, Gender, Colour and Class and the Anti-Racist Struggle*, London: Routledge.

Arendt, H. (1973) *The Origins of Totalitarianism*, Boston, MA: Houghton Mifflin Harcourt.

Ashcroft, Lord (2016) 'How the United Kingdom voted on Thursday and Why', Lord Ashcroft [poll] 24 June. Available from: https://lordashcroftpolls.com/2016/06/how-the-united-kingdom-voted-and-why/ [Accessed 2 February 2020].

Ashcroft, R.T. and Bevir, M. (2018) 'Multiculturalism in contemporary Britain: policy, law and theory', *Critical Review of International Social and Political Philosophy*, 21(1): 1–21.

Asthana, A. (2017) 'Corbyn on Brexit: UK can be better off out of the EU', *The Guardian*, 10 January. Available from: https://www.theguardian.com/politics/2017/jan/09/jeremy-corbyn-uk-is-better-off-out-of-eu-with-managed-migration [Accessed 2 February 2020].

Asthana, A. and Stewart, H. (2017) 'Dominic Grieve says he has had death threats after Brexit rebellion', *The Independent*, 14 December. Available from: https://www.theguardian.com/politics/2017/dec/14/dominic-grieve-says-he-has-had-death-threats-after-brexit-rebellion [Accessed 2 February 2020].

Asthana, A., Stewart, H. and Boffey, D. (2018) 'May "double cherry-picking" on Brexit, says leaked EU report', *The Guardian*, 6 March. Available from: https://www.theguardian.com/politics/2018/mar/06/theresa-may-conservative-politics-brexit-solutions-leaked-eu-report [Accessed 2 February 2020].

Back, L. (1996) *New Ethnicities and Urban Culture: Racisms and Multiculture in Young Lives*, London: Routledge.

Bailey, D. (2017) 'Class struggle after Brexit', *Capital & Class*, 41(2): 333–5.

Baker, D., Gamble, A. and Seawright, D. (2002) 'Sovereign nations and global markets: modern British conservatism and hyperglobalism', *The British Journal of Politics and International Relations*, 4(3): 399–428.

Baker, T. (2019) 'JFC: Tories criticised after depicting Jeremy Corbyn as chicken', *Evening Standard*, 6 September. Available from: https://www.standard.co.uk/news/politics/jfc-tories-criticised-after-depicting-jeremy-corbyn-as-chicken-a4231021.html [Accessed 1 March 2020].

Bale, T. (2016) *The Conservative Party: From Thatcher to Cameron*, Bristol: Policy Press.

Balzacq, T. (2005) 'The three faces of securitization: political agency, audience and context', *European Journal of International Relations*, 11(2): 171–201.

Banks, A. (2017) *The Bad Boys of Brexit: Tales of Mischief, Mayhem and Guerrilla Warfare from the Referendum Frontline*, London: Biteback Publishing.

Barker, A. (2018) 'Barnier warns Britain to stop playing hide and seek', *Financial Times*, 26 May. Available from: https://www.ft.com/content/262ef6da-60c6-11e8-a39d-4df188287fff [Accessed 2 February 2020].

Barnett, A. (2016) 'Press regulation in Britain: a step forward – and a step back', *The Conversation*, [online] 25 October. Available from: http://theconversation.com/press-regulation-in-britain-a-step-forward-and-a-step-back-67582 [Accessed 2 February 2020].

Barnier, M. (2016) 'Introductory comments by Michel Barnier', European Commission, [press briefing] 6 December. Available from: https://ec.europa.eu/info/news/introductory-comments-michel-barnier-2016-dec-06_en [Accessed 2 February 2020].

Barnier, M. (2017a) Berlin Security Conference speech, The European Commission, [speech] 29 November, Berlin. Available from: https://ec.europa.eu/commission/presscorner/detail/en/SPEECH_17_5021 [Accessed 2 February 2020].

Barnier, M. (2017b) European Economic and Social Committee, [speech] 6 July, Brussels. Available from: https://www.ifa.ie/speech-by-michel-barnier-at-the-eesc-06-july/ [Accessed 2 February 2020].

Barnier, M. (2018) 'An ambitious partnership with the UK after Brexit', *European Commission*, [op-ed] 2 August. Available from: https://ec.europa.eu/commission/news/ambitious-partnership-uk-after-brexit-2018-aug-02_en [Accessed 2 February 2020].

Barth, C. and Bijsmans, P. (2018) 'The Maastricht Treaty and public debates about European integration: the emergence of a European public sphere?', *Journal of Contemporary European Studies*, 26(2): 215–31.

BBC Today Programme (2017) 'EU trade deal "easiest in human history"', *BBC News*, 20 July. Available from: https://www.bbc.com/news/av/uk-40667879/eu-trade-deal-easiest-in-human-history [Accessed 2 February 2020].

Bean, E. (2017) 'Keir Starmer: Labour has six tests for Brexit – if they're not met we won't back the final deal in parliament', *Labour List*, 27 March. Available from: https://labourlist.org/2017/03/keir-starmer-labour-has-six-tests-for-brexit-if-theyre-not-met-we-wont-back-the-final-deal-in-parliament/ [Accessed 1 March 2020].

Beck, U. (2000) 'The cosmopolitan perspective: sociology of the second age of modernity', *British Journal of Sociology*, 51(1): 79–105.

Beckett, M. (2019) 'Labour must support a second referendum or risk becoming history', *The Observer*, [article] 22 June. Available from: https://www.theguardian.com/politics/2019/jun/22/labour-must-back-peoples-vote-or-isk-becoming-hisotyr-margaret-beckett-brexit [Accessed 2 February 2020].

Belam, M. (2019) 'Surrender, humbug: key heated exchanges in Commons debate', *The Guardian*, 26 September. Available from: https://www.theguardian.com/politics/2019/sep/26/surrender-humbug-most-heated-exchanges-in-commons-debate [Accessed 2 February 2020].

Bellamy, A. (2003) *The Formation of Croatian National Identity: A Centuries-Old Dream*, Manchester: Manchester University Press.

Benton, T. (2017) 'Beyond neoliberalism, or life after capitalism? A red–green debate', in B. Jones and M. O'Donnell (eds) *Alternatives to Neoliberalism: Towards Equality and Democracy*, Bristol: Policy Press, pp 59–79.

Bhambra, G.K. (2017) 'Locating Brexit in the pragmatics of race, citizenship and empire', in O. William (ed) *Brexit: Sociological Responses*, London: Anthem Press, pp 153–82.

Bienkov, A. (2016) 'John McDonnell backs Brexit as "enormous opportunity" for Britain', Politics.co.uk, 15 November. Available from: https://www.politics.co.uk/news/2016/11/15/john-mcdonnell-backs-brexit-enormous-opportunity-britain [Accessed 2 February 2020].

Blackford, I. (2018) *Hansard*, Engagements Volume 642, [speech] 13 June. Available from: https://hansard.parliament.uk/Commons/2018-06-13/debates/F47BCB09-741E-4518-B46C-63391962F87B/Engagements [Accessed 2 February 2020].

Blake, R. (2011) *The Conservative Party from Peel to Major*, London: Faber.

Block, P. (2018) 'EU citizens didn't jump the queue, Prime Minister: they exercised their fundamental rights', *New Statesman*, 20 November. Available from: https://www.newstatesman.com/politics/staggers/2018/11/eu-citizens-didn-t-jump-queue-prime-minister-they-exercised-their [Accessed 2 February 2020].

Boffey, D. (2017a) 'British MEPs who voted to delay trade talks "facing witch-hunt"', *The Guardian*, 17 October. Available from: https://www.theguardian.com/politics/2017/oct/17/british-meps-voted-delay-trade-talks-witch-hunt-verhofstadt-davis [Accessed 2 February 2020].

Boffey, D. (2017b) 'Irish report shows lack of respect in EU for UK's handling of Brexit', *The Guardian*, 23 November. Available from: https://www.theguardian.com/politics/2017/nov/23/irish-report-shows-eu-lack-of-respect-for-uk-handling-of-brexit [Accessed 2 February 2020].

Boffey, D. and Helm, T. (2016) 'Vote Leave embroiled in race row over Turkey security threat claims', *The Guardian*, 22 May. Available from: https://www.theguardian.com/politics/2016/may/21/vote-leave-prejudice-turkey-eu-security-threat [Accessed 2 February 2020].

Boffey, D. and Stewart, H. (2018) 'Theresa May tells EU leaders: you are putting lives at risk over Brexit', *The Guardian*, 28 June. Available from: https://www.theguardian.com/politics/2018/jun/28/uks-cabinet-split-is-bad-for-brexit-negotiations-says-juncker [Accessed 2 February 2020].

Boffey, D. and Walker, P. (2018) 'May's Brexit transition demand "would penalise EU citizens"', *The Guardian*, 18 February. Available from: https://www.theguardian.com/politics/2018/feb/18/theresa-may-brexit-transition-demand-demonise-eu-citizens-verhofstadt [Accessed 2 February 2020].

Bourdieu, P. (1990a) *The Logic of Practice*, Stanford, CA: Stanford University Press.

Bourdieu, P. (1990b) *In other Words: Essays Towards a Reflexive Sociology*, Cambridge: Polity Press.

Bourdieu, P. (1995) *Sociology in Question*, London: SAGE.

Bourne, J. (2007) 'In defence of multiculturalism', Institute for Race Relations [Briefing Paper No. 2], 21 February. Available from: https://www.bl.uk/collection-items/in-defence-of-multiculturalism [Accessed 6 April 2020].

Boyle, N. (2017) 'The problem with the English: England doesn't want to be just another member of a team', *The New European*, 17 January. Available from: https://www.theneweuropean.co.uk/top-stories/the-problem-with-the-english-england-doesn-t-want-to-be-just-another-member-of-a-team-1-4851882 [Accessed 2 February 2020].

Brown, G. (2007) Speech at a seminar on Britishness at the Commonwealth Club, London, 27 February. Available from: https://www.theguardian.com/politics/2007/feb/27/immigrationpolicy.race [Accessed 2 February 2020].

Brown, G. (2019) 'The very idea of a United Kingdom is being torn apart by toxic nationalism', *The Guardian*, 10 August. Available from: https://www.theguardian.com/commentisfree/2019/aug/10/very-idea-of-a-united-kingdom-being-torn-apart-by-toxic-nationalism [Accessed 2 February 2020].

Brown, W. (2015) *Undoing the Demos: Neoliberalism's Stealth Revolution*, Cambridge, MA: MIT Press.

Brubaker, R. (2017) 'Why populism?' *Theory and Society*, 46(5): 357–85.

Buchan, L. (2017) 'Tory MP Anna Soubry reports threats to police after "Brexit mutineer" story', *The Independent*, [online] 15 November. Available from: https://www.independent.co.uk/news/uk/politics/anna-soubry-threats-brexit-mutineer-police-report-tory-mp-rebel-daily-telegraph-a8056441.html [Accessed 2 February 2020].

Buchan, L. (2018) 'Brexit: Labour MP accuses colleague of "sounding like Jacob Rees-Mogg" amid party splits on leaving EU', *The Independent*, 10 June. Available from: https://www.independent.co.uk/news/uk/politics/brexit-latest-labour-party-split-chris-leslie-caroline-flint-jacob-rees-mogg-a8392071.html [Accessed 2 February 2020].

Busby, M. (2019) 'Tories deny plan to compromise workers' rights after Brexit', *The Guardian*, 26 October. Available from: https://www.theguardian.com/politics/2019/oct/26/tories-deny-compromise-workers-rights-after-brexit [Accessed 2 February 2020].

Bush, S. (2017) 'Vote Leave can't hide their responsibility for the Brexit mess', *New Statesman*, 18 September. Available from: https://www.newstatesman.com/politics/staggers/2017/09/vote-leave-cant-hide-their-responsibility-brexit-mess [Accessed 2 February 2020].

Butcher, J. (2019) 'Brexit working-class revolt or middle-class outlook?' *Discover Society*, 3 July. Available from: https://discoversociety.org/2019/07/03/brexit-working-class-revolt-or-middle-class-outlook/ [Accessed 2 February 2020].

Cadwalladr, C. (2017) 'Interview: Arron Banks: "Brexit was a war. We won. There's no turning back now"', *The Guardian*, 2 April. Available from: https://www.theguardian.com/politics/2017/apr/02/arron-banks-interview-brexit-ukip-far-right-trump-putin-russia [Accessed 2 February 2020].

Cameron, D. (2009) Conservative National Conference speech, 8 October. Available from: https://www.theguardian.com/politics/2009/oct/08/david-cameron-speech-in-full [Accessed 2 February 2020].

Cammaerts, B. (2016) 'Our report found that 75% of press coverage misrepresents Jeremy Corbyn – we can't ignore media bias anymore', *The Independent*, 19 July. Available from: https://www.independent.co.uk/voices/jeremy-corbyn-media-bias-labour-mainstream-press-lse-study-misrepresentation-we-cant-ignore-bias-a7144381.html [Accessed 2 February 2020].

Cap, P. (2017) *The Language of Fear: Communicating Threat in Public Discourse*, London and New York: Palgrave Macmillan.

Carl, N., Dennison, J. and Evans, G. (2019) 'European but not European enough: an explanation for Brexit', *European Union Politics*, 20(2): 282–304.

Carrell, S. (2019) 'Sturgeon outlines new Scottish independence referendum plans', *The Guardian*, 24 April. Available from: https://www.theguardian.com/politics/2019/apr/24/sturgeon-outlines-new-scottish-independence-referendum-plans [Accessed 2 February 2020].

Cash, W. (2017) *Hansard*, Volume 620, Col 836–7, [speech] 31 January. Available from: https://hansard.parliament.uk/Commons/2017-01-31/debates/C2852E15-21D3-4F03-B8C3-F7E05F2276B0/EuropeanUnion(NotificationOfWithdrawal)Bill [Accessed 2 February 2020].

Castle, S. (2017) 'Tony Blair calls for people to "rise up" against Brexit', *New York Times*, 17 February. Available from: https://www.nytimes.com/2017/02/17/world/europe/tony-blair-uk-brexit.html [Accessed 6 April 2020].

Cecil, N. (2019) 'Brexit news latest: poll of polls says Britain is now against leaving EU as most want to stay', *Evening Standard*, 10 October. Available from: https://www.standard.co.uk/news/politics/brexit-news-latest-britain-against-leaving-eu-as-poll-of-polls-says-most-now-want-to-stay-a4257476.html [Accessed 2 February 2020].

Centre on Constitutional Change (2018) 'Press release: May's "Precious Union" has little support in Brexit Britain', 8 October. Available from: https://www.centreonconstitutionalchange.ac.uk/news_opinion/press-release-mays-precious-union-has-little-support-brexit-britain [Accessed 2 February 2020].

Ceyhan, A. and Tsoukala, A. (2002) 'The securitization of migration in Western societies: ambivalent discourses and policies', *Alternatives*, 27(1, suppl.): 21–39.

Chakelian, A. (2017) 'Vince Cable: Theresa May's Tory conference speech "could have been taken out of *Mein Kampf*"', *New Statesman*, 5 July. Available from: https://www.newstatesman.com/politics/uk/2017/07/vince-cable-theresa-may-s-tory-conference-speech-could-have-been-taken-out-mein [Accessed 2 February 2020].

Chalmers, D. (2017) 'Brexit and the renaissance of parliamentary authority', *The British Journal of Politics and International Relations*, 19(4): 663–79.

Chambers, S. (2009) 'Rhetoric and the public sphere: has deliberative democracy abandoned mass democracy?', *Political Theory*, 37(3): 323–50.

Charter, D. (2016) 'Brexit spells end of western political civilisation, says Tusk', *The Times*, 13 June. Available from: https://www.thetimes.co.uk/article/brexit-spells-the-end-of-western-political-civilisation-says-tusk-sndcrfw93 [Accessed 2 February 2020].

Charteris-Black, J. (2005) *Politicians and Rhetoric: The Persuasive Power of Metaphor*, London: Palgrave Macmillan.

Chessum, M. (2019) 'Full report: what happened at Labour Conference?', Another Europe is Possible, [online] 1 October. Available from: https://www.anothereurope.org/full-report-what-happened-at-labour-conference/ [Accessed 2 February 2020].

Chilton, P. (2004) *Analysing Political Discourse: Theory and Practice*, London and New York: Routledge.

Chilton, P. and Schäffner, C. (1997) 'Discourse and politics', in T. van Dijk (ed) *Discourse as Social Interaction*, London: Sage, pp 206–30.

Chrisafis, A. and Rankin, J. (2017) 'Macron lays out vision for "profound" changes in post-Brexit EU', *The Guardian*, 26 September. Available from: https://www.theguardian.com/world/2017/sep/26/profound-transformation-macron-lays-out-vision-for-post-brexit-eu [Accessed 2 February 2020].

Christie, L. (2019) 'Majority of Scots favour independence, poll finds', *Irish Times*, 5 August. Available from: https://www.irishtimes.com/news/world/uk/majority-of-scots-favour-independence-poll-finds-1.3977776 [Accessed 2 February 2020].

Chu, B. (2017) 'The left-wing argument for Brexit is embarrassingly flimsy', *The Independent*, 13 August. Available from: https://www.independent.co.uk/voices/jeremy-corbyn-europe-lexit-brexit-a7890421.html [Accessed 2 February 2020].

Clarke, H., Whiteley, P., Borges, W., Sanders, D. and Stewart, M. (2016) 'Modelling the dynamics of support for a right-wing populist party: the case of UKIP', *Journal of Elections, Public Opinion and Parties*, 26(2): 135–54.

Clarke, K. (2017) *Hansard*, Volume 620, Col 831, 31 January. Available from: https://hansard.parliament.uk/Commons/2017-01-31/debates/C2852E15-21D3-4F03-B8C3-F7E05F2276B0/EuropeanUnion(NotificationOfWithdrawal)Bill [Accessed 2 February 2020].

Clegg, N. (2017) *How to Stop Brexit (And Make Britain Great Again)*, London: The Bodley Head.

Clery, E., Curtice, J. and Harding, R. (2016) 'British social attitudes: the 34th report', London: NatCen Social Research.

Cohen, S. (1995) *The Symbolic Construction of Community*, London and New York: Routledge.

Cohen, P. (2002) *Folk Devils and Moral Panics* (3rd edn), London: Routledge.

Cooper, C. and Ariès, Q. (2017) 'Michel Barnier: UK must choose European rules if it wants trade', *Politico*, 11 September. Available from: https://www.politico.eu/article/michel-barnier-wilbur-ross-brexit-uk-must-choose-european-rules-if-it-wants-trade/ [Accessed 6 April 2020].

Corbyn, J. (2017) Speech to Trades Union Congress, 12 September. Available from: https://www.tuc.org.uk/speeches/jeremy-corbyns-speech-tuc-congress-2017 [Accessed 2 February 2020].

Corbyn, J. (2018a) 'Built in Britain', [speech] 24 July. Available from: https://labourlist.org/2018/07/build-it-in-britain-again-corbyns-full-speech/ [Accessed 2 February 2020].

Corbyn, J. (2018b) 'Labour could do a better Brexit deal. Give us the chance', *The Guardian*, [article] 6 December. Available from: https://www.theguardian.com/commentisfree/2018/dec/06/jeremy-corbyn-general-election-brexit-labour-theresa-may [Accessed 2 February 2020].

Corbyn, J. (2018c) Progress on EU Exit Negotiations, *Hansard*, Volume 649, Col 1098, 15 November. https://hansard.parliament.uk/Commons/2018-11-15/debates/8595BA5C-B515-4BD3-A9FE-38345E6AE2B4/EUExitNegotiations#contribution-3993AB86-8C92-4A57-8696-A35861D8324B [Accessed 2 February 2020].

Corbyn, J. (2019a) 'Corbyn tells members: Labour backs Remain against no deal or Tory deal', *Labour List*, 9 July. Available from: https://labourlist.org/2019/07/corbyn-tells-members-labour-backs-remain-against-no-deal-or-tory-deal/ [Accessed 2 February 2020].

Corbyn, J. (2019b) Labour Conference speech, 24 September. Available from: https://www.politicshome.com/news/uk/political-parties/labour-party/jeremy-corbyn/news/106805/read-full-jeremy-corbyns-speech [Accessed 2 February 2020].

Cortes, M. (2018) 'Only Labour can save Britain from this disastrous Brexit', *The Guardian*, 18 October. Available from: https://www.theguardian.com/commentisfree/2018/oct/18/labour-save-britain-disastrous-brexit-transition-deal [Accessed 2 February 2020].

Cowburn, A. (2018) 'Nicola Sturgeon says she will "restart" debate on Scottish independence in coming weeks', *The Independent*, 20 May. Available from: https://www.independent.co.uk/news/uk/politics/scottish-independence-debate-referendum-independent-scotland-a8360131.html [Accessed 2 February 2020].

Cowburn, A. (2019) 'General election result: nearly twice as many Labour voters defected over Jeremy Corbyn's leadership than party's Brexit stance, poll finds', *The Independent*, 14 December. Available from: https://www.independent.co.uk/news/uk/politics/general-election-result-jeremy-corbyn-brexit-labour-boris-johnson-a9246046.html [Accessed 2 February 2020].

Cowley, P. and Kavanagh, D. (2018) *The British General Election of 2017*, London: Palgrave Macmillan.

Crisp, J. (2017) 'Chief Brexit negotiator Michel Barnier says free trade deal is "impossible" and warns UK it has "more to lose" than EU', *The Telegraph*, 19 June. Available from: https://www.telegraph.co.uk/news/2017/07/06/eu-brexit-negotiator-michel-barnier-warns-uk-will-lose-no-deal/ [Accessed 2 February 2020].

Crouch, C. (2017) 'Neoliberalism and social democracy', in J. Bryn and M. O' Donnell (eds) *Alternatives to Neoliberalism: Towards Equality and Democracy*, Bristol: Policy Press, pp 195–208.

Crowson, N.J. (2011) *Britain and Europe: A Political History since 1918*, New York: Routledge.

Cruddas, J. (2019) 'Labour can't afford to lose its working-class heartlands by backing Remain', *The Guardian*, 26 June. Available from: https://www.theguardian.com/commentisfree/2019/jun/26/labour-working-class-heartlands-remain-brexit [Accessed 2 February 2020].

Daddow, O., Gifford, C. and Wellings, B. (2019) 'The battle of Bruges: Margaret Thatcher, the foreign office and the unravelling of British European policy', *Political Research Exchange*, 1(1): 1–24.

Daily Mail Comment (2016) 'A PM on the ropes', *Mail Online*, 20 February. Available from: https://www.dailymail.co.uk/debate/article-3455467/DAILY-MAIL-COMMENT-PM-ropes.html [Accessed 2 February 2020].

Daily Mail Comment (2018) 'Saboteurs endangering our nation', *Mail Online*, 23 October. Available from: https://www.dailymail.co.uk/debate/article-6305601/DAILY-MAIL-COMMENT-Saboteurs-endangering-nation.html [Accessed 3 March 2020].

Dallison, P. (2017) 'Yanis Varoufakis: I told Jeremy Corbyn to be a radical Remainer', *Politico*, 9 January. Available from: https://www.politico.eu/article/yanis-varoufakis-i-told-jeremy-corbyn-to-be-a-radical-remainer/ [Accessed 2 February 2020].

Dallison, P. (2019) 'Nigel Farage launches Brexit Party: "No more Mr. Nice Guy"', *Politico*, 4 April. Available from: https://www.politico.eu/article/nigel-farage-launches-brexit-party-no-more-mr-nice-guy/ [Accessed 2 February 2020].

Dathan, M. (2015) 'Anti-EU protesters create fake firm to heckle David Cameron during CBI speech', *The Independent*, 9 November. Available from: https://www.independent.co.uk/news/uk/politics/anti-eu-protesters-created-fake-firm-to-heckle-david-cameron-during-cbi-speech-a6727041.html [Accessed 2 February 2020].

Dathan, M. and Clark, N. (2018) 'Fox on the hunt: Liam Fox accuses EU of behaving like gangsters in its threat to punish Britain for Brexit', *The Sun*, 8 March. Available from: https://www.thesun.co.uk/news/5756473/liam-fox-eu-gangsters-threat-brexit/ [Accessed 2 February 2020].

Davidson, L. (2018) 'Corb Limey: Jeremy Corbyn accused of bringing back 1970s-style protectionism as he launched a Britain first "manufacturing revolution"', *The Sun*, 25 July. Available from: https://www.thesun.co.uk/news/6858166/jeremy-corbyn-manufacturing-revolution/ [Accessed 2 February 2020].

Davidson, S. and Elstub, S. (2014) 'Deliberative and participatory democracy in the UK', *British Journal of Politics and International Relations*, 16: 367–85.

Delanty, G. (1996) 'Beyond the nation-state: national identity and citizenship in a multicultural society – a response to Rex', *Sociological Research Online*, 1(3): 1–8.

Denham, J. and Kenny, M. (2016) 'Who speaks to England? Labour's English challenge' [report], London: Fabian Society.

Denham, J. (2019) 'Nationalism in England is not just a rightwing nostalgia trip', *The Guardian*, 13 August. Available from: https://www.theguardian.com/commentisfree/2019/aug/13/english-nationalism-brexit-remain-and-reform [Accessed 2 February 2020].

Dennison, J. (2018) 'The rug pulled from under them: UKIP and the Greens', *Parliamentary Affairs*, 71(1): 91–108.

De Vries, C.E. (2017) 'Benchmarking Brexit: how the British decision to leave shapes EU public opinion', *Journal of Common Market Studies*, 55: 38–53.

Dietrich, D. (2014) *Rebellious Conservatives: Social Movements in Defense of Privilege*, New York: Palgrave Macmillan.

Donovan, T. and Redlawsk, D. (2018) 'Donald Trump and right-wing populists in comparative perspective', *Journal of Elections, Public Opinion and Parties*, 28(2): 190–207.

Dorling, D. (2016) 'Brexit: the decision of a divided country', *British Medical Journal*, 354:i3697. Available from: https://www.bmj.com/content/354/bmj.i3697 [Accessed 5 March 2020].

Dorling, A. and Tomlinson, S. (2019) *Rule Britannia: Brexit and the End of Empire*, London: Biteback Publishing.

Drury, C. (2019) 'Brexit march: how a summer of regional rallies turned the tide in the fight for a second referendum', *The Independent*, 18 October. Available from: https://www.independent.co.uk/news/uk/home-news/brexit-march-peoples-vote-second-referendum-north-midlands-regions-london-rally-a9159336.html [Accessed 2 February 2020].

Dryzek, J.S. (2010) 'Rhetoric in democracy: a systemic appreciation', *Political Theory*, 38(3): 319–39.

Dryzek, J.S. and Niemeyer, S. (2006) 'Reconciling pluralism and consensus as political ideals', *American Journal of Political Science*, 50: 634–49.

Duncan Smith, I. (2019) 'The Reformation was the making of modern Britain. Brexit is a similar opportunity', *The Telegraph*, 2 August. Available from: https://www.telegraph.co.uk/politics/2019/08/02/reformation-making-modern-britain-brexit-similar-opportunity/ [Accessed 2 February 2020].

Dunleavy, P. (1993) 'The political parties', in P. Dunleavy (ed), *Developments in British Politics*, vol. 4, London: Macmillan.

Eaton, G. (2012) 'John Bright: statesman, orator, agitator', *New Statesman*, 9 January. Available from: https://www.newstatesman.com/books/2012/01/john-bright-cash-england-corn [Accessed 2 February 2020].

Eaton, G. (2016) 'What is Labour's official Brexit policy?', *New Statesman*, 15 November. Available from: https://www.newstatesman.com/politics/uk/2016/11/what-labours-official-brexit-policy [Accessed 2 February 2020].

Economist (2016) 'Post-truth politics: art of the lie', 10 September. Available from: https://www.economist.com/leaders/2016/09/10/art-of-the-lie [Accessed 2 February 2020].

Edwards, J. (2013) 'Play and democracy: Huizinga and the limits of agonism', *Political Theory*, 41(1): 90–115.

Ekström, M. and Morton, A. (2017) 'The performances of right-wing populism: populist discourse, embodied styles and forms of news reporting', in M. Ekström and J. Firmstone (eds) *The Mediated Politics of Europe: A Comparative Study of Discourse*, Cham: Palgrave Macmillan, pp 289–318.

Elgot, J. (2018) 'Chequers deal could be undone after Britain leaves EU, claims Gove', *The Guardian*, 17 September. Available from: https://www.theguardian.com/politics/2018/sep/16/chequers-deal-undone-after-britain-leaves-eu-michael-gove-brexit [Accessed 2 February 2020].

Elgot, J. and Sabbagh, D. (2019) 'May to woo Labour with law giving UK workers same rights as in EU', *The Guardian*, 6 February. Available from: https://www.theguardian.com/politics/2019/feb/06/may-to-woo-labour-with-law-giving-uk-workers-same-rights-as-in-eu [Accessed 2 February 2020].

Ellison, J. (2012) 'Is Britain more European than it thinks?', *History Today*, 62(2). Available from: https://www.historytoday.com/archive/britain-more-european-it-thinks [Accessed 1 March 2020].

Elwes, J. (2014) 'Ukip's appeal – it's all about identity', Prospect Magazine blog, 10 October. Available from: https://www.prospectmagazine.co.uk/blogs/prospector-blog/ukips-appeal-its-all-about-identity [Accessed 2 February 2020].

Embury-Dennis, T. and Buncombe, A. (2018) 'Nigel Farage threatens to return as UKIP leader unless Brexit is put "back on track"', *The Independent*, 9 July. Available from: https://www.independent.co.uk/news/uk/politics/brexit-latest-nigel-farage-ukip-leader-article-50-chequers-theresa-may-a8439436.html [Accessed 2 February 2020].

Erikson, K. (1995) 'Notes on trauma and community', in C. Caruth (ed) *Trauma Explorations in Memory*, Baltimore, MD: Johns Hopkins University Press, pp 183–99.

Fairclough, N. (1989) *Language and Power*. London: Longman.

Fairclough, N. (2003) *Analysing Discourse: Textual Analysis for Social Research*, London and New York: Routledge.

Farage, N. (2017) Address to the European Parliament, [video clip] 5 April. Available from: https://www.itv.com/news/2017-04-05/nigel-farage-mafia-gangsters-brexit-heckled-over-mafia-remark-so-calls-meps-gangsters-instead/ [Accessed 2 February 2020].

Farrar, M. (2012) '"Interculturalism" or "critical multiculturalism": which discourse works best?', in M. Farrar (ed) *Debating Multiculturalism*, London: The Dialogue Society, pp 89–100.

Favell, A. (2017) 'European Union versus European society: sociologists on "Brexit" and the "failure" of Europeanization', in W. Outhwaite (ed) *Brexit: Sociological Responses*, London and New York: Anthem Press, pp 193–9.

Fekete, L. (2017) 'Flying the flag for neoliberalism', *Race & Class*, 58(3): 3–22.

Fischer, J. (2017) 'Brexit to nowhere?' *Social Europe*, [online article] 13 July. Available from: https://www.socialeurope.eu/brexit-to-nowhere [Accessed 2 February 2020].

Ford, R. and Goodwin, M. (2014) *Revolt on the Right: Explaining Support for the Radical Right in Britain*, Abingdon: Routledge.

Forester, J. (1999) 'Dealing with deep value differences', in Lawrence Susskind (ed) *The Consensus Building Handbook*, Thousand Oaks, CA: Sage, pp 463–93.

Foucault, M. (2002) *The Archaeology of Knowledge*, London and New York: Routledge.

Foucault, M. (2003) *Society Must Be Defended: Lectures at the Collège de France, 1975–76*, New York: Picador.

Foucault, M. (2008) *The Birth of Biopolitics: Lectures at the Collège de France 1978–1979*, New York: Palgrave Macmillan.

Fourastié, J. (1979) *Les Trente Glorieuses, ou la révolution invisible de 1946 à 1975*, Paris: Fayard.

Fox, L. (2017) 'Outside the EU, Britain should be an evangelist for world trade', *The Guardian*, 11 December. Available from: https://www.theguardian.com/commentisfree/2017/dec/11/outside-eu-britain-evangelist-world-trade-brexit-britain [Accessed 2 February 2020].

Fox, S. and Pearce, S. (2018) 'The generational decay of Euroscepticism in the UK and the EU referendum', *Journal of Elections, Public Opinion and Parties*, 28(1): 19–37.

Fraser, N. (1992) 'Rethinking the public sphere: a contribution to the critique of actually existing democracy', in C. Calhoun (ed) *Habermas and the Public Sphere*, Cambridge, MA: MIT Press, pp 109–42.

Freeden, M. (2017) 'After the Brexit referendum: revisiting populism as an ideology', *Journal of Political Ideologies*, 22(1): 1–11.

Freire, P. (1994) *Pedagogy of Hope: Reliving Pedagogy of the Oppressed*, New York: Continuum.

Fromage, D. and van den Brink, T. (2018) 'Democratic legitimation of EU economic governance: challenges and opportunities for European legislatures', *Journal of European Integration*, 40(3): 235–48.

Fukuyama, F. (1992) *The End of History and the Last Man*, New York: Free Press.

Fung, A. (2003) 'Recipes for public spheres', *Journal of Political Philosophy*, 11: 338–67.

Gaitskell, H. (1962) Labour national conference speech, 3 October. Available from: https://www.cvce.eu/content/publication/1999/1/1/05f2996b-000b-4576-8b42-8069033a16f9/publishable_en.pdf [Accessed 2 February 2020].

Gamble, A. (2017) 'British politics after Brexit', *Political Insight*, 8(1): 4–6.

Gambles, A. (1998) 'Rethinking the politics of protection: conservatism and the corn laws, 1830–52', *The English Historical Review*, 113(453): 928–52.

Gans, H.J. (2011) 'Multiperspectival news revisited: journalism and representative democracy', *Journalism*, 12(1): 3–13.

Garland, D. (2008) 'On the concept of moral panic', *Crime, Media, Culture*, 4(1), 9–30.

Garside, L., Osborne, H. and MacAskill, E. (2017) 'Brexiters who put their money offshore', *The Guardian*, 9 November. Available from: https://www.theguardian.com/news/2017/nov/09/brexiters-put-money-offshore-tax-haven [Accessed 2 February 2020].

Gee, J.P. (2011) *How to Do Discourse Analysis*, London: Routledge.

Gellner, E. (1983) *Nations and Nationalism*, Oxford: Basil Blackwell.

George, S. (1998) *An Awkward Partner: Britain in the European Community* (3rd edn), Oxford: Oxford University Press.

Giddens, A. (1995) 'Brave new world: the new context for politics', in D. Miliband (ed) *Reinventing the Left*, Cambridge: Polity Press, pp 21–38.

Giddens, A. (2014) *Turbulent and Mighty Continent: What Future for Europe?* Cambridge: Polity Press.

Giddens, A. and Pierson, C. (1998) *Conversations with Anthony Giddens: Making Sense of Modernity*, Stanford, CA: Stanford University Press.

Gilroy, P. (2004) *After Empire: Melancholia or Convivial Culture?* London: Routledge.

Goffman, E. (1956) *The Presentation of Self in Everyday Life*. New York: Doubleday.

Goodhart, D. and Kaufmann, E. (2016) 'A respectable Englishness', Fabian Society, 16 August. Available from: https://fabians.org.uk/a-respectable-englishness/ [Accessed 2 February 2020].

Gough, J. (2017) 'Brexit, xenophobia and left strategy now', *Capital & Class*, 41(2): 366–72.

Gourtsoyannis, P. (2018) 'Poll: Leave voters want Brexit even if it breaks up UK', *The Scotsman*, 19 June. Available from: https://www.scotsman.com/news/politics/poll-leave-voters-want-brexit-even-if-it-breaks-up-uk-1-4756562 [Accessed 2 February 2020].

Gove, M. (2016a) 'EU "needs to think again"', *The Andrew Marr Show*, BBC, [video clip] 8 May. Available from: https://www.bbc.co.uk/programmes/p03thvx4 [Accessed 2 February 2020].

Gove, M. (2016b) 'The facts of life say leave', Vote Leave, [speech] 19 April. Available from: http://www.voteleavetakecontrol.org/michael_gove_the_facts_of_life_say_leave.html [Accessed 2 February 2020].

Gray, M. and Barford, J. (2018) 'The depths of the cuts: the uneven geography of local government austerity', *Cambridge Journal of Regions, Economy and Society*, 11(3): 541–63.

Green, D. (2018) 'Behaviour of many in cabinet has been bizarre, inexcusable and deeply disloyal says former deputy PM Damian Green', *Daily Mail*, 1 July. Available from: https://www.dailymail.co.uk/news/article-5905217/Damian-Green-Behaviour-Cabinet-bizarre-inexcusable.html [Accessed 2 February 2020].

Griffin, A. (2016) 'Brexit legal challenge: Nigel Farage says parliament has "no idea what anger they will provoke" if Article 50 blocked', *The Independent*, 3 November. Available from: https://www.independent.co.uk/news/uk/politics/brexit-legal-challenge-latest-nigel-farage-updates-ukip-article-50-parliament-huge-anger-political-a7395006.html [Accessed 2 February 2020].

Gross, N. (2008) *Richard Rorty: The Making of An American Philosopher*, Chicago: University of Chicago Press.

Groves, J. (2017) 'Proud of yourselves?' *Daily Mail*, 14 December. Available from: https://www.newstatesman.com/politics/media/2017/12/proud-yourselves-internet-s-best-alternative-daily-mail-front-pages [Accessed 2 February 2020].

Guinan, J. and Hanna, T. (2017) 'Lexit: the EU is a neoliberal project, so let's do something different when we leave it', *New Statesman*, 20 July. Available from: https://www.newstatesman.com/politics/brexit/2017/07/lexit-eu-neoliberal-project-so-lets-do-something-different-when-we-leave-it [Accessed 2 February 2020].

Habermas, J. (1989) *The Structural Transformation of the Public Sphere: An Inquiry into a Category of Bourgeois Society*, Cambridge, MA: Thomas Burger.

Habermas, J. (1996) *Between Facts and Norms: Contributions to a Discourse Theory of Law and Democracy*, Cambridge, MA: MIT Press.

Habermas, J. (2001a) 'Warum braucht Europa eine Verfassung?' [Why Does Europe Need a Constitution?], *Zeit*, 28 June. Available from: https://www.zeit.de/2001/27/Warum_braucht_Europa_eine_Verfassung_/komplettansicht [Accessed 2 February 2020].

Habermas, J. (2001b) *On the Pragmatics of Social Interaction*, trans B. Fultner, Cambridge, MA: MIT Press.

Habermas, J. (2009) *Europe: The Faltering Project*, Cambridge: Polity Press.

Habermas, J. (2012) *The Crisis of the European Union: A Response*, Cambridge: Polity Press.

Hacked Off (2018) 'Thrown to the wolves', [online report]. Available from: https://hackinginquiry.org/wp-content/uploads/2018/09/ThrowntotheWolves.pdf [Accessed 2 February 2020].

Hague, W. (2001) Speech to Conservative rally in Brighton, 29 May. Available from: https://conservative-speeches.sayit.mysociety.org/speech/601083 [Accessed 2 February 2020].

Harding, L. (2017) 'MP calls for inquiry into Arron banks and "Dark Money" in EU referendum', *The Guardian*, 9 October. Available from: https://www.theguardian.com/politics/2017/oct/19/mp-calls-for-inquiry-into-arron-banks-and-dark-money-in-eu-referendum [Accessed 2 February 2020].

Hawken, A. and Matthews, A. (2016) 'Nigel Farage says British women will be at risk of mass sex attacks by gangs of migrants if we vote to stay in the EU', *Daily Mail*, 4 June. Available from: https://www.dailymail.co.uk/news/article-3625475/Nigel-Farage-says-security-Britain-risk-stay-EU-ISIS-promise-flood-Continent-jihadists.html [Accessed 2 February 2020].

Heath, A. (1998) *The Course of My Life: The Autobiography of Edward Heath*, London: Hodder & Stoughton.

Helm, T. (2019) 'Poll shows Conservative party 15 points ahead of Labour', *The Guardian*, 6 October. Available from: https://www.theguardian.com/politics/2019/oct/06/poll-shows-conservative-party-15-points-ahead-of-labour [Accessed 2 February 2020].

Helm, T. and Walker, P. (2019) 'Brexit countdown: inside Boris Johnson's terrible week', *The Guardian*, 28 September. Available from: https://www.theguardian.com/politics/2019/sep/28/boris-johnson-terrible-week-supreme-court-jennifer-arcuri [Accessed 2 February 2020].

Hearn, J. (2017) 'Nationalism, globalization and the balance of power in the making of Brexit', in W. Outhwaite (ed) *Brexit: Sociological Responses*, London and New York: Anthem Press, pp 91–100.

Henley, J. (2017a) 'Brexit weekly briefing: talks stall as negotiators trade verbal blows', *The Guardian*, 5 September. Available from: https://www.theguardian.com/politics/2017/sep/05/brexit-weekly-briefing-talks-stall-as-negotiators-trade-verbal-blows [Accessed 2 February 2020].

Henley, J. (2017b) 'Britain's cake-and-eat-it Brexit routine wears thin with Barnier', *The Guardian*, 31 August. Available from: https://www.theguardian.com/politics/2017/aug/31/britain-cake-and-eat-it-brexit-routine-michel-barnier [Accessed 2 February 2020].

Henley, J. (2018) 'Brexit weekly briefing: the crunchiest crunch time yet', *The Guardian*, 2 July. Available from: https://www.theguardian.com/politics/2018/jul/02/brexit-weekly-briefing-the-crunchiest-crunch-time-yet [Accessed 2 February 2020].

Henley, J. and Elgot, J. (2017) 'Brexit weekly briefing: UK rift widens as May names article 50 day', *The Guardian*, 21 March. Available from: https://www.theguardian.com/politics/2017/mar/21/brexit-weekly-briefing-uk-rift-widens-as-may-names-article-50-day [Accessed 2 February 2020].

Henley, J. and Rice-Oxley, M. (2019) 'Fight for Europe – or the wreckers will destroy it', *The Guardian*, 25 January. Available from: https://www.theguardian.com/commentisfree/2019/jan/25/fight-europe-wreckers-patriots-nationalist [Accessed 2 February 2020].

Henley, J. and Walker, P. (2017a) 'Brexit weekly briefing: May's last-minute diplomacy falls flat', *The Guardian*, 16 October. Available from: https://www.theguardian.com/politics/2017/oct/16/brexit-weekly-briefing-mays-last-minute-diplomacy-falls-flat [Accessed 2 February 2020].

Henley, J. and Walker, P. (2017b) 'May manages to further alienate EU with Trump as her Brexit best buddy', *The Guardian*, 31 January. Available from: https://www.theguardian.com/politics/2017/jan/31/theresa-may-further-alienate-eu-donald-trump-brexit-best-buddy [Accessed 2 February 2020].

Heppell, T. and Hill, M. (2005) 'Ideological typologies of contemporary British conservatism', *Political Studies Review*, 3(3): 335–55.

Herring, E. and Robinson, P. (2014) 'Deception and Britain's road to war in Iraq', *International Journal of Contemporary Iraqi Studies*, 8: 213–32.

Herzog, B. (2016) *Discourse Analysis as Social Critique*, London: Palgrave Macmillan.

Hewitt, R. (2005) *White Backlash and the Politics of Multiculturalism*, New York: Cambridge University Press.

Heywood, A. (2015) *Political Theory: An Introduction* (4th edn), Basingstoke: Palgrave.

Higley, J. (2017) 'Can elites contain and manage the crisis?', *Corvinus Journal of Sociology and Social Policy*, 8(3): 7–16.

Hobolt, S.B. (2016) 'The Brexit vote: a divided nation, a divided continent', *Journal of European Public Policy*, 23(9): 1259–77.

Hogan, P. (2018) Speech by Commissioner Phil Hogan at Brexit event, Rosslare Port, Ireland, [speech] 11 June. Available from: https://trade.ec.europa.eu/doclib/press/index.cfm?id=2088 [Accessed 2 February 2020].

Holehouse, M. (2014) 'Jose Manuel Barroso: nearly impossible for Scotland to join EU', *The Telegraph*, 16 February. Available from: https://www.telegraph.co.uk/news/uknews/scotland/10641833/Jose-Manuel-Barroso-nearly-impossible-for-Scotland-to-join-EU.html [Accessed 2 February 2020].

Hughes, L. (2019) 'Jo Swinson rules out Lib Dems helping Corbyn into number 10', *Financial Times*, 13 November. Available from: https://www.ft.com/content/454c1ed0-060b-11ea-9afa-d9e2401fa7ca [Accessed 2 February 2020].

Hughes, L. and Parker, G. (2019) 'Farage claims Tories dangled titles for Brexit party support', *Financial Times*, 14 November. Available from: https://www.ft.com/content/2c8bb0a8-06fc-11ea-a984-fbbacad9e7dd [Accessed 2 February 2020].

Hunt, D. (2018) Speech to Conservative national conference, 30 September. Available from: https://www.conservativehome.com/parliament/2018/09/never-mistake-british-politeness-for-british-weakness-hunts-conference-speech-full-text.html [Accessed 2 February 2020].

Huntington, S.P. (2012) 'The clash of civilizations?', in F.J. Lechner and J. Boli (eds) *The Globalization Reader*, Chichester: Wiley-Blackwell, pp 37–44.

Inglehart, R.F. and Norris, P. (2016) 'Trump, Brexit, and the rise of populism: economic have-nots and cultural backlash', HKS Working Paper No. RWP16-026, Harvard Kennedy School. Available from: https://www.hks.harvard.edu/publications/trump-brexit-and-rise-populism-economic-have-nots-and-cultural-backlash [Accessed 2 February 2020].

Jacobs, M. (2017) *Panic at the Pump: The Energy Crisis and the Transformation of American Politics in the 1970s*, New York: Farrar, Straus and Giroux.

Jankowicz, M. (2019) 'Vince Cable: Swinson's revoke Article 50 promise is a "distraction"', *The New European*, 30 November. Available from: https://www.theneweuropean.co.uk/top-stories/vince-cable-on-revoking-article-50-lib-dems-1-6402454 [Accessed 2 February 2020].

Johnson, B. (2016a) 'Boris Johnson exclusive: there is only one way to get the change we want – vote to leave the EU', *The Telegraph*, 16 March. Available from: https://www.telegraph.co.uk/opinion/2016/03/16/boris-johnson-exclusive-there-is-only-one-way-to-get-the-change/ [Accessed 2 February 2020].

Johnson, B. (2016b) 'Boris Johnson: UK and America can be better friends than ever Mr Obama… if we LEAVE the EU', *The Sun*, 22 April. Available from: https://www.thesun.co.uk/archives/politics/1139354/boris-johnson-uk-and-america-can-be-better-friends-than-ever-mr-obama-if-we-leave-the-eu/ [Accessed 2 February 2020].

Johnson, B. (2018) Brexit speech, *The Spectator*, [speech] 14 February. Available from: https://blogs.spectator.co.uk/2018/02/full-text-boris-johnsons-brexit-speech/ [Accessed 2 February 2020].

Johnson, B. (2019a) Speech to national Conservative Party Conference, 2 October. Available from: https://www.theguardian.com/politics/ng-interactive/2019/oct/02/boris-johnsons-speech-to-the-tory-party-conference-annotated [Accessed 2 February 2020].

Johnson, B. (2019b) 'No more fake Brexit deadlines: we must leave the EU on 31st October, come what may', *Brexit Central*, 7 July. Available from: https://brexitcentral.com/no-more-fake-brexit-deadlines-we-must-leave-the-eu-on-31st-october-come-what-may/ [Accessed 2 February 2020].

Johnson, B. (2019c) Priorities for Government, *Hansard*, 25 July, Volume 663. Available from: https://hansard.parliament.uk/Commons/2019-07-25/debates/D0290128-96D8-4AF9-ACFD-21D5D9CF328E/PrioritiesForGovernment [Accessed 2 February 2020].

Johnson, B. (2019d) Prime Minister's Questions Live, Facebook. Available from: https://www.facebook.com/borisjohnson/ [Accessed 2 February 2020].

Johnson, B. (2019e) Prime Minister's Update, *Hansard*, 25 September, Volume 664. Available from: https://hansard.parliament.uk/Commons/2019-09-25/debates/AD2A07E5-9741-4EBA-997A-97776F80AA38/PrimeMinisterSUpdate [Accessed 2 February 2020].

Johnson, B. (2019f) G7 Update, *Hansard*, 3 September, Volume 664. Available from: https://hansard.parliament.uk/Commons/2019-09-03/debates/9C6A36DF-1CCF-4C07-9F81-DD16B8564D0C/G7Summit [Accessed 2 February 2020].

Johnson, B. (2019g) European Union (Withdrawal Agreement) Bill, *Hansard*, 20 December, Volume 669. Available from: https://hansard.parliament.uk/commons/2019-12-20/debates/FE5B9762-F298-457B-8306-98D2D1D3519B/EuropeanUnion(WithdrawalAgreement)Bill [Accessed 2 February 2020].

Johnson, P. (2008) 'Globalizing democracy: reflections on Habermas's radicalism', *European Journal of Social Theory*, 11(1): 71–86.

Jones, D. (2012) *Masters of the Universe: Hayek, Friedman, and the Birth of Neoliberal Politics*, Princeton, NJ: Princeton University Press.

Kalberg, S. (1980) 'Max Weber's types of rationality: cornerstones for the analysis of rationalization processes in history', *The American Journal of Sociology*, 85(5): 1145–79.

Kaldor, M. (2018) 'Jeremy Corbyn should offer pro-EU hope, not more fears about Brexit', *The Guardian*, 8 March. Available from: https://www.theguardian.com/commentisfree/2018/mar/08/jeremy-corbyn-offer-pro-eu-hope-brexit-fears [Accessed 2 February 2020].

Kaufman, E. (2018) *Whiteshift: Populism, Immigration and the Future of White Majorities*, London: Allen Lane.

Kavanagh, T. (2016) 'With project fear in full flight, the Brexit "catastrophe" is a Hitler-style big lie', *The Sun*, 18 April. Available from: https://www.thesun.co.uk/news/opinion/trevor-kavanagh/1197502/with-project-fear-in-full-flight-the-brexit-catastrophe-is-a-hitler-style-big-lie/ [Accessed 2 February 2020].

Kelley, R. and Tuck, S. (2015) *The Other Special Relationship: Race, Rights and Riots in Britain and the United States*, Basingstoke: Palgrave Macmillan.

Khan, M. (2017) 'Barnier denies trying to lecture UK over Brexit', *Financial Times*, 4 September. Available from: https://www.ft.com/content/cf9e045c-ff12-3389-90d6-9ec2e6b2463f [Accessed 2 February 2020].

Kirkup, J. (2019) 'The genius of Boris's Brexit slogan', *The Spectator* blogs, 30 September. Available from: https://blogs.spectator.co.uk/2019/09/the-genius-of-boriss-brexit-slogan/ [Accessed 2 February 2020].

Klos, F. (2018) *Churchill's Last Stand: The Struggle to Unite Europe*, London and New York: I.B. Tauris.

Koselleck, R. (2004) *Futures Past: On the Semantics of Historical Time*. New York: Columbia University Press.

Krzyżanowski, M. (2019) 'Brexit and the imaginary of "crisis": a discourse-conceptual analysis of European news media', *Critical Discourse Studies*, 16(4): 465–90.

Kuhn, T. (1962) *The Structure of Scientific Revolutions* (1st edn), Chicago: University of Chicago Press.

Kumar, K. (2003) *The Making of English National Identity*, Cambridge: Cambridge University Press.

Kundnani, A. (2007) *The End of Tolerance: Racism in 21st Century Britain*, London: Pluto Press.

Kwarteng, K., Patel, P., Raab, D. Skidmore, C. and Truss, E. (2012) *Britannia Unchained: Global Lessons for Growth and Prosperity*, Basingstoke: Palgrave Macmillan.

Labour List (2018) 'Labour's Brexit composite motion in full', *Labour List*, 26 September. Available from: https://labourlist.org/2018/09/labours-brexit-composite-motion-in-full/ [Accessed 6 April 2020].

Laclau, E. and Mouffe, C. (2001) *Hegemony and Socialist Strategy: Towards a Radical Democratic Politics*, London: Verso.

Ladson-Billings, G. and Gillborn, D. (eds) (2004) *The RoutledgeFalmer Reader in Multicultural Education*, New York: RoutledgeFalmer.

Lammy, D. (2019) European Union (Withdrawal) Act, *Hansard*, Volume 652, 10 January. Available from: https://hansard.parliament.uk/Commons/2019-01-10/debates/159740E3-991B-4DF4-A29C-D04B2F1CE10F/EuropeanUnion(Withdrawal)Act [Accessed 2 February 2020].

Lapavitsas, C. (2018) *The Left Case Against the EU*, Bristol: Policy Press.

Lawson, N. (2016) 'Brexit gives us a chance to finish the Thatcher revolution', *Financial Times*, 24 September. Available from: https://www.ft.com/content/6cb84f70-6b7c-11e6-a0b1-d87a9fea034f [Accessed 2 February 2020].

Leahy, P. (2016) 'Four out of five Irish voters say UK was wrong to leave EU', *Irish Times*, 7 July. Available from: https://www.irishtimes.com/news/politics/four-out-of-five-irish-voters-say-uk-was-wrong-to-leave-eu-1.2712755 [Accessed 2 February 2020].

Leroux, M. and Baldwin, L. (2018) 'Arron Banks and Brexit's offshore secrets', *Open Democracy*, [online] 18 April. Available from: https://www.opendemocracy.net/en/dark-money-investigations/brexit-s-offshore-secrets-0/ [Accessed 2 February 2020].

Letta, E. (2016) 'EU: relaunch or die', *Politico*, 8 August. Available from: https://www.politico.eu/article/the-eu-must-relaunch-or-die-brexit-consequences-reform-europe-future/ [Accessed 2 February 2020].

Levitas, R. (1998) *The Inclusive Society? Social Exclusion and New Labour*, Basingstoke: Palgrave Macmillan.

Levy, D., Aslan, B. and Bironzo, D. (2016) 'The press and the referendum campaign', in D. Jackson, E. Thorsen and D. Wring (eds) *EU Referendum Analysis 2016: Media, Voters and the Campaign Early Reflections from Leading UK Academics*, Bournemouth: Centre for the Study of Journalism, Culture and Community (Bournemouth University), Centre for Politics and Media Research (Bournemouth University), Centre for Research in Communication and Culture (Loughborough University) and PSA The Media and Politics Group, pp 33–4.

Lewis, P. and Hilder, P. (2018) 'Cambridge Analytica misled MPs over work for Leave.EU, says ex-director', *The Guardian*, 23 March. Available from: https://www.theguardian.com/news/2018/mar/23/cambridge-analytica-misled-mps-over-work-for-leave-eu-says-ex-director-brittany-kaiser [Accessed 2 February 2020].

Lis, J. (2017) 'Brexit: Corbyn is playing a clever long game that could benefit us all', Politics.co.uk, 28 December. Available from: https://www.politics.co.uk/comment-analysis/2017/12/28/brexit-corbyn-is-playing-a-clever-long-game-that-could-benef [Accessed 2 February 2020].

Lis, J. (2019) 'The language of Brexit "betrayal" is poisoning politics', *The Guardian*, 21 September. Available from: https://www.theguardian.com/commentisfree/2019/sep/21/brexit-betrayal-politics-culture-war [Accessed 2 February 2020].

Llewellyn, C. and Cram, L. (2016) 'The results are in and the UK will #Brexit: What did social media tell us about the UK's EU referendum?', in D. Jackson, E. Thorsen and D. Wring (eds) *EU Referendum Analysis 2016: Media, Voters and the Campaign Early Reflections from Leading UK Academics*, Bournemouth: Centre for the Study of Journalism, Culture and Community (Bournemouth University), Centre for Politics and Media Research (Bournemouth University), Centre for Research in Communication and Culture (Loughborough University) and PSA The Media and Politics Group, pp 90–1.

Loughborough University (2019) 'Press hostility to Labour reaches new levels in 2019 election campaign', [press release] 19 December. Available from: https://www.lboro.ac.uk/news-events/news/2019/december/press-hostility-to-labour-reaches-new-levels/ [Accessed 2 February 2020].

Lowe, J. (2016) 'EU's Martin Schulz casts doubt on UK free movement deal', *Newsweek*, 23 September. Available from: https://www.newsweek.com/brexit-martin-schulz-eu-speech-free-movement-immigration-european-parliament-502033 [Accessed 6 April 2020].

Lucardie, P. (2000) 'Prophets, purifiers and prolocutors: towards a theory on the emergence of new parties', *Party Politics*, 6(2): 175–85.

MacShane, D. (2016) *Brexit: How Britain Left Europe*, London: I.B.Tauris.

MacShane, D. (2017) *Brexit, No Exit: Why (in the End) Britain Won't Leave Europe*, London: I.B.Tauris.

McSmith, A. (2016) 'Brexit: Jeremy Corbyn undermined and sabotaged Remain campaign, claims Peter Mandelson', *The Independent*, 7 August. Available from: https://www.independent.co.uk/news/uk/politics/brexit-jeremy-corbyn-peter-mandelson-remain-campaign-eu-referendum-7176551.html [Accessed 2 February 2020].

Maidment, J. (2017) 'Jeremy Corbyn's "soft Brexit" U-turn will cause Leave voters to abandon Labour and return to Ukip, MP warns', *The Telegraph*, 28 August. Available from: https://www.telegraph.co.uk/news/2017/08/28/jeremy-corbyns-soft-brexit-u-turn-will-cause-leave-voters-abandon/ [Accessed 2 February 2020].

Mairs, N. (2017) 'David Davis "pushed" Theresa May into holding snap election, new book claims', *Politics Home*, [online] 10 September. Available from: https://www.politicshome.com/news/uk/political-parties/conservative-party/news/88857/david-davis-%E2%80%98pushed%E2%80%99-theresa-may-holding [Accessed 2 February 2020].

Malik, K. (2019) 'This Brexit poll found we want to believe the worst of ourselves', *The Guardian*, 27 October. Available from: https://www.theguardian.com/commentisfree/2019/oct/27/brexit-poll-found-we-want-to-believe-the-worst-of-ourselves [Accessed 2 February 2020].

Mallet, V. (2019) 'French minister vows to overcome resistance to Macron's EU plans', *Financial Times*, 31 July. Available from: https://www.ft.com/content/ea51cab0-adfa-11e9-8030-530adfa879c2 [Accessed 2 February 2020].

Mansfield, K. (2017) '"Naive and irresponsible" German president Frank-Walter Steinmeier rips into Brexit', *The Express*, 4 April. Available from: https://www.express.co.uk/news/world/787693/brexit-frank-walter-steinmeier-european-union-parliament-populism-germany [Accessed 2 February 2020].

Marr, A. (2016) Penny Mordaunt interviewed by Andrew Marr, BBC, [video clip] 22 May. Available from: https://www.bbc.co.uk/programmes/p03vxlks [Accessed 2 February 2020].

Marr, A. (2017) Corbyn interviewed by Andrew Marr, BBC, [transcript] 23 July. Available from: http://news.bbc.co.uk/2/shared/bsp/hi/pdfs/23071701.pdf [Accessed 2 February 2020].

Martin, K. (2016) 'Eurosceptic genie is out of the bottle', *Financial Times*, 24 June. Available from: https://www.ft.com/content/68cdbdc9-c8ee-339e-b70e-e0ee4d5bfd29 [Accessed 2 February 2020].

Mason, P. (2019a) 'Corbynism is now in crisis: the only way forward is to oppose Brexit', *The Guardian*, 27 May. Available from: https://www.theguardian.com/commentisfree/2019/may/27/corbynism-crisis-oppose-brexit-jeremy-corbyn-labour [Accessed 2 February 2020].

Mason, P. (2019b) 'Labour's best tactic to beat Boris Johnson? A popular front', *The Guardian*, 2 August. Available from: https://www.theguardian.com/commentisfree/2019/aug/02/labour-boris-johnson-progressive-pact-greens-lib-dems [Accessed 2 February 2020].

Mason, R. (2016) 'Labour voters in the dark about party's stance on Brexit, research says', *The Guardian*, 30 May. Available from: https://www.theguardian.com/politics/2016/may/30/labour-voters-in-the-dark-about-partys-stance-on-brexit-research-says [Accessed 2 February 2020].

Mason, R. (2019) 'Labour chair: some Remainers are sneering at ordinary people', *The Guardian*, 29 May. Available from: https://www.theguardian.com/politics/2019/may/29/labour-chair-peoples-vote-backers-sneering-ordinary-people-ian-lavery [Accessed 2 February 2020].

Mason, R. and Asthana, A. (2016) 'David Cameron: Leave vote would be economic bomb for UK', *The Guardian*, 6 June. Available from: https://www.theguardian.com/politics/2016/jun/06/david-cameron-brexit-would-detonate-bomb-under-uk-economy [Accessed 2 February 2020].

Mason, R., Elgot, J. and Syal, R. (2016) 'Osborne on ropes after "punishment budget" plan infuriates Tory MPs', *The Guardian*, 15 June. Available from: https://www.theguardian.com/politics/2016/jun/15/osborne-britain-eu-more-important-career-tory-mps [Accessed 2 February 2020].

Mason, R. and Stewart, H. (2016) 'Corbyn's defence of immigration splits shadow cabinet', *The Guardian*, 28 September. Available from: https://www.theguardian.com/uk-news/2016/sep/28/corbyn-defence-of-immigration-splits-shadow-cabinet-labour [Accessed 2 February 2020].

Maton, K. (2003) 'Pierre Bourdieu and the epistemic conditions of social scientific knowledge', *Space and Culture*, 6(1): 52–65.

May, S. and Sleeter, C. (2010) *Critical Multiculturalism: Theory and Praxis*, New York: Routledge.

May, T. (2016a) Theresa May's Conservative party conference speech, Conservative Conference, [speech] 5 October. Available from: https://www.independent.co.uk/news/uk/politics/theresa-may-speech-tory-conference-2016-in-full-transcript-a7346171.html [Accessed 2 February 2020].

May, T. (2016b) *Hansard*, European Council [Statement], Volume 618, Col 1185, 19 December. Available from: https://hansard.parliament.uk/Commons/2016-12-19/debates/605D7654-DF44-4B82-A2A5-C07448B2FCD6/EuropeanCouncil2016 [Accessed 2 February 2020].

May, T. (2017a) *Hansard*, Article 50 [Statement], Volume 624, Col 251, 29 March. Available from: https://hansard.parliament.uk/Commons/2017-03-29/debates/A6DFE4A0-6AB1-4B71-BF25-376F52AF3300/Article50 [Accessed 2 February 2020].

May, T. (2017b) Lancaster House speech, 17 January. Available from: https://time.com/4636141/theresa-may-brexit-speech-transcript/ [Accessed 2 February 2020].

May, T. (2018) Mansion House speech, 2 March. Available from: https://www.gov.uk/government/speeches/pm-speech-on-our-future-economic-partnership-with-the-european-union [Accessed 2 February 2020].

Mazza, C. (2019) 'Exiled by Trump, Steve Bannon could be about to rise again in Europe', *Newsweek*, 25 May. Available from: https://www.newsweek.com/steve-bannon-trump-european-elections-1434592 [Accessed 2 February 2020].

Merrick, R. (2018) 'Theresa May's post-Brexit customs plan for EU is "completely cretinous", Jacob Rees-Mogg says', *The Independent*, 24 April. Available from: https://www.independent.co.uk/news/uk/politics/brexit-uk-customs-deal-eu-trade-theresa-may-jacob-rees-mogg-a8320446.html [Accessed 2 February 2020].

Merrick, R. (2019) 'Brexit: hardline Tories to back Boris Johnson's agreement to pave way for no-deal exit next year, one reveals', *The Independent*, 18 October. Available from: https://www.independent.co.uk/news/uk/politics/brexit-boris-johnson-no-deal-transition-brexiteers-delay-eu-a9161616.html [Accessed 2 February 2020].

Mikhailova, A. (2019) '"What an earthquake we have created": Read in full Boris Johnson's victory speech at Tory headquarters', *The Telegraph*, 13 December. Available from: https://www.telegraph.co.uk/politics/2019/12/13/earthquake-have-created-boris-johnsons-victory-speech-tory-headquarters/ [Accessed 2 February 2020].

Mnookin, R., Peppet, S. and Tulumello, A. (1996) 'The tension between empathy and assertiveness', *Negotiation Journal*, 12: 217–30.

Modood, T. (2012) 'New paradigms in public policy post-immigration "difference" and integration: the case of Muslims in Western Europe', a report for the British Academy, London: British Academy Policy Centre.

Moffitt, B. (2016) *The Global Rise of Populism: Performance, Political Style and Representation*, Stanford, CA: Stanford University Press.

Moore, M. and Ramsey, G. (2017) 'UK media coverage of the 2016 EU referendum campaign', London: Kings College Centre for the Study of Media, Communication and Power. Available from: https://www.kcl.ac.uk/policy-institute/assets/cmcp/uk-media-coverage-of-the-2016-eu-referendum-campaign.pdf [Accessed 1 March 2020].

Morphet, J. (2017) *Beyond Brexit? How to Assess the UK's Future*, Bristol: Policy Press.

Morris, S. (2018) 'New Plaid Cymru leader vows to guide Wales to independence', *The Guardian*, 28 September. Available from: https://www.theguardian.com/politics/2018/sep/28/new-plaid-cymru-leader-adam-price-leanne-wood-wales-independence [Accessed 2 February 2020].

Moskal, M. (2016) 'Spaces of not belonging: inclusive nationalism and education in Scotland', *Scottish Geographical Journal*, 132(1): 85–102.

Mouffe, C. (1999) 'Deliberative democracy or agonistic pluralism?', *Social Research*, 66: 745–58.

Mouffe, C. (2005) *On the Political*, London and New York: Routledge.

Mouffe, C. (2016) 'Democratic politics and conflict: an agonistic approach', *Política común*, 9(1). Available from: https://quod.lib.umich.edu/p/pc/12322227.0009.011/--democratic-politics-and-conflict-an-agonistic-approach?rgn=main;view=fulltext [Accessed 1 March 2020].

Mudde, C. (2010) 'The populist radical right: a pathological normalcy', *West European Politics*, 33(6): 1167–86.

Mudde, C. and Kaltwasser, C. (2013) 'Exclusionary vs. inclusionary populism: comparing contemporary Europe and Latin America', *Government and Opposition*, 48(2): 147–74.

Mudde, C. and Kaltwasser, C. (2017) *Populism: A Very Short Introduction*, Oxford: Oxford University Press.

Muthoo, A. (2019) 'Random acts of madness: all the things that Dominic Cummings is getting wrong about game theory', *The Independent*, 16 September. Available from: https://www.independent.co.uk/voices/brexit-dominic-cummings-game-theory-boris-johnson-parliament-supreme-court-a9106926.html [Accessed 2 February 2020].

Nelson, F. (2016) 'The deceptions behind George Osborne's Brexit report', *The Spectator* blogs, 18 April. Available from: https://blogs.spectator.co.uk/2016/04/the-deceptions-behind-george-osbornes-brexit-report/ [Accessed 1 March 2020].

Oborne, P. (2012) 'The right-wing agitators out to get David Cameron', *The Telegraph*, 18 April. Available from: https://www.telegraph.co.uk/news/politics/conservative/9211677/The-Right-wing-agitators-out-to-get-David-Cameron.html [Accessed 2 February 2020].

Oliver, C. (2016) *Unleashing Demons: The Inside Story of Brexit*, London: Hodder and Stoughton.

Osborne, G. (2016) 'Decision to leave EU comes at a price: it is £4,300 per family', *The Times*, 18 April. Available from: https://www.thetimes.co.uk/article/decision-to-leave-eu-comes-at-a-price-it-is-4-300-per-family-zfs372lf3 [Accessed 2 February 2020].

Pap, A. (2017) *Democratic Decline in Hungary: Law and Society in an Illiberal Democracy*, New York: Routledge.

Parker, A. (2016) 'Donald Trump, in Scotland, calls "Brexit" result "a great thing"', *New York Times*, 24 June. Available from: https://www.nytimes.com/2016/06/25/us/politics/donald-trump-scotland.html [Accessed 2 February 2020].

Parris, M. (2016) 'Six reasons to keep calm and vote Remain', *The Spectator*, 11 June. Available from: https://www.spectator.co.uk/2016/06/the-six-best-reasons-to-vote-in/ [Accessed 2 February 2020].

Parvin, P. (2018) 'Representing the people: British democracy in an age of political ignorance', *Political Studies Review*, 16(4): 265–78.

Patel, P. (2016) Speech to Women for Britain, 8 March. Available from: https://www.businessinsider.com/priti-patel-launches-women-for-britain-2016-3 [Accessed 2 February 2020].

Patel, P. (2019) Conservative conference speech, 1 October. Available from: https://www.conservativehome.com/parliament/2019/10/priti-patel-i-will-give-the-police-the-powers-they-need-to-defeat-crime-full-text-of-her-conference-speech.html [Accessed 2 February 2020].

Patten, C. (2019) 'Is Britain becoming a failed state?', *Project Syndicate*, 20 August. Available from: https://www.project-syndicate.org/commentary/britain-brexit-failed-state-by-chris-patten-2019-08?barrier=accesspaylog [Accessed 2 February 2020].

Payne, A. (2017) 'EU Parliament tells May: improve your offer to EU citizens or we'll block the Brexit deal', *Business Insider*, 10 July. Available from: https://uk.news.yahoo.com/eu-parliament-tells-may-improve-083905642.html [Accessed 2 February 2020].

Peck, T. (2017a) 'Arlene Foster writes to 27 EU leaders to categorically reject Northern Ireland staying in Customs Union', *The Independent*, 25 November. Available from: https://www.independent.co.uk/news/uk/politics/arlene-foster-brexit-customs-union-northern-ireland-dup-conference-a8075576.html [Accessed 2 February 2020].

Peck, T. (2017b) 'Nigel Farage would "pick up a rifle" if Brexit is not delivered', *The Independent*, 17 May. Available from: https://www.independent.co.uk/news/uk/politics/nigel-farage-brexit-rifle-pick-up-uk-eu-withdrawal-ukip-leader-liberal-democrat-a7741331.html [Accessed 2 February 2020].

Peston, R. (2017) Interview with Chris Patten, ITV, 16 July. Available from: https://www.youtube.com/watch?v=8ukvrr7wSjU [Accessed 2 February 2020].

Pettifor, A. (2016) 'Brexit and its consequences', *Globalizations*, 14(1): 1–6.

Phillips, J. (2019) 'Boris Johnson has unleashed a monstrous politics of fear, and only the people can stop him', *The Independent*, 2 September. Available from: https://www.independent.co.uk/voices/brexit-referendum-boris-johnson-parliament-final-say-jess-phillips-a9088241.html [Accessed 2 February 2020].

Phipps, C. (2016) 'EU referendum morning briefing: what we learned from Sturgeon v Johnson', *The Guardian*, 10 June. Available from: https://www.theguardian.com/politics/2016/jun/10/eu-referendum-morning-briefing-what-we-learned-sturgeon-johnson [Accessed 2 February 2020].

Piketty, T. (2014) *Capital in the Twenty-First Century*, Cambridge, MA: Belknap Press.

Plato (2009) *Gorgias, Menexenus, Protagoras*, ed. M. Schofield and trans. T. Griffith, Cambridge Texts in the History of Political Thought, Cambridge: Cambridge University Press.

Polanyi, K. (1944) *The Great Transformation: The Political and Economic Origins of Our Time*, Boston, MA: Beacon Press.

Powell, J. (2018) 'Northern Ireland could be the issue over which Brexit talks collapse', *The Independent*, 19 March. Available from: https://www.independent.co.uk/voices/brexit-northern-ireland-border-talks-collapse-uk-eu-david-davis-barnier-theresa-may-a8263731.html [Accessed 2 February 2020].

Press Association (2016) 'Nigel Farage: "Dawn is breaking over independent UK"', *The Telegraph*, 24 June. Available from: https://www.telegraph.co.uk/news/2016/06/24/nigel-farage-dawn-is-breaking-over-independent-uk/ [Accessed 1 March 2020].

Press Association (2019) 'Dominic Grieve: PM's rhetoric led directly to death threats', *The Guardian*, 17 August. Available from: https://www.theguardian.com/politics/2019/aug/17/dominic-grieve-pm-boris-johnson-rhetoric-led-directly-to-death-threats [Accessed 2 February 2020].

Proctor, K. (2019) 'Cameron accuses Johnson and Gove of behaving appallingly over Brexit', *The Guardian*, 13 September. Available from: https://www.theguardian.com/politics/2019/sep/13/david-cameron-accuses-boris-johnson-and-michael-gove-of-behaving-appallingly-over-brexit [Accessed 2 February 2020].

Pugh, M. (2010) *Speak for Britain! A New History of the Labour Party*, London: Bodley Head.

Quinn, B. (2019) 'Just 7% of UK public think government has handled Brexit well – study', *The Guardian*, 26 March. Available from: https://www.theguardian.com/politics/2019/mar/26/public-think-government-has-not-handled-brexit-well-study [Accessed 2 February 2020].

Ramet, S. and Adamovic, L. (1995) *Beyond Yugoslavia: Politics, Economics, and Culture in a Shattered Community*, Boulder, CO: Westview Press.

Ramsey, A. (2019) 'National Crime Agency finds "no evidence" of crimes committed by Arron Banks's Brexit campaign', *Open Democracy*, 25 September. Available from: https://www.opendemocracy.net/en/dark-money-investigations/national-crime-agency-finds-no-evidence-of-crimes-committed-by-arron-bankss-brexit-campaign [Accessed 2 February 2020].

Randerson, J. (2018) 'Donald Tusk: UK Brexit position is "pure illusion"', *Politico*, 23 February. Available from: https://www.politico.eu/article/donald-tusk-uk-brexit-position-is-pure-illusion/ [Accessed 2 February 2020].

Rayner, G. and Swinford, S. (2017) 'Theresa May accuses EU of trying to "deliberately" interfere in election', *The Telegraph*, 3 May. Available from: https://www.telegraph.co.uk/news/2017/05/03/theresa-may-accuses-eu-trying-deliberately-interfere-election/ [Accessed 2 February 2020].

Reid, A. and Dotto, C. (2019) 'Thousands of misleading Conservative ads side-step scrutiny thanks to Facebook policy', *First Draft*, [online] 6 December. Available from: https://firstdraftnews.org/latest/thousands-of-misleading-conservative-ads-side-step-scrutiny-thanks-to-facebook-policy/ [Accessed 2 February 2020].

Reisigl, M. and Wodak, R. (2009) 'The discourse-historical approach (DHA)', in R. Wodak and M. Meyer (eds) *Methods for Critical Discourse Analysis* (2nd revised edn), London: Sage, pp 87–121.

Rex, J. (1996) *Ethnic Minorities in the Modern Nation State*, London: Macmillan Press.

Richardson, J. and Ryder, A. (2012) *Gypsies and Travellers: Accommodation, Empowerment and Inclusion in British Society*, Bristol: Policy Press.

Ridge, S. (2019) Interview with Baroness Chakrabarti, *Sophy Ridge on Sunday*, Sky News, 8 September. Available from: https://www.youtube.com/watch?v=Pwkd4BE6JPk [Accessed 2 February 2020].

Rifkind, M. (2019) 'Times letters: Boris Johnson's threat to defy a no-confidence vote', *The Times*, 7 August. Available from: https://www.thetimes.co.uk/article/times-letters-johnson-s-threat-to-defy-a-no-confidence-vote-dgmcqppmt [Accessed 2 February 2020].

Rigby, H. (2018) 'For people suffering under austerity Corbyn is the answer, not the EU', *The Guardian*, 22 November. Available from: https://www.theguardian.com/commentisfree/2018/nov/22/austerity-corbyn-eu-brexit-peoples-vote [Accessed 2 February 2020].

Robinson, E. (2016) 'Radical nostalgia, progressive patriotism and Labour's "English problem"', *Political Studies Review*, 14(3): 378–87.

Rose, R. (2018) 'Referendum challenges to the EU's policy legitimacy – and how the EU responds', *Journal of European Public Policy*, 26(2): 207–25.

Rosman, A. and Rubel, P. (2006) 'Ethnonationalism, nationalism, empire: their origins and their relationship to power, conflict and culture building', *Global Bioethics*, 19(1): 55–71.

Ross, T. (2016) 'Nigel Farage: migrants could pose sex attack threat to Britain', *The Telegraph*, 4 June. Available from: https://www.telegraph.co.uk/news/2016/06/04/nigel-farage-migrants-could-pose-sex-attack-threat-to-britain/ [Accessed 2 February 2020].

Rousseau, J. (1762/2014) *The Social Contract*, London: Penguin Classics.

Ryder, A. (2017) *Sites of Resistance: Gypsies, Roma and Travellers in School, Community and the Academy*, London: Trentham Press.

Ryder, A. (2019) 'Brexit – time to pause, reflect and take a deep breath', *Open Labour*, [online] 21 September. Available from: https://openlabour.org/brexit-time-to-pause-reflect-and-take-a-deep-breath/ [Accessed 2 February 2020].

Ryder, A. and Taba, M. (2018) 'Roma and a social Europe: the role of redistribution, intervention and emancipatory politics', *The Journal of Poverty and Social Justice*, 26(1): 59–75.

Sabbagh, D. and Rankin, J. (2019) 'Boris Johnson wrongly denies stirring Turkey fears in Brexit campaign', *The Guardian*, 18 January. Available from: https://www.theguardian.com/politics/2019/jan/18/boris-johnson-falsely-denies-issuing-turkey-warning-in-brexit-campaign [Accessed 2 February 2020].

Saes, E. and Zucman, G. (2014) 'Wealth inequality in the United States since 1913: evidence from capitalized income tax data, National Bureau of Economic Research', Working Paper 20625. Available from: https://gabriel-zucman.eu/files/SaezZucman2014.pdf [Accessed 2 February 2020].

Said, E. (1978) *Orientalism*, New York: Pantheon Books.

Salter, B. (2018) 'When intellectuals fail? Brexit and hegemonic challenge', *Competition & Change*, 22(5): 467–87.

Sarup, M. (1991) 'Education and the ideologies of racism', in D. Gillborn and L. Billings (eds) *The RoutledgeFalmer Reader in Multicultural Education*, New York and London: Routledge and Falmer.

Saunders, R. (2018) 'A device of dictators and demagogues: renegotiation to referendum', in R. Saunders (ed) *Yes to Europe!: The 1975 Referendum and Seventies Britain*, Cambridge: Cambridge University Press, pp 63–98.

Savage, M. (2019) 'Civil war within people's vote campaign could derail a second referendum', *The Guardian*, 3 November. Available from: https://www.theguardian.com/politics/2019/nov/03/civil-war-in-peoples-vote-puts-at-risk-tactical-voting-for-referendum [Accessed 2 February 2020].

Schaap, A. (2006) 'Agonism in divided societies', *Philosophy & Social Criticism*, 32(2): 255–77.

Schaart, T. (2019) 'Donald Tusk: "Special place in hell" for those who backed Brexit with no plan', *Politico*, 2 June. Available from: https://www.politico.eu/article/__trashed-21/ [Accessed 2 February 2020].

Schelling, T. (1960) *The Strategy of Conflict*, Cambridge, MA: Harvard University Press.

Schindler, J. (2018) Interview with Jeremy Corbyn: 'We can't stop Brexit', *Der Spiegel*, 9 November. Available from: https://www.spiegel.de/international/europe/interview-with-labour-leader-corbyn-we-can-t-stop-brexit-a-1237594.html [Accessed 2 February 2020].

Scotto, T., Sander, D. and Reifler, J. (2017) 'The consequential nationalist–globalist policy divide in contemporary Britain: some initial analyses', *Journal of Elections, Public Opinion and Parties*, 28(1): 38–58.

Sculthorpe, T. (2016) 'Nigel Farage dismisses fury over his pro-Brexit immigration poster and claims it only sparked such a row because Labour MP Jo Cox was KILLED', *Daily Mail*, 19 June. Available from: https://www.dailymail.co.uk/news/article-3648946/I-shuddered-Michael-Gove-slams-Ukip-s-racist-poster-warning-immigration-breaking-point-defends-Vote-Leave-claims-Turkey-birth-rate.html [Accessed 2 February 2020].

Sculthorpe, T. (2017) 'An historic mistake: Sir John Major slams Brexit', *Daily Mail*, 27 February. Available from: https://www.dailymail.co.uk/news/article-4265008/Sir-John-Major-slams-Brexit-historic-mistake.html [Accessed 2 February 2020].

Seidler, V. (2018) *Making Sense of Brexit: Democracy, Europe and Uncertain Futures*, Bristol: Policy Press.

Shipman, T. (2016) *All Out War: The Full Story of How Brexit Sank Britain's Political Class*, London: Harper Collins.

Shipman, T. (2017) *Fall Out: A year of Political Mayhem*, London: HarperCollins Publishers.

Simmel, G. (1957) 'Fashion', *American Journal of Sociology*, 62(6): 541–58.

Singh, A. (2018) 'Business secretary reassures Tory Brexit hardliners after PM warned of election failure by Jacob Rees-Mogg', *The Independent*, 27 January. Available from: https://www.independent.co.uk/news/uk/politics/brexit-european-union-theresa-may-jacob-rees-mogg-david-davis-2022-general-election-latest-a8180911.html [Accessed 2 February 2020].

Skidelsky, R. (2015) 'George Osborne's cunning plan: how the chancellor's austerity narrative harmed recovery', *New Statesman*, 29 April. Available from: https://www.newstatesman.com/politics/2015/04/george-osborne-s-cunning-plan-how-chancellors-austerity-narrative-has-harmed [Accessed 2 February 2020].

Sky News (2016) Interview with Michael Gove by Faisal Islam, 3 June. Available from: https://www.youtube.com/watch?v=GGgiGtJk7MA [Accessed 1 March 2020].

Slack, J. (2016) 'Enemies of the people: fury over "out of touch" judges who have "declared war on democracy" by defying 17.4m Brexit voters and who could trigger constitutional crisis', *Daily Mail*, 3 November. Available from: https://www.dailymail.co.uk/news/article-3903436/Enemies-people-Fury-touch-judges-defied-17-4m-Brexit-voters-trigger-constitutional-crisis.html [Accessed 2 February 2020].

Smith, D.A. (1991) *National Identity*, London: Penguin.

Smith, G. (2000) 'Citizens' juries and deliberative democracy', *Political Studies*, 48: 51–65.

Smith, M. (2018) '"Britain was the only loser in World War II" says Nigel Farage', *Daily Mirror*, 18 April. Available from: https://www.mirror.co.uk/news/politics/britain-only-loser-world-war-12387975 [Accessed 2 February 2020].

Smith, M. and Jones, R. (2015) 'From big society to small state: conservatism and the privatisation of government', *British Politics*, 10(2): 226–48.

Smyth, P. (2017) 'Brexiteers are hooked on brinkmanship – and have been since the beginning', *Irish Times*, 19 October. Available from: https://www.irishtimes.com/news/world/europe/brexiteers-are-hooked-on-brinkmanship-and-have-been-since-the-beginning-1.3260731 [Accessed 2 February 2020].

Soubry, A. (2018) *Hansard*, Volume 642, Col 770, European Withdrawal Bill, [speech] 12 June. Available from: https://hansard.parliament.uk/Commons/2018-06-12/debates/3AC9EE4B-A84C-47D1-9519-80CEA3653807/EuropeanUnion(Withdrawal)Bill [Accessed 2 February 2020].

Starmer, K. (2018) Speech to Labour Party Conference, 25 September. Available from: https://labour.org.uk/press/keir-starmer-speaking-labour-party-conference-today/ [Accessed 2 February 2020].

Stewart, H. (2017) 'Michel Barnier raises UK hackles with speech about Isis and Brexit', *The Guardian*, 29 November. Available from: https://www.theguardian.com/politics/2017/nov/29/michel-barnier-raises-uk-hackles-with-speech-about-isis-and-brexit [Accessed 2 February 2020].

Stewart, H. (2018) 'Brexit: May to urge MPs not to "break faith" by demanding people's vote', *The Guardian*, 17 December. Available from: https://www.theguardian.com/politics/2018/dec/16/brexit-pm-to-urge-parliament-not-to-break-faith-with-the-people [Accessed 1 March 2020].

Stewart, H. and Elgot, J. (2018) 'Pro-Brexit Labour MPs expose rift over EEA membership', *The Guardian*, 11 June. Available from: https://www.theguardian.com/politics/2018/jun/11/pro-brexit-labour-mps-expose-partys-divisions-over-eea-membership [Accessed 2 February 2020].

Stiglitz, J. (1998) 'Redefining the role of the state – what should it do? How should it do it? And how should these decisions be made?' MITI Research Institute, [presentation] 17 March.

Stone, J. (2017a) 'Theresa May accuses Nicola Sturgeon of playing a "game" with second Scottish independence referendum', *The Independent*, 13 March. Available from: https://www.independent.co.uk/news/uk/politics/scottish-independence-referendum-second-nicola-sturgeon-theresa-may-response-a7627496.html [Accessed 2 February 2020].

Stone, J. (2017b) '"Britain is backtracking" on its Brexit divorce bill commitments, EU's chief negotiator warns', *The Independent*, 7 September. Available from: https://www.independent.co.uk/news/uk/politics/brexit-eu-divorce-bill-payment-michel-barnier-david-davis-backtracking-brussels-a7934296.html [Accessed 2 February 2020].

Stone, J. (2017c) 'EU "will not step back one millimetre" from defending citizens' rights during Brexit', *The Independent*, 30 August. Available from: https://www.independent.co.uk/news/uk/politics/brexit-eu-parliament-president-antonio-tajani-citizens-rights-to-remain-a7920681.html [Accessed 2 February 2020].

Stone, J. (2018a) 'Brexit: Tony Blair attacks right-wing press "cartel" over EU coverage', *The Independent*, 1 March. Available from: https://www.independent.co.uk/news/uk/politics/brexit-tony-blair-right-wing-press-cartel-eu-single-market-thatcherite-revolution-a8234836.html [Accessed 2 February 2020].

Stone, J. (2018b) 'Ukip to team up in "unholy alliance" with Steve Bannon's new far right European movement', *The Independent*, 28 July. Available from: https://www.independent.co.uk/news/uk/politics/steve-bannon-movement-ukip-brexit-a8464846.html [Accessed 2 February 2020].

Stone, J. (2019) 'Brexit will not get done by 2021, EU chief negotiator admits in leaked recording that blows hole in Boris Johnson promise', *The Independent*, 11 December. Available from: https://www.independent.co.uk/news/uk/politics/brexit-delay-boris-johnson-deal-general-election-eu-barnier-leak-deadline-a9242346.html [Accessed 2 February 2020].

Sturgeon, N. (2016) Plan to keep Scotland in the European Union, [speech] 28 June. Available from: https://www.commonspace.scot/articles/8711/full-speech-nicola-sturgeon-sets-out-plan-keep-scotland-european-union [Accessed 2 February 2020].

Sturgeon, N. (2017a) Nicola Sturgeon's statement on EU negotiations and Scotland's future, SNP, 27 June. Available from: https://www.snp.org/nicola-sturgeon-s-statement-on-eu-negotiations-and-scotland-s-future/ [Accessed 2 February 2020].

Sturgeon, N. (2017b) 'To limit the harm done by Brexit, stay in the EU single market', *The Guardian*, 2 December. Available from: https://www.theguardian.com/commentisfree/2017/dec/02/limit-brexit-harm-stay-single-market-theresa-may-confront-arch-brexiteers [Accessed 2 February 2020].

Sturgeon, N. (2018) Conference Speech, Glasgow, [speech] 9 October. Available from: https://www.bbc.com/news/av/uk-politics-45798267/in-full-nicola-sturgeon-s-speech-to-2018-snp-conference [Accessed 2 February 2020].

Sturgeon, N. (2019) Nicola Sturgeon's EU manifesto launch address, 17 May. Available from: https://www.snp.org/nicola-sturgeons-eu-manifesto-launch-address/ [Accessed 2 February 2020].

Sullivan, A. (2019) 'Boris's blundering brilliance', *New York Magazine*, 6 December. Available from: http://nymag.com/intelligencer/2019/12/boris-johnson-brexit.html [Accessed 2 February 2020].

Supreme Court Judgement (2019) (on the application of Miller) (Appellant) v The Prime Minister (Respondent) Cherry and others (Respondents) v Advocate General for Scotland (Appellant) (Scotland). 24 September. Available from: https://www.supremecourt.uk/cases/docs/uksc-2019-0192-judgment.pdf [Accessed 2 February 2020].

Susen, S. (2017) 'No exit from Brexit?', in W. Outhwaite (ed) *Brexit: Sociological Responses*, London and New York: Anthem Press, pp 153–82.

Sweeting, D. and Copus, C. (2012) 'Whatever happened to local democracy?' *Policy and Politics*, 40(1): 21–37.

Swinford, S. (2017) 'The Brexit mutineers: at least 15 Tory MPs rebel against leave date with threat to join forces with Labour', *The Telegraph*, 14 November. Available from: https://www.telegraph.co.uk/news/2017/11/14/nearly-20-tory-mps-threaten-rebel-against-brexit-date-brutal/ [Accessed 2 February 2020].

Syal, R. (2019a) 'Hammond voices concern PM may be trying to dupe MPs into backing no deal', *The Guardian*, 18 October. Available from: https://www.theguardian.com/politics/2019/oct/18/no-deal-brexit-still-possible-under-new-agreement-says-mp [Accessed 2 February 2020].

Syal, R. (2019b) 'Dominic Cummings accused of lying to undermine MPs', *The Guardian*, 2 October. Available from: https://www.theguardian.com/politics/2019/oct/02/dominic-cummings-accused-of-lying-to-undermine-mps-boris-johnson-benn-act-pmqs [Accessed 2 February 2020].

Syal, R. and O'Carroll, L. (2018) 'David Davis calls on ministers to rebel against Brexit deal', *The Guardian*, 14 October. Available from: https://www.theguardian.com/politics/2018/oct/14/david-davis-calls-on-ministers-to-rebel-against-brexit-deal [Accessed 2 February 2020].

Taggart, P. (2000) *Populism*, Buckingham: Open University Press.

Taggart, P. and Szczerbiak, A. (2018) 'Putting Brexit into perspective: the effect of the Eurozone and migration crises and Brexit on Euroscepticism in European states', *Journal of European Public Policy*, 25(8): 1194–1214.

Tajtel, H. and Turner, J.C. (1979) 'An integrative theory of intergroup conflict', in W.G. Austin and S. Worchel (eds) *The Social Psychology of Intergroup Relations*, Monterey, CA: Brooks/Cole Pub. Co.

Taylor, A. (2016) 'Obama's support for the E.U. is driving some Brits mad', *Washington Post*, 22 April. Available from: https://www.washingtonpost.com/news/worldviews/wp/2016/04/21/why-obamas-support-for-the-e-u-is-driving-some-brits-mad/ [Accessed 2 February 2020].

Taylor, R. (2017) 'Brexit is a prize within reach for the British left', London School of Economics and Political Science, [blog] 6 August. Available from: Stevens, Simon (2016) 'Brexit will put NHS at risk', BBC [News] [videoclip] 22 May. Available from: https://www.bbc.co.uk/programmes/p03vxmnv [Accessed 2 February 2020].

The Telegraph (2017) 'Brexit is a chance to set the wealth creators free', 30 March. Available from: https://www.telegraph.co.uk/opinion/2017/03/30/brexit-chance-set-wealth-creators-free/ [Accessed 6 April 2020].

Thompson, B. and Pickard, J. (2017) 'Concerns remain over how "Henry VIII powers" will affect Brexit', *Financial Times*, 12 September. Available from: https://www.ft.com/content/3e667c06-93d4-11e7-a9e6-11d2f0ebb7f0 [Accessed 2 February 2020].

Thrasher, M., Goodwin, M., Rallings, C. and Borisyuk, G. (2018) *Mobilising the 'People's Army' at the Grassroots: Examining Support for the UK Independence Party (UKIP) in English Local Elections*, Oxford: Oxford University Press.

Tilford, S. (2017a) 'The British and their exceptionalism', Centre of European Reform, [online] 3 May. Available from: https://www.cer.eu/insights/british-and-their-exceptionalism [Accessed 2 February 2020].

Tilford, S. (2017b) 'The limits to Labour's "constructive ambiguity" over Brexit', *Centre of European Reform*, [online] 6 July. Available from: https://www.cer.eu/insights/limits-labours-constructive-ambiguity-over-brexit [Accessed 2 February 2020].

Timothy, N. (2018) 'This is your Brexit Boudicca moment, Theresa… it's time to say: "On Your Way, Barnier" like "Up Yours, Delors"', *The Sun*, 5 October. Available from: https://www.thesun.co.uk/news/7501794/this-is-your-brexit-boudicca-moment-theresa-its-time-to-say-on-your-way-barnier-like-up-yours-delors/ [Accessed 2 February 2020].

Treanor, J. (2017) 'Darling: Brexit would not have happened without banking crisis', *The Guardian*, 13 September. Available from: https://www.theguardian.com/business/2017/sep/13/darling-brexit-banking-crisis [Accessed 2 February 2020].

Truger, A. (2013) 'Austerity in the Euro area: the sad state of economic policy in Germany and the EU', Working Paper 22/2013, IPE Working Papers, Institute for International Political Economy, HWR Berlin. Available from: https://econpapers.repec.org/paper/zbwipewps/222013.htm [Accessed 2 February 2020].

Tusk, D. (2016) Speech by President Donald Tusk at the European Policy Centre conference, European Commission, [speech] 13 October. Available from: https://www.consilium.europa.eu/hu/press/press-releases/2016/10/13/tusk-speech-epc/ [Accessed 2 February 2020].

Tusk, D. (2018) Speech by President Donald Tusk on receiving lifetime membership of the UCD Law Society in Dublin, European Council, 10 April. Available from: https://www.consilium.europa.eu/en/press/press-releases/2018/04/10/speech-by-president-donald-tusk-at-the-university-college-dublin-law-society/ [Accessed 2 February 2020].

UKIP (2015) *Believe in Britain*: UKIP manifesto. Available from: https://www.slideshare.net/miquimel/the-ukip-manifesto-2015-believe-in-britain [Accessed 6 April 2020].

UK Statistics Authority (2016) UK Statistics Authority statement on the use of official statistics on contributions to the European Union, 27 May. Available from: https://www.statisticsauthority.gov.uk/news/uk-statistics-authority-statement-on-the-use-of-official-statistics-on-contributions-to-the-european-union/ [Accessed 1 March 2020].

Umunna, C. (2017) 'Single market membership is crucial to Labour's mission', *Prospect*, 27 June. Available from: https://www.prospectmagazine.co.uk/politics/single-market-membership-is-a-win-win-for-britain [Accessed 3 March 2020].

Van Dijk, T. (1998) 'What is political discourse analysis?', *Belgian Journal of Linguistics*, 11: 11–52.

Varoufakis, Y. (2017) 'A new deal to save Europe', *Social Europe*, [online] 25 January. Available from: https://www.socialeurope.eu/new-deal-save-europe [Accessed 2 February 2020].

Virdee, S. and McGeever, B. (2018) 'Racism, crisis, Brexit', *Ethnic and Racial Studies*, 41(10): 1802–19.

Waever, O. (1995) 'Securitization and de-securitization', in R. Lipschutz (ed) *On Security*, New York: Columbia University Press, pp 46–86.

Wagstyl, S. (2017) 'Angela Merkel warns Britain over Brexit "illusions"', *Financial Times*, [online] 27 April. Available from: https://www.ft.com/content/4deb1d40-2b3c-11e7-9ec8-168383da43b7 [Accessed 2 February 2020].

Walker, P. (2019) 'PM's Brexit speech changed after Welsh devolution claim disproved', *The Guardian*, 14 January. Available from: https://www.theguardian.com/politics/2019/jan/14/theresa-may-claim-that-all-parties-accepted-welsh-devolution-questioned [Accessed 2 February 2020].

Walker, P., O'Carroll, L. and Asthana, A. (2018) 'Irish prime minister dismisses Theresa May's border idea', *The Guardian*, 5 March. Available from: https://www.theguardian.com/politics/2018/mar/05/post-brexit-irish-border-could-be-like-us-canada-says-may [Accessed 2 February 2020].

Wall, S. (2008) *A Stranger in Europe: Britain and the EU from Thatcher to Blair*. Oxford: Oxford University Press.

Wallerstein, I. (2000) *The Essential Wallerstein*, New York: The New York Press.

Walsh, J. (2014) 'A British politician lost her job over a tweet: how to explain it to someone outside the UK', *The Guardian*, 21 November. Available from: https://www.theguardian.com/politics/2014/nov/21/emily-thornberry-resignation-explain-outside-britain [Accessed 2 February 2020].

Waterson, J. (2019) 'Media plans drawn: the battle to influence the UK electorate', *The Guardian*, 7 November. Available from: https://www.theguardian.com/politics/2019/nov/07/media-plans-drawn-the-battle-to-influence-the-uk-electorate [Accessed 2 February 2020].

Watt, N. (2012) 'David Cameron becomes Britain's new Harold Wilson over EU referendum', *The Guardian*, 2 July. Available from: https://www.theguardian.com/politics/wintour-and-watt/2012/jul/02/davidcameron-eu [Accessed 2 March 2020].

Watts, J. (2016) 'Theresa May's UK Brexit talks fall flat as Nicola Sturgeon brands them "deeply frustrating"', *Belfast Telegraph*, 24 October. Available from: https://www.independent.co.uk/news/uk/politics/brexit-theresa-may-nicola-sturgeon-uk-talks-eu-withdrawal-a7378036.html [Accessed 2 February 2020].

Watts, J. (2017a) 'Boris Johnson warns UK could become a "vassal state" if it accepts EU's Brexit plans', *The Independent*, 17 December. Available from: https://www.independent.co.uk/news/uk/politics/boris-johnson-brexit-latest-vassal-state-philip-hammond-a8115041.html [Accessed 2 February 2020].

Watts, J. (2017b) 'Michael Heseltine: hard Brexiteers have "betrayed" the achievements of Conservative governments', *The Independent*, 17 December. Available from: https://www.independent.co.uk/news/uk/politics/brexit-latest-michael-heseltine-betrayed-hard-eu-brussels-mutineers-a8115111.html [Accessed 2 February 2020].

Watts, J. (2017c) 'British politics "is going badly wrong"! As MPs face abuse and death threats, warns Nicky Morgan', *The Independent*, 18 December. Available from: https://www.independent.co.uk/news/uk/politics/uk-politics-mp-death-threats-abuse-media-newsppaers-nicky-morgan-brexit-remain-tory-conservative-a8116156.html [Accessed 2 February 2020].

Weaver, M. and Waterson, J. (2018) 'Leave.EU fined £70,000 over breaches of electoral law: campaign's chief officer referred to police after inquiry finds it broke referendum spending limit', *The Guardian*, 11 May. Available from: https://www.theguardian.com/politics/2018/may/11/leaveeu-fined-70k-breaches-of-electoral-law-eu-referendum [Accessed 2 February 2020].

Weber, M. (1958) 'The three types of legitimate rule', *Berkeley Publications in Society and Institutions*, 4(1): 1–11.

Weekes, J. (1990) 'The value of difference', in J. Rutherford (ed) *Identity: Community, Culture, Difference*, London: Lawrence and Wishart, pp 88–100.

Westlake, M. (2017) 'The increasing inevitability of that referendum', in W. Outhwaite (ed) *Brexit: Sociological Responses*, London and New York: Anthem Press, pp 3–18.

Whyman, P. (2018) *The Left Case for Brexit: Active Government for an Independent UK*, London: Civitas.

Widdecombe, A. (2019) Address to the European Parliament, [speech] 4 July, Strasbourg. Available from: https://www.theguardian.com/politics/2019/jul/04/ann-widdecombe-likens-brexit-to-emancipation-of-slaves [Accessed 2 February 2020].

Wiener, A. (2017). 'The impossibility of disentangling integration', in W. Outhwaite (ed) *Brexit: Sociological Responses*, London and New York: Anthem Press, pp 139–52.

Wiesner, C., Haapala, T. and Palonen, K. (2017) *Debates, Rhetoric and Political Action: Practices of Textual Interpretation and Analysis*, London: Palgrave Macmillan.

Wilkins, J. (2018) 'Junker and Tusk: Britain could still change its mind on Brexit', *Politics Home*, 16 January. Available from: https://www.politicshome.com/news/europe/eu-policy-agenda/brexit/news/92106/juncker-and-tusk-britain-could-still-change-its-mind [Accessed 2 February 2020].

Wilkinson, R. and Pickett, K. (2009) *The Spirit Level: Why More Equal Societies Almost Always Do Better*, London: Allen Lane.

Williams, B. (2017) 'Theresa May's premiership: continuity or change?', *Political Insight*, 8(1): 10–13.

Williams, B. (2018) 'Brexit: the links between domestic and foreign policy', *Political Insight*, 9(2): 36–9.

Williams, M.C. (2011) 'Securitization and the liberalism of fear', *Security Dialogue*, 42(4–5): 453–63.

Williams, Z. (2016) 'Paddy Ashdown: I turned to my wife and said, it's not our country anymore', *The Guardian*, 16 September. Available from: https://www.theguardian.com/politics/2016/sep/16/paddy-ashdown-i-turned-to-my-wife-and-said-its-not-our-country-any-more [Accessed 2 February 2020].

Winlow, S., Hall, S. and Treadwell, J. (2016) *The Rise of the Right: English Nationalism and the Transformation of Working-Class Politics*, Bristol: Bristol University Press.

Wintour, P. (2018) 'German ambassador: Second World War image of Britain has fed Euroscepticism', *The Guardian*, 29 January. Available from: https://www.theguardian.com/politics/2018/jan/29/german-ambassador-peter-ammon-second-world-war-image-of-britain-has-fed-euroscepticism [Accessed 2 February 2020].

Wodak, R. (2015) *The Politics of Fear*, Thousand Oaks, CA: Sage

Wodak, R. (2018) 'Discourse and European integration', Working Paper, Freie Universität Berlin. Available from: https://www.polsoz.fu-berlin.de/en/v/transformeurope/publications/working_paper/wp/wp86/WP_86_Wodak_Druck_und_Web.pdf [Accessed 6 April 2020].

Wodak, R. and Meyer, M. (eds) (2001) *Methods of Critical Discourse Analysis*, London: Sage.

Wood, M., Corbett, J. and Flinders, M. (2016) 'Just like us: everyday celebrity politicians and the pursuit of popularity in an age of anti-politics', *The British Journal of Politics and International Relations*, 18(3): 581–98.

Woodcock, A. (2019) 'Brexit: UK faces "full blown constitutional crisis" if no deal forced through', *The Independent*, 5 October. Available from: https://www.independent.co.uk/news/uk/politics/brexit-no-deal-leave-eu-boris-johnson-dominic-cummings-jeremy-corbyn-a9040521.html [Accessed 2 February 2020].

Woodward, K. (ed) (2000) *Questioning Identity: Gender, Class, Nation*, London and New York: Routledge.

Woodward, K. (2002) *Identity and Difference*, London: Sage.

Wright, O. and Coates, S. (2018) 'Theresa May's Chequers plan is hated more than the poll tax, says Justine Greening', *The Times*, 3 September. Available from: https://www.thetimes.co.uk/article/theresa-mays-chequers-plan-is-hated-more-than-the-poll-tax-says-justine-greening-sfj0z7k6s [Accessed 2 February 2020].

Young, D. and McHugh, M. (2018) 'Juncker warns Irish border agreement must be part of Britain's Brexit deal', *The Irish News*, 21 June. Available from: https://www.irishnews.com/news/brexit/2018/06/21/news/no-brexit-deal-without-border-agreement-says-simon-coveney-1361572/ [Accessed 2 February 2020].

Young, J. (1999) *The Exclusive Society: Social Exclusion, Crime and Difference in Late Modernity*, London: Sage.

Young, J. (2011) 'Moral panics and the transgressive other', *Crime, Media, Culture*, 7(3): 245–58.

Zagar, I. (2010) 'Topoi in critical discourse analysis', *Lodz Papers in Pragmatics*, 6(1): 3–27.

Zarefsky, D. (2011) 'History of public discourse studies', in A. Lunsford, K. Lunsford, W. Eberly and R. Eberly (eds) *The Sage Handbook of Rhetorical Studies*, New York and Delhi: Sage.

Zelizer, B. (2018) 'Resetting journalism in the aftermath of Brexit and Trump', *European Journal of Communication*, 33(2): 140–56.

Zimmerman, D. (2017) 'This is what we really think about Brexit in Germany', *The Independent*, 10 August. Available from: https://www.independent.co.uk/voices/brexit-germany-germans-reaction-britain-uk-scotland-leaving-european-union-nationalism-separation-a7885931.html [Accessed 1 March 2020].

Index

Note: Page numbers for tables appear in italics.

9/11 terror attacks 29

A
abuse 116, 135
academics 174
Adamovic, L. 110
ad hominem *12*, 76, 154
age, effect of, on Leave vote 31
Aggregate IQ 55, 56
agonism 169, 171, 172
Allen, Heidi 171
Ammon, Peter 132
anomic anxiety 36
Another Europe is Possible 101
anti-racism 29
antithesis *12*, 103
anxiety 8, 34, 35, 36, 37, 45
anxiety trauma 24
Arendt, Hannah 36, 163
argumentation 9–10
argumentative topoi *11*
Article 50 58, 63, 90, 122, 159
Ashcroft, Lord 29, 127, 157
Ashdown, Paddy 1
assimilation 28
audit culture 26
austerity 24, 29–30, 37, 59, 107, 176, 177
  and the EU 39, 143
Austria 130
authoritarianism 35, 84, 152
authoritarian populism 166–7
authoritarians 33
autonomy 27, 43, 60, 64, 66, 126, 140
  and civil society 173
  and EU 133, 134

B
the backstop 80, 81–2, 137, 146, 149
Baker, Steve 71
Balzacq, T. 8
Banks, Arron 1, 44, 49, 55, 56
Bannon, Steve 36, 125, 140, 177
Barnier, Michel 130, 131, 132, 133–4, 135, 136, 162–3
  cherry picking is not an option 137
  on no deal 139
  on unity of EU 140
Baron, John 148
Barroso, José Manuel 117
Batten, Gerard 123–4
BBC 55
Beck, U. 3
Beckett, Margaret 105
Benn, Tony 20, 88
Benn Act 149–50
Bevin, Ernest 87
Bickerstaffe, Rodney 5
Big Society 30
biography 27
Blackford, Ian 115–16
Black Wednesday 21
Blair, Tony 29, 38, 88, 91, 97–8
Blake, R. 63–4
Bloomsberg speech 65
bombast 36
bomb metaphor 47
bonding rhetoric 167–8
border, Irish 60, 80, 81, 94, 119, 137
Boudicca 79
boundaries 43
Bourdieu, Pierre 3, 27
Boyle, N. 23
Bradshaw, Ben 56

Brady, Sir Graham 82–3
'breaking point' poster 51–2, 122
Bretton Woods agreement 25
Brexit 26, 31, 35, 66–85, 90–107, 111, 127
　and Northern Ireland 118–19
　and Scotland 114, 115–17
　and Wales 117–18
Brexiteers 115, 135, 136
Brexit nationalism 27, 36, 40, 126, 162, 179
Brexit negotiations 14, 134–40, 155
Brexit Party 109, 111, 124–5, 146, 157, 160, 175
　2019 election result 161
　and European elections 104
　and Labour 89, 105
Brexit referendum 22, 23, 41–57, 112
Brexit withdrawal agreement 80–2
Bridgen, Andrew 92
bridging rhetoric 167–8
Bright, John 168
Britannia Unchained (Kwarteng et al) 148
British democracy, state of 52–7
British exceptionalism *see* exceptionalism
British identity 64, 88, 120, 175
　see also identity
British imperialism 120, 121, 127
Britishness 29, 32–3
British Social Attitudes survey 33
British sovereignty *see* sovereignty
Brown, Gordon 65, 88, 153, 175
Brubaker, R. 2
Bruges speech, 1988 20
burden 28, 29, 93
Burke, Edmund 37
Butcher, J. 32

C
Cable, Vince 70, 159
Cambridge Analytica 55
Cameron, David 22, 38, 39–40, 42, 44, 85, 134
　and Big Society 30
　and one nation approach 65
　on prorogation 150
　and Remain campaign 45, 46–7
　resigned 53
candidate selection processes 171
Cardiff University 157
Cash, Sir William 72
Central East European states 29, 130

Central European University 179
centre left 22
centre right 22, 162
centrist Labour MPs 151–2
Ceyhan, A. 7
chains of equivalence 173
Chakrabarti, Baroness Shami 122, 153
Change UK 104
chauvinism 29, 35
Chequers' proposal 78–80, 123, 139
cherry picking 137, 138
'chicken game' 145
Chilcot Inquiry 38
Chilton, P. 50
Christians, fundamentalist 172
Chu, Ben 96
Churchill, Winston 17–18
citizenship, inclusive 112
citizens' rights 136–7
civic education 173–4
civic nationalism 111, 112, 113, 175
civil society 8, 173, 179
Clarke, Kenneth 76–7, 149
class 31–2
　see also working class
Clean Break Brexiteers 66, 71–5, 78, 80, 81–2, 83, 84, 137
Clegg, Nick 121
Cleverly, James 151
cliff edge metaphor 76
coal 18, 20
coalition government 29–30
coercion 10, 167
Coffey, Ann 53
Cohen, P. 27
collective identity 27–33
colonies 19, 27
common market 18
'Common Market 2' 97
communitarianism 30
community action 30
Confederation of British Industry (CBI) 44, 102, 166
connotation 12
Conservative government 18
Conservative Home 78
Conservative Party 5, 20–2, 42, 60, 63–85, 160–1
Conservatives
　Scottish 114
　and Stronger In 45
Conservatives for Managed Migration 93
Conservative supporters 31

constructive ambiguity 94, 101, 107
contextualization 10, *12*, 46, 47, 74, 94, 130
continental model 171
Cooper, Yvette 178
Corbyn, Jeremy 22, 73, 88, 89–93, 95, 99, 147
  and Blair 98
  on Brexit 106–7
  on customs union 94
  on EU Withdrawal Bill 102
  and no-confidence motion against 53
  on 'race to the bottom' 153–4
  as Remainer 46
  and second referendum 158–9
  on unity government 155–6
  won leadership contest 58, 178
Corbynite left 151–2
core countries 26
core Europe 142
Corns Laws, repeal of, 1846 63
corporate elites 90
Cortes, M. 102–3
cosmopolitanism 106, 110, 111, 129
Council of Europe (CoE) 17
counternarratives 82, 173
counter-public sphere 8, 55
COVID-19 180–1
Cox, Jo 52, 152
crisis 24, 25, 26, 162
crisis of legitimation 35
critical consciousness 8
critical discourse analysis (CDA) 9–10, *12*, 177
critical multiculturalism 175
critical pedagogy 180
critical thinking/critical thought 6, 174
Crosby, Lynton 5, 45, 59
Cruddas, Jon 105–6
cultural nationalism 112
cultural trauma 34
culture 27, 118
Cummings, Dominic 43–4, 52, 55, 58, 85, 146, 150
customs union 58, 60, 66, 68, 84, 93–4
  and Northern Ireland 137, 151
Czech Republic 38, 140

D

Daily Mail 42, 51, 58, 59, 77, 82
Daily Telegraph 77

danger 47, 81, 105, 152
dark money 56
Darling, Alistair 24
Davis, David 14, 57, 58–9, 78, 81
decentralization 30
decolonialization 19
de Gaulle, General Charles 19
deindustrialization 89
Delanty, G. 110
delegitimization 10, *12*
deliberative democracy 169–72
Delors, Jacques 20, 21
Deltapoll 78
demagoguery 5
democracy 37, 52–7, 76, 100, 168–70
Democratic Unionist Party (DUP) 60, 81, 118
Denham, John 175
Denmark 113
Dennison, J. 120
deregulation 25, 69, 70
Der Spiegel 103
desecuritization 8
de Zoete, Henry 55
difference *13*
discourse analysis 9–14
discourse historical approach *12*
disintegration, European 130
diversity 28, 29, 30
'dog whistle politics' 54
doing and not just saying *12*
donations, political 174
Dorling, Danny 31
'Double Movement' 24
DUP (Democratic Unionist Party) 82, 118–19, 151

E

economic crisis 6, 24, 25, 40, 64, 84, 142
  see also financial crisis, 2008
economic dangers 46–7
economic elites 25, 26, 45, 74
economic fears 45
economic inequality 176
economic justice 24
economic nationalism 92
The Economist 54
Eden, Anthony 19
education, effect of, on Leave vote 31, 32
EEC (European Economic Community) 18, 19–20, 87, 88
Egypt 19

225

Electoral Commission 44, 45, 56
elites 8, 35, 45, 53, 69, 70, 73
   corporate 90
   economic 25, 26, 45, 74
   European 131
   metropolitan liberal 30, 45, 149
   political 23–4, 35, 36, 38, 39, 110, 141
   and Tea Party 85
elitism 36, 150
Elwes, J. 121
empire 23, 32, 75–6, 121
   see also imperialism
employment 25
'end of history' 26
England, and exclusionary nationalism 112
English Defence League 30
English exceptionalism *see* exceptionalism
English identity 32–3
   see also identity
English nationalism 69, 89, 120, 165, 175
Englishness 33, 165
entrepreneurialism 25
the establishment 44–5
ethnic groups 28–9
ethnicity 28
ethos *12*
EU (European Union) 38–40, 129–43
   agreed to an extension to Brexit 155
   on the backstop 82
   Brexit negotiations 134–40
   and Brexit withdrawal agreement 80
   and coronavirus 181
   and corporate elites 90
   as folk devils 35
   frustrated by the British Government's procrastination 78
   image of in Leave campaign 49
   and left Euroscepticism 95–6
   and Northern Ireland 119
   political elites 131
   project to create a European federal state 69
   rejected Chequers' proposal 79
   and Scotland 117
   and social Europe 177
   as supranationalist project 111
   and Thatcherites 64

EU citizens' rights 136–7
euro currency 88
European Coal and Steel Community (ECSC) 18
European Communities Act 1972 58, 61
European disintegration 130
European elections 104, 124
European elites 131
European Exchange Rate Mechanism 21
European Fiscal Compact 38
European Free Trade Association (EFTA) 18
European identity 33
European Parliament 38
European Project 39, 133
European Research Group (ERG) 71, 82, 148
European Union Withdrawal Bill 58, 61, 80–1, 102, 103, 115–16, 155
   and Cash 72
   and Johnson 147, 163
Europe as a future direction 76
Europhiles 32
Euroscepticism 23, 62, 65, 95
Eurosceptic market liberals 64–5
Eurosceptics 21–2, 32
eurozone 21, 30, 130
exceptionalism 29, 32, 127, 132, 162, 165, 175
   and imperialism 120
   and loss of empire 23
   and Second World War 18
exclusion 110, 153
exclusionary nationalism 111, 112, 119–21
exigency *12*
Exiting the EU Select Committee 84
expression structures *12*
extremism 82, 157

F
Facebook 158
face work *12*
fair play 175
Farage, Nigel 1, 44, 51, 52–3, 56, 120–3, 124
   withdrew Brexit Party candidates in Conservative-held seats 157, 160
far-right political groupings 28
fascism 24, 36, 110
Favell, A. 2–3

INDEX

fear 8, 45, 46, 50, 139
fecklessness 25, 30
feminism 31
field 3
Field, Frank 97
fill in 12
financial costs, personal, and Brexit 47
financial crisis, 2008 24, 26, 29, 37–8, 111, 130
  and Greece 96
  legacy of in COVID-19 pandemic 180
financial political donations 174
First Draft 158
Fiscal Compact 38
Fischer, Joschka 34, 60
Fixed Term Parliament Act 155
Flint, Caroline 97
folk devils 34, 35
foodbanks 30
Foot, Michael 88, 170
Forester, J. 171–2
former Yugoslavia 110–11
Foster, Arlene 118
Foucault, M. 8, 9
Fourastié, Jean 25
four freedoms 133, 137, 138
Fox, Liam 57, 74–5
frames 6–7, 8, 46
France 19, 87, 130, 141
Fraser, N. 173
freedom of movement 39–40, 42, 71, 93, 101, 138, 148–9
free market 64
free trade 64, 73–4, 77
Freire, Paulo 180
Fukuyama, Francis 26, 110
full employment 25
fundamentalist Christians 172

G
Gaitskell, Hugh 87
Gamal Abdel Nasser 19
game theory 145–6, 160, 161
Gans, H.J. 173
GDP 47–8
Gellner, E. 110
General Elections
  2015 112
  2017 58–60, 114
  2019 155, 157–61, 165
genre 12
Germany 23, 24, 38, 96, 130, 142
'get Brexit done' 150, 152, 158, 162

Giddens, A. 33–4, 38, 107
Girling, Julie 85
'global Britain' 69
globalism 126
globalization 110, 130
global tax 176
Glorious Thirty 4, 25, 172, 176
Goffman, E. 111
Good Friday Agreement 80, 137
Gorgias (Plato) 167
Gove, Michael 42–3, 44, 48–9, 53, 57, 62, 148
  on Turkey 51
Great Depression, 1930s 24
Greece 30, 96
Green, Damian 78
Greenland 113
Greens 160
Grieve, Dominic 77, 152
Gross, N. 3
'in' group 43
growth, economic 25, 49, 172, 176
Guardian 44, 115
Guinan, J. 95
Gunster, Gerry 55
Gypsies 4–5

H
Habermas, Jürgen 8, 35, 38–9, 131, 170, 172, 179
Hacked Off 173
Hague, William 21, 65
Hammond, Philip 148, 149
Hanna, T. 95
hard border 60, 94, 119, 137
hard Brexit 60, 109, 123, 135, 138, 139, 155
  and Blair 98
  and Clean Break Brexiteers 71
  and Confederation of British Industry 102
  and Labour 90
  and one nation Conservatives 75
  and Scotland 113, 117
  and Sinn Fein 118
  and Soubry 76
hard Brexiteers 136, 146
Hardheaded Brexiteers 66–71
Harman, Harriet 45
hate crimes 53
having one's cake and eating it 137–8
Heath, Edward 19–20
hegemonic power 8, 9

hegemony 22, 26, 85, 107, 140, 168, 180
　Germany 23, 38, 96
'Henry VIII powers' 61
Heseltine, Michael 21, 76
hierarchicalism 123, 125
hierarchy 36, 43, 48, 79
history 124, 146, 153
HIV/AIDS care 172
Hodge, Margaret 53
Hoey, Kate 97, 99
Hogan, Phil 135, 142
household income 47–8
House of Commons Exiting the EU Select Committee 84
housing 25
Howard, Michael 5, 21–2, 65
human rights 24
Human Rights Act 1998 175
Hungarian Academy of Science 179
Hungary 2, 6, 130, 140, 179–80
Hunt, David 79
Huntington, S.P. 110
hyperglobalism 6, 68–70, 73–4, 148, 176
hysteria 34, 35

I
identarianism 111
identity 8, 27–33, 37, 85, 109–10, 129–30, 174–5
　British 64, 88, 120
　and migrants 7
　national 36, 70–1, 76
　and social identity theory 112–13
　working class 89
ideological fervour 64
idioms 13, 137–8
idleness 30
immigration 50, 54
　see also migration
immigration crisis, 2015 39, 42, 51–2
imperialism 120, 121, 127
　see also empire
inclusion 110
inclusive citizenship 112
income, household 47–8
independence, Scottish 113–14, 127
The Independent 152
Independent Press Standards Organisation (IPSO) 173
indicative votes 84
individualism 35, 64, 98
inflation 25, 64, 69

insinuation 12, 50, 130–1
integration 29
integrity 68, 78, 162
interdiscursivity 12
internationalism 96
International Monetary Fund 26
Iraq 38
Ireland
　Northern 60, 80, 94, 118–19, 137, 146, 151
　Republic 80, 137, 141
irony 12, 52–3, 56, 58, 76, 102–3
Islamophobia 29
Israel 25
Italy 126, 142

J
Jenkins, Roy 28, 41
jingoism 36
'jobs-first Brexit' 91
Johnson, Alan 45–6
Johnson, Boris 42–3, 52, 53, 73, 135, 145–8, 149–52
　and 2019 election result 161, 165
　appointed Foreign Secretary 57
　appointed Prime Minister 85
　on the backstop 81
　on Brexit in wake of COVID-19 pandemic 181
　on Brexit withdrawal agreement 81
　and Clean Break Brexiteers 71, 72
　and Corbyn 153–4
　desire to 'reunite' the country 163
　and 'get Brexit done' 157–8, 162
　on hung parliament 159
　on Obama 48
　resigned from May's government 78
　on scrapping of the social chapter 74
　sought Brexit extension 155
　on Turkey 51
　and Vote Leave 44
Juncker, Jean-Claude 59, 135, 136, 137, 138–9, 141
justice 74, 106, 116

K
kairos 13, 106
Kaiser, Brittany 55
Kaldor, Mary 98–9
Kaufman, E. 29
Kavanagh, Trevor 48
Kennedy, President 19

INDEX

Keynesian economics 25
Kinnock, Neil 20, 88
Kinnock, Stephen 97
Koselleck, R. 34
Kuhn, Thomas 2

L

labour, low-skilled and low-paid 29
Labour Europhiles 89, 97–8
Labour government 18, 21–2
Labour Party 4, 5–6, 20, 30, 58, 59–60, 87–107
   2019 election result 160, 161
   agreed to election 157
   no-confidence motion against Jeremy Corbyn 53
   remain campaign group 45–6
   and second referendum 158–9
   on unity government 155–6
Laclau, E. 168, 173
Lammy, David 100
language 10, 13–14
Lavery, Ian 99, 104–5
Lawson, Nigel 176
leap into the dark 46, 47
Leave campaign 50–2, 55
   see also Vote Leave
Leave.EU 44–5, 50, 51, 55, 56, 120
Leavers 46, 48–9, 53
Leave vote 29, 31, 32, 33, 89, 127, 157
left Euroscepticism 20, 22, 95
left nationalism 96
legal rationalism 142
legitimation *13*, 99, 100
legitimization 10
Leonard, Richard 113
Le Pen, Marine 130
lessons learnt 124, 153
Letta, Enrico 141–2
Letwin, Sir Oliver 154–5
level playing field commitments 80, 139, 147
Leveson, Lord 173
Levido, Isaac 158
Lexiteers 22, 88, 95–7, 105
Leyen, Ursula von der 177
LGBTQ activists 172
liberal democracy 26, 28
Liberal Democrats 65, 104, 151–2, 156, 157, 159, 160
   2019 election result 161
liberal metropolitan elite 30, 45, 149
liberal representative democracy 56–7
liberal values 121
liberal world order 24–5
libertarians 33
Lis, Jonathan 94, 167
Lisbon Treaty 133
living standards 25
logos *13*
Loughborough University Centre for Research in Communication and Culture 159
low-skilled and low-paid labour 29
Lucardie, P. 162

M

Maastricht Treaty 21, 64
MacDonald, Ramsay 84
Macmillan, Harold 19
Macron, Emmanuel 141, 142
MacShane, D. 54
'madman theory' 145–6
Mair, Thomas 52
Major, John 21, 35, 64
managed migration 93, 97
Manichaean dichotomies *13*, 34, 35, 43, 118, 124
the market 37, 64
market fundamentalism 26
market globalism 126
marketization 26
market liberals 64
Marr, Andrew 92–3
Mason, Paul 105, 106, 156–7
May, Theresa 57–8, 59, 61, 62, 66, 69–71, 134
   on Article 50 63
   and Brexit/EU Withdrawal Bill 80–1, 102, 103
   and Chequers' proposal 78–9, 139
   and Clean Break Brexiteers 74
   and customs union 93–4
   and DUP 60, 118
   and EU negotiations 135, 137
   and Farage 123
   and Labour 90
   Lancaster House speech 67–8
   resignation announcement 84
   and SNP 113
   vote of confidence 83
McCluskey, Len 102, 104–5
McDonald, Mary Lou 118
McDonnell, John 88, 90, 102, 104
McGrory, James 159
McVey, Esther 81
meaningful votes (MV) 82, 83–4

means testing 30
media 8, 20, 21, 37, 45, 77, 172–3
   attacked Cameron's deal 42
   on Corbyn 159
   on Europe 131
   and moral panics 35
   referendum campaign coverage 54–5
   tabloids 5, 21, 45, 59, 131
meritocracy 70
Merkel, Angela 134
metaphors *13*, 43, 48, 102, 138
   bomb 47
   cliff edge 76
   suicide vest 81–2
metropolitan liberal elite 30, 45, 149
'Mexican Standoff' 160
Meyer, M. 3
middle class 32
migrants 7, 31, 35
migration 27–8, 30, 37, 42–3, 57, 71, 137
   crisis in Europe 39
   in the EU 40
   and Labour 92–3, 103–4
   and Leave campaign 29, 33, 50, 51–2
   and Patel 149
   post Brexit 166
   and Remain 45
   and UKIP 120
migration crisis, 2015 39, 42, 51–2
Miliband, Ed 107
Miller, Gina 58
Milne, Seumas 105
misrepresentation, and language 10
modals *13*
modernity 33–4
modernization 20, 76, 111, 121
Momentum 101
monetary union 64
Monnet, Jean 18
monoculturalism 27, 32, 111, 129, 132, 165, 175
   and Englishness 33
   and May 70–1
moral panics 34, 35
moral values 64
Moran, Layla 125
Mordaunt, Penny 51
Morgan, Nicky 77
Mouffe, C. 168, 171, 173
'The Movement' 125, 177

multiculturalism 28, 29, 30, 31, 126, 127, 174
   and identity 175
Murphy, Karie 105
Muslims 29, 31, 51
mythopoesis 147

N
NatCen 103
National Crime Agency (NCA) 56
National Front 28
national identity 36, 70–1, 76, 109–10
nationalism 20, 92, 96, 109–27, 129
   Brexit 31, 35, 179
   English 69, 89, 165, 175
nationalist populism 36, 125–6, 174, 176
nationalists 151–2
national populist right 162
national uniqueness 18–19, 22
nationhood 8
nations 110
nativism 29, 35, 36, 62, 120, 132, 175
   and May 71
   and speech acts 37
   and working class 31, 89
negotiations, EU 60–1, 134–40
neo-functionalists 141
neoliberalism 25–6, 30, 39, 64, 65, 69, 129, 162
   and nationalist populism 176
   prone to instability 24
   and representative democracy 37
Netherlands 130, 141
New Labour 4, 21–2, 88
new neoliberal turn 176
next steps (NS) 83
NHS 47, 49
no deal 79, 81, 90, 106, 139, 148
   and Johnson 145, 146, 149
'the normal pathology thesis' 162
Northern Ireland 60, 80, 94, 118–19, 137, 146, 151
Norway Plus 70
nostalgia 67, 69, 132, 162

O
Obama, President 48
oil embargo 25
Oliver, Craig 41, 45, 49–50, 53, 57
Oliver, Tim 42
one nation Conservatives 22, 64, 65, 75–8, 83, 151–2

One Nation Europhiles 66
Opinium 159
oppression, language of 125
Orbán, Viktor 179
ordoliberalism 38–9, 177
Organization of Arab Petroleum Exporting Countries 25
Orientalism 50, 51
orientation to difference *13*, 28, 29, 70, 112, 114
Orwellian manipulation 76
Osborne, George 30, 45, 47, 48
othering 50–1
out-group 43, 171

P
Paradise Papers 56
paranoia 36
parliamentary sovereignty 66
Parris, Matthew 62
Patel, Priti 74, 85, 148–9
'pathological normalcy' 162
pathos *13*, 76, 82, 125, 135
Patten, Chris 75, 76, 154, 169
pedagogy, critical 180
People's Vote campaign 159–60
Phillips, Jess 152
Pickett, K. 172
Piketty, Thomas 176
Plaid Cymru 117–18
Plato 167
plebiscitary rhetoric 167, 168, 172–3
Poland 2, 140
Polanyi, Karl 24, 26, 84, 98, 176
political class 37–8, 53–4, 56
political donations 174
political elites 23–4, 35, 36, 38, 39, 110, 141
    EU 131
political speech acts 50
politicking 113
politics building 139
Pompidou, President 19
the poor 25, 30, 32
populism 2, 35–7, 40, 53, 57, 125–6, 166–7, 178–9
    and Clean Break Brexiteers 72–3
    and the Conservatives 85
    and Farage 52, 121
    and identity 174
    and migration 39
    and neoliberalism 176
    and Taggart 62
populist nationalist rhetoric 125

populist radical right 162
populist right 162
post-truth politics 37, 54
poverty 29, 74
Powell, Enoch 28
power, hegemonic 8, 9
pragmatism 64
Price, Adam 118
print media 55, 159, 172, 173
'Prisoner's Dilemma' 160
private sphere 8
privatization 25
progressive social reform 172
'Project Fear' 49
proportional representation 171
prorogation 150
public discourse 10
public spending cuts 29–30
public sphere 8, 172–4, 179

R
Raab, Dominic 81, 85, 148
race 37, 57
'race to the bottom' 153, 154
racism 28, 50, 52
radical democracy 168–9, 170
radical left 22, 23
Radical Left Europhiles 89, 98–101
radical right 22, 23, 130
Ramet, S. 110
rationalism 133, 142
rationalization *13*
rational legitimation 99
Rayner, Angela 92
recklessness 47
'red lines' 60, 139
Rees-Mogg, Jacob 71, 73
Reeves, Rachel 92
referendums
    1975 20, 88
    Brexit 22, 23, 41–57, 112
    Scottish independence 112, 113, 114, 116–17
    see also second Brexit referendum
reflexive modernity 33–4
reflexivity 3–6
refugee crisis 39, 42, 51–2
regional English identities 175
reification 123
reifying *13*
Remain campaign 45–8, 49, 52, 55
Remainers 31, 50, 60, 66, 89, 95
Remain parties 161

Remain vote 32, 53, 112, 113, 127, 157, 160
renegotiation, EU membership 42–3
repetition 13
representation, language 10
representative judgement 67–8, 76, 100, 169–70
'reverse Greenland' option 113
revolutionary fervour 72–3
rhetoric 9, 10, 13–14, 53–4, 62, 72, 167–8
   government 30
   plebiscitary 172–3
   populist nationalist 125
Rifkind, Malcolm 153
right Euroscepticism 22
right-wing populism 125–6
rigour, lack of moral 154
risk 34–5
risk society 34
'rivers of blood' speech 28
Robinson, Tommy 124, 163
Rome Treaty 18, 133
Rousseau, J. 73
Royal Prerogative 58
Rudd, Amber 70, 149
Rudd, Roland 159–60

S
Saatchi & Saatchi 54
Salmond, Alex 112
Salzburg Summit 79
scapegoating 35
Scargill, Arthur 96
Schäffner, C. 50
Schelling, Thomas 145
Schmitt, Carl 169
Schulz, Martin 138
Schuman Plan 18, 20
Scottish civic nationalism 175
Scottish independence 113–14, 127
   see also SNP (Scottish National Party)
second Brexit referendum 68, 84, 97, 105
   and Labour 101–2, 103, 104, 107, 158–9
Second World War 18, 110, 132
securitization 6–8
self-conception 3
self-determination 112
semi-periphery countries 26
services, pressure on 29
sexual assault 51

Sherriff, Paula 152
Simmel, G. 27
Single European Act 133
single market 20, 64, 66, 68, 88, 94, 101
   and Barnier 131, 134
   and EU negotiations 137
   and May 57–8
Single Market Act 64
Sinn Fein 118
Sked, Alan 119
Skinner, Dennis 96
Slovakia 38, 140
Smith, Iain Duncan 21, 65, 72
Smith, Will 45
Snell, Gareth 99
SNP (Scottish National Party) 109, 111–17, 157
social chapter 21, 74, 88
social class 31–2
   see also working class
social conservativism 64
social Europe 177
social housing 25
social identity theory 112–13
social justice 91, 99, 129
social media 55–6, 172, 173
social movement theory 85
social nationalism 112
social reform, progressive 172
social renters 32
socio-economic discourse 129–30
soft Brexit 71, 73, 84, 95, 97, 123, 155
Soros, George 179
Soubry, Anna 76, 77, 104
sovereignty 21, 49, 55, 64, 67, 77
   and hyperglobalists 69
   parliamentary 66
Soviet Union 25–6
Spain 117
'Special Relationship' 18, 19
speech acts 9, 10, 13, 41, 42, 50, 54
   nativist 37
   and populism 36
   and securitization 7, 8
The Spirit Level (Wilkinson and Pickett) 172
Stability and Growth Pact 177
Starmer, Keir 90, 102, 158, 163
the state, role of 64, 69
state intervention 25, 92
state ownership 25
statism 64, 129
steel 18, 20

INDEX

Steinmeier, Frank-Walter 132
Stiglitz, Joseph 26
Stronger In 45, 46
Stuart, Gisela 51
Sturgeon, Nicola 112, 113–14, 115, 116–17
Suez Crisis 19, 75–6
suicide vest metaphor 81
Sullivan, Andrew 161–2
The Sun 5, 21, 59, 75, 88
suppression 28, 169
supranational institutions 126
supranationalism 110, 111
Supreme Court 58, 150
Swinson, Jo 156, 160
Switzerland 133
syntax 13
Syrian refugee crisis 42, 130

T

tabloids 5, 21, 45, 59, 131
 see also media
Taggart, P. 62
Tajani, Antonio 136
'take back control' 67, 73, 134, 138, 149
targeted messaging 55
taxation 25, 47, 92, 176
Taylor, Richard 96
Tea Party 85
The Telegraph 59, 74
terrorist attacks 29, 59, 130
Thatcher, Margaret 20–1, 37, 64
Thatcherites 64
Third Reich 34
third way 30, 107
Thornberry, Emily 30
threat 105, 152
'three circles' doctrine 18
Tilford, S. 19
timeliness 106
Timothy, Nick 59, 70, 79
tolerance 28, 175
topoi 10, *11*, 22
totalitarianism 36
trade talks 148
trade unionism 64
tradition 67
trauma 34, 35
Travellers 4–5
treaties, EU
 Lisbon 133
 Maastricht 21, 64
 Rome 18, 133

Les Trente Glorieuses 4, 25, 172, 176
triumphalism 26
Trump, Donald 1, 36, 44, 54, 72, 125
 and Johnson 153, 154
Truss, Liz 148
trust 154–5, 162
Tsoukala, A. 7
Turkey 50, 51
Tusk, Donald 1, 131–2, 138, 142
Twitter 55
two-speed Europe 21, 22

U

UKIP (UK Independence Party) 44, 55, 89, 109, 111, 119–22
 and Conservatives 22, 42
 and monoculturalism 175
UK Referendum Party 22
Umunna, Chuka 104
unemployed people 32
unemployment 25
uniqueness, national 18–19
United Nations 24
United States 18, 19, 25, 85, 91, 139, 140
'United States of Europe' 18
unity government 155–6
Universal Declaration of Human Rights 24
university, role of 180
utopianism 20

V

Varoufakis, Yanis 93, 142
Verhofstadt, Guy 125, 136, 137, 140
Vietnam War 25
volunteering 30
Vote Leave 43–4, 49, 50, 55, 56, 120
vote of confidence in May 83

W

Wales 117–18
Wall Street Crash 24
war, effect of 18, 32, 110
Washington Consensus 74
wealth 24, 25, 91, 126
Weber, Manfred 140
Weber, Max 133, 142
Weberian legal rationalism 133
Weekes, J. 27
welfare 129, 176–7
welfare states 25
welfare system 25, 30
Welsh Nationalists 160

Westminster model 67, 171
white communities 28–9, 30–1, 126
Widdecombe, Anne 124–5
Wilders, Geert 130
Wilkinson, R. 172
will of the people 36, 149
Wilson, Harold 20, 87, 88
'Winds of Change' 19
Winlow et al 30
Withdrawal Agreement *see* European Union Withdrawal Bill
Wodak, R. 3, 35
Wollaston, Sarah 171
Wood, Leanne 117–18

workers' rights 81
working class 31, 32, 90, 98, 99–100, 105, 165
   identity 30, 89
   white communities 29, 126
World Bank 26
world-systems theory 26, 91

X
xenophobia 36, 70

Y
Yom Kippur War 25
YouGov poll 78
Yugoslavia, former 110–11

www.ingramcontent.com/pod-product-compliance
Lightning Source LLC
Chambersburg PA
CBHW070921030426
42336CB00014BA/2477